Cognitive Insights into Discourse Markers and Second Language Acquisition

Cognitive Insights into Discourse Markers and Second Language Acquisition

Iria Bello, Carolina Bernales, Maria Vittoria Calvi and Elena Landone (eds)

PETER LANG
Oxford • Bern • Berlin • Bruxelles • New York • Wien

Bibliographic information published by Die Deutsche Bibliothek
Die Deutsche Bibliothek lists this publication in the Deutsche Nationalbibliografie; detailed bibliographic data is available on the Internet at http://dnb.d-nb.de

A catalogue record for this book is available at the British Library.

Library of Congress Cataloging-in-Publication Data. A CIP catalog record for this book has been applied for at the Library of Congress.

Cover design by Brian Melville.

ISBN 978-1-78707-891-8 (print) • ISBN 978-1-78707-892-5 (ePDF)
ISBN 978-1-78707-908-3 (ePub) • ISBN 978-1-78707-909-0 (mobi)

Published by Peter Lang Ltd, International Academic Publishers,
52 St Giles, Oxford, OX1 3LU, United Kingdom
oxford@peterlang.com, www.peterlang.com

Printed in Germany

Contents

Figures

Tables

IRIA BELLO, CAROLINA BERNALES, MARIA VITTORIA CALVI AND ELENA LANDONE

Introduction
Insights into Discourse Markers: Cognition and Acquisition

This volume brings together a selected group of empirical studies about the interconnections of Discourse Markers (henceforth DMs) and Second Language Acquisition (henceforth SLA). As a matter of fact, DMs' cognitive processing and SLA reveal a research space that has continued to develop in methodological terms. As a matter of fact, whereas early studies often focused on the grammar of Discourse Markers (Weydt 1979, Martín Zorraquino 1998), current research treats them as a functional class and resorts to proposals stemming from different theories of communication and discourse, mainly from Argumentation Theory (Anscombre and Ducrot 1983; Anscombre, Rodríguez and Gómez-Jordana 2012), Relevance Theory (Sperber and Wilson 1995) or Cognitive Linguistics (Sweetser 1990; Langacker 1991, 2001). Corpus (Gast 2006; Aijmer 2013; Zufferey and Degand 2013; Gast and Rzymski 2015; Polat 2011) and experimental studies have proved that empirical methodologies are useful for the description of discourse markers (Loureda, Cruz, and DPKog 2013, 2014, 2015; Loureda et al. 2015; Zufferey, Mak, Degand, and Sanders 2015; Loureda, Nadal, and Recio 2016a, 2016b; Nadal, Cruz, Recio, and Loureda 2016; Nadal, Recio, Rudka, and Loureda 2017; Zufferey and Gygax 2017; Loureda, Recio, Nadal, and Cruz forthcoming) and different approaches have been used to describe them (Maschler and Schiffrin 2015). These include theoretical (Schiffrin 1987 [1982]; Foolen 1996; Blakemore 2004; Fischer 2006; Landone 2009), descriptive (König 1991; Dimroth and Klein 1996; Panders and Sanders 2006; Traugott 2006) and contrastive perspectives (Andersen, Brizuela, Dupuy, and Gonnerman 1999; Bouma, Hendricks, and Hoeksema 2007; Gast and van der Auwera 2011; Liu

2013; Borreguero Zuloaga and Gómez 2015; Loureda, Parodi, Rudka, and Salameh forthcoming).

In applied linguistics, specifically in second and foreign language acquisition studies, DMs have been a growing research topic (Meng and Strömqvist 1999; Müller 2006; Bini and Pernas 2007; Hellermann and Vergun 2007; Andorno 2008; Piedehierro 2009; De la Fuente 2009; Djigunovic and Vickov 2010; Fuentes Rodríguez 2010; Loureda 2010; Hernández 2011; House 2013; Pihler Ciglic 2014; Guil 2015; Heidari Tabrizi and Vaezi 2015; Jafrancesco 2015; Van Silfhout, Evers-Vermeul, and Sanders 2015; Zufferey et al. 2015; Andorno and Rossi 2016; Thörle and Borreguero Zuloaga 2016; Fant 2016). Undoubtedly, DMs are a difficult category to define, because it includes a large group of heterogeneous words which only share a functional purpose. Moreover, the functions they can fulfill actually cover many patterns of human communication, which results in a really high frequency of use. Therefore, they are pragmatically complex and communicatively frequent, and that is challenging for a foreign/second language learner, especially concerning input comprehension, stages of acquisition and questions of form and content processing in second language acquisition (Long 1981; Van Patten 1984, 1990; Chaudron 1985; Færch and Kasper 1986; Sharwood Smith 1986; Yule 1986; Danesi 1987; Ellis 1990; Schimdt 1990; Van Patten and Cadierno 1993; Johnston 1995). On the contrary, DMs are easily learnt in bilingual contexts because of their communicative relevance. L2 DMs are acquired early and are even used in L1 speech as tag switches or emblematic code-switching, that is, emblems of the bilingual character of a monolingual sentence, stressing affiliation, dual identities, etc. (Poplack 1980). Some studies suggest that L2 markers first enter L1 speech as emblematic codeswitches, then they become established borrowings, and even lead to the loss of the native marking system (Goss and Salmons 2000; Maschler 2000; Matras 2000; Calvi 2016; Hlavac 2006; Rocchi 2008).

The insights that we can gather on the nature of this pragmatic family through a cognitive processing lens lead us to focus those peculiarities of DMs that could cast light on language acquisition. The study of the process and the results of acquisition of DMs offer the opportunity to focus on those 'acquisitional incidents' that may reveal new insights into the nature of these particles: Why are they so difficult to learn? Why is a semantic approach not successful? Why are they overused and misused by learners? Moreover, it seems that only those learners who achieve a high proficiency level in a L2 are able to master the use of DMs (Charaudeau and Maingueneau 2005: 373), which confirms the proposition that DMs are linguistically relevant units and, at the same time, they are communicatively and cognitively very difficult to learn.

All the chapters in this book adopt a different but complementary focus and share insights on cognition and foreign or second language acquisition, with the exception of Chapter 1, which deals with native speakers' use of DMs and can be considered our starting point as it sets a baseline to understand their use. DMs are very efficient means to handle speech and interaction and to guide the listener's comprehension and inferential processes, but it is not always easy to understand the reasons that lead speakers to select among different DMs which are functionally similar. Even in native speakers, the complexity and over-availability of DMs can sometimes generate confusion and misunderstanding. From this point of view, the learning of a second or a foreign language increases the complexity of the pragmatic system already acquired in L1, and pragmatics is definitely the linguistic level in which it is more difficult for non-native speakers to develop native-like competence.

The contrastive approach which in Chapter 1 is internal to one language becomes interlingual in the other chapters. Each one of them is devoted to a different combination of native and target language. The foreign and second languages investigated are English, Italian and Spanish; the relationship between L1 and L2 also differ: in some cases they are closely related (Spanish to Italian in Chapter 7; Brazilian Portuguese, Spanish and Catalan to Italian in Chapter 8) and in other cases they are more distant languages (Spanish to English in Chapters 2 and 4; German to English in Chapter 3; German to Spanish in Chapter 5; Dutch to Spanish in Chapter 6); in Chapter 9, Italian is the target language for learners with different native languages (Ukrainian, Sinhalese, Pular, Wolof and Polish). Even if some space is devoted to comparative analysis, the approach is mostly contrastive, as far as cognitive processes are involved, both in native speakers and in foreign/second language learners. Thanks to the cognitive focus of each chapter, many results are equally applicable to different foreign languages.

This volume sheds light on similarities and differences between DMs processing in L1/L2 and gives some responses to the questions on the difficulties for learners. In some chapters, namely Chapter 4, the aim is precisely to compare the pragmatic processing in native and non-native, although highly proficient, English speakers. But the problem is also to highlight the factors which can influence the process and guide the learners to achieve better or even almost native-like proficiency. The status of the interlanguage can obviously have an effect on the level of proficiency in DMs' use, but the acquisition process is not linear and can be influenced by different aspects, such as the immersion in the target language. In natural environments, the search for social integration is a very strong pulling factor. In foreign language learning, the acquisition of DMs seems to be facilitated by the adoption of teaching techniques which promote participative involvement and metalinguistic awareness in action. In general, explicit attention must be paid to these units, all along the learning process, stressing on functional properties more than the construction of formal repertoires.

Common theoretical sources and empirical basis contribute to reinforce the results of these intertwined studies, which offer a wide range of methodological approaches and techniques: recorded or video recorded storytelling (Chapter 5), oral narratives (Chapter 6), role-play interactions (Chapter 7) and sociolinguistic interviews (Chapter 9); reading experiment monitored by eye-trackers (Chapters 2, 3 and 4); ethnographic observation (Chapter 8). The stress on oral expression is also dominating.

Chapter 1 by Eugenia Sainz ('Evidentiality, intersubjectivity and ownership of the information: The evidential utterances with *así que* and *que* in Spanish') focuses on the meaning and function of Spanish evidentials and discusses presumption of relevance and emotional involvement. Using a similar perspective, Elisa Narváez García and Lourdes Torres, in 'Processing causality in Spanish-speaking L2 English: An experimental approach to the study of *therefore*' (Chapter 2) study the inferential guide that causal connectives offer. The authors conducted an eye-tracking reading experiment and their conclusions support the recurrent observation on the rigidity of the procedural meaning that causal connectives embody. In Chapter 3 ('Pragmatic processing in second language: What can focus operators tell us about cognitive performance in L2?'), Olga Ivanova and Iria Bello Viruega highlight the scientific debate on language processing in L1 and L2. The authors conclude that the differences between native and non-natives speakers in cognitive processing depends on the different way in processing semantic and pragmatic information rather than to differences in native and non-native language systems. They show that pragmatic processing in L2, albeit native-like in comprehension, is not as sensitive to subtle inferential contrasts. In Chapter 4 ('Processing focus operators and pragmatic scales: An eye-tracking study on information processing in English L2'), Iria Bello Viruega and Carolina Bernales apply the same empirical methodology to cast light on the inferential process and the cognitive effort that focus operators involve in non-native speakers of English. Once more we see that pragmatics is the key to correctly comprehend and interpret Discourse Markers in a second language.

In Chapter 5, Britta Thörle and Christian Koch study 'The discourse markers *sí, claro* and *vale* in Spanish as a Foreign Language' and observe that learners acquire affirmation markers according to their proficiency level and that, in low proficiency, learners overuse them in a multifunctional way; besides the affirmative use, they assign the DM interactional, metadiscursive, and cognitive functions. Using a more communicative focus, in Chapter 6 ('A pilot study on the use of discourse markers in the oral discourse of language learners of Spanish'), An Vande Casteele and Kim Collewaert examine the use of discourse markers in oral narratives produced by language learners of Spanish and contrast the results with the findings of a control group of Spanish native speakers to show their importance in the interpretation of language learners' discourse.

In Chapter 7 ('Expressing agreement in L2 Italian: Strategies and discourse markers in Spanish learners'), Margarita Borreguero Zuloaga observes that there is not a clear path for the acquisition of Discourse Markers and that they may indeed undergo fossilization and code-switching processes. She concludes that learners overuse these markers from very early stages of acquisition because of the reduced set of lexical units at their disposal, which contrasts sharply with their communicational needs. In Chapter 8 ('The appropriation of discourse markers by students of Italian as a Foreign Language in a sequence of action-oriented learning tasks'), Marilisa Birello and Roberta Ferroni demonstrate that input enhancement offers the students the possibility to reflect on the uses and functions of the Discourse Markers and to re-use them naturally. Finally, Patrizia Giuliano, Rosa Russo, Simona Anastasio (Chapter 9, 'Discourse markers, interlanguage level and social integration: The immigrant learners in the Naples area') observe that interaction markers are more frequent than the meta-textual ones in the interlanguage of immigrant learners and that meta-textual markers are less used by those with a lower proficiency level; they also found that, in this group, the meta-textual markers can be used in a non-native way.

All the contributions included in this edited volume explore different approaches and methods that complement existing theoretical claims and that had been applied only partially until now. In conjunction, these studies arrive to very relevant conclusions for our understanding of DMs and we wish that this specialized book will be of interest for scholars who study Discourse Markers in general, and for those who investigate their acquisition from a cognitive perspective. Finally, we would like to thanks all the authors who contributed their very relevant and interesting work to this book.[1,2]

Bibliography

Aijmer, Karin, *Understanding Pragmatic Markers. A Variational Pragmatic Approach* (Edinburgh: Edinburgh University Press, 2013).

1 Our special thanks to the the reviewers for their helpful feedback.
2 This book project was carried out partly as a co-operation effort within the CONICYT International co-operation project No. 201150058.

Andersen, Elaine, Maquela Brizuela, Beatrice Dupuy and Laura Gonnerman, 'Cross-Linguistic Evidence for the Early Acquisition of Discourse Markers as Register Variables', *Journal of Pragmatics 31*/10 (1999), 1339–1351.

Andorno, Cecilia, 'Entre énoncé et interaction: le role des particules d'affirmation et négation dans les lectes d'apprenants', *Acquisition et interaction en langue étrangère 26* (2008), 173–190.

Andorno, Cecilia, and Fabiana Rosi, 'Confirming or Asserting?: Conflicting Values and Cross-Linguistic Influence in the Use of *yes/no* Particles in L2 Italian', in Margarita Borreguero and Britta Thörle, eds, *Discourse Markers in Second Language Acquisition – Studies on French and Italian as L2. Language, Acquisition and Interaction (Special Issue)* 7/1 (2016), 17–43.

Anscombre, Jean-Claude, and Oswald Ducrot, *L'argumentation dans la langue* (Bruxelles: Mardaga, 1983).

Anscombre, Jean-Claude, Amalia Rodríguez Somolinos, Sonia Gómez-Jordana Ferary, dirs, *Voix et marqueurs du discours: des connecteurs à l'argument d'autorité* (Lyon: ENS Éd., 2012).

Bini, Milena, and Almudena Pernas, 'Marcadores discursivos en los primeros estadios de adquisición del italiano L2'. *25 años de lingüística aplicada en España: Hitos y Retos* (Murcia: Universidad de Murcia, 2007), 25–36.

Blakemore, Diane, 'Discourse Markers', in Laurence R. Horn and Gregory Ward, eds, *The Handbook of Pragmatics* (Oxford: Blackwell Publishing, 2004), 221–240.

Borreguero Zuloaga, Margarita and Sonia Gómez Jordana, *Marqueurs du discours dans les langues romanes: une approche contrastive* (Limoges: Lambert-Lucas, 2015).

Bouma, Gosse, Petra Hendricks and Jack Hoeksema, 'Focus Particles inside Prepositional Phrases: A Comparison of Dutch, English and German'. *Journal of Comparative Germanic Linguistics 10* (2007), 1–24.

Calvi, Maria Vittoria, 'La alternancia *anche/también* en el español hablado por inmigrantes hispanoamericanos en Italia', in Eugenia Sainz González, Inmaculada Solís García, Florencio del Barrio de la Rosa, and Ignacio Arroyo Hernández, eds, *Geométrica explosión: Estudios de lengua y literatura en homenaje a René Lenarduzzi* (Venice: Edizioni Ca' Foscari, 2016), 147–160.

Charaudeau, Patrick, and Dominique Maingueneau, *Diccionario de análisis del discurso* (Buenos Aires: Amorrortu, 2005).

Chaudron, Craig, 'Intake: On Models and Methods for Discovering Learner's Processing of Input', *Studies in Second Language Acquisition* 7/1 (1985), 1–14.

Danesi, Marcel, 'Practical Application of Current Brain Research to the Teaching of Italian', *Italica 64* (1987), 377–392.

De la Fuente, María José, 2009, 'The Role of Pedagogical Tasks and Focus on Form in Acquisition of Discourse Markers by Advanced Language Learners', *Georgetown University Round Table on Languages and Linguistics* (2009), 211–221.

Dimroth, Christine, and Wolfgang Klein, 'Fokuspartikeln in Lernervarietäten. Ein Analyserahmen und einige Beispiele', *Zeitschrift für Literaturwissenschaft und Linguistik 104* (1996), 73–114.

Djigunovic, Jelena, and Gloria Vickov, 'Acquisition of Discourse Markers: Evidence from EFL Writing', *Studia Romanica et Anglica Zagrabiensia 55* (2010), 255–278.

Ellis, Rod, *Instructed Second Language Acquisition* (Oxford, Blackwell, 1990).

Færch, Claus, and Kasper, Gabriele, 'The Role of Comprehension in Second-Language Learning', *Applied Linguistics 7/3* (1986), 257–274.

Fant, Lars, 'Pragmatic Markers in High-Level Second Language Use', in K. Hyltenstam, ed., *Advanced Proficiency and Exceptional Ability in Second Languages* (Berlin: de Gruyter Mouton, 2016), 15–42.

Fischer, Kerstin (ed.), *Approaches to Discourse Particles* (Amsterdam: Elsevier, 2006).

Foolen, Ad, 'Pragmatic Particles', in Jef Verschueren, Jan-Ola Östman, Jan Blommaert, and Chris Bulcaen, eds, *Handbook of Pragmatics* (Amsterdam: Benjamins, 1996), 1–24.

Fuentes Rodríguez, Catalina, Los marcadores del discurso y la lingüística aplicada, in Óscar Loureda Lamas and Esperanza Acín Villa, eds, *Los estudios sobre marcadores del discurso en español, hoy* (Madrid: Arco Libros, 2010), 689–746.

Gast, Volker, 'The Distribution of *also* and *too*: a Preliminary Corpus Study', *Zeitschrift für Anglistik und Amerikanistik 54/2* (2006), 163–176.

Gast, Volker, and Christoph Rzymski, 'Towards a Corpus-Based Analysis of Evaluative Scales Associated with eve', *Linguistik Online 71* (2015), 2–15.

Gast, Volker, and Jan van der Auwera, 'Scalar Additive Operators in the Languages of Europe', *Language 87/1* (2011), 2–54.

Goss, Emily L., and Joseph C. Salmons, 'The Evolution of a Bilingual Discourse Marking System: Modal Particles and English Markers in German-American dialects', *International Journal of Bilingualism 4/4* (2000), 469–484.

Guil, Pura, 'Marcadores discursivos en la interlengua de aprendices de italiano L2', in Margarita Borreguero Zuloaga and Sonia Gómez-Jordana Ferary, eds, *Les marqueurs du discours dans les langues romanes: une approche contrastive* (Limoges, Lambert-Lucas, 2015), 373–386.

Heidari, Tabrizi Heidari, and Ramin Vaezi, 'The Pedagogical Influence of Interpersonal and Cognitive Discourse Markers on Iranian Intermediate EFL Learners' Listening Comprehension', *Theory and Practice in Language Studies 5/8* (2015), 1570–1577.

Hellermann, John, and Andrea Vergun, 'Language which is not Taught: The Discourse Marker Use of Beginning Adult Learners of English', *Journal of Pragmatics 39/1* (2007), 157–179.

Hernández, Todd A., 'Re-Examining the Role of Explicit Instruction and Input Flood on the Acquisition of Spanish Discourse Markers', *Language Teaching Research 15/2* (2011), 159–182.

Hlavac, Jim, 'Bilingual Discourse Markers: Evidence from Croatian–English Code-Switching', *Journal of Pragmatics 38*/11 (2006), 1870–1900.

House, Juliane, 'Developing Pragmatic Competence in English as a Lingua Franca: Using Discourse Markers to Express (Inter)subjectivity and Connectivity', *Journal of Pragmatics 59* Part A (2013), 57–67.

Jafrancesco, Elisabetta, 'L'acquisizione dei segnali discorsivi in italiano L2', *Italiano LinguaDue 1* (2015), 1–36.

Johnston, Malcolm, *Stages of Acquisition of Spanish as a Second Language* (NLLIA/LARC, University of Western Sidney, Macarthur, 1995).

König, Ekkehard, *The Meaning of Focus Particles: A Comparative Perspective* (London and New York: Routledge, 1991).

Landone, Elena, *Los marcadores del discurso y la cortesía verbal en español* (Bern: Peter Lang, 2009).

Langacker, Ronald W., *Foundations of Cognitive Grammar*, vol. 2, Descriptive Application (Stanford, CA: Stanford University Press, 1991).

Langacker, Ronald W., 'Discourse in Cognitive Grammar', *Cognitive Linguistics 12* (2001), 143–188.

Liu, Binmei, 'Effect of First Language on the Use of English Discourse Markers by L1 Chinese Speakers of English', *Journal of Pragmatics 45*/1 (2013), 149–172.

Long, Michael, 'Input, Interaction and Second Language Acquisition', Native Language and Foreign Language Acquisition, *Annals of the New York Academy of Sciences 379*/1 (1981), 259–278.

Loureda Lamas, Óscar, 'Marcadores del discurso, pragmática experimental y traductología: Horizontes para una nueva línea de investigación (I)', *Pragmalingüística 18* (2010), 74–107.

Loureda, Óscar, Adriana Cruz, and DPKog research group, 'Aproximación experimental sobre los costes de procesamiento de las partículas focales del español también e incluso', in Maria Vittoria Calvi and Antonio Briz, eds, *Nuevas tendencias en la lingüística del discurso*, Sección monográfica de Cuadernos AISPI. *Estudios de lenguas y literaturas hispánicas 2* (2003), 75–98.

Loureda, Óscar, Adriana Cruz, and DPKog research group, 'En los márgenes del léxico: las partículas focales del español (incluso, también) y el análisis experimental', in Luis Luque Toro and Rocío Luque, eds, *Léxico Español Actual, Vol. IV* (Venice: Cafoscarina, 2014), 85–104.

Loureda, Óscar, Adriana Cruz, Martha Rudka, Laura Nadal, Inés Recio and Margarita Borreguero Zuloaga, 'Focus Particles in Information Processing: An Experimental Study on Pragmatic Scales with Spanish incluso', in Anna María De Cesare and Cecilia Andorno, eds, *Linguistik online 71*, 2/15 Focus particles in the Romance and Germanic languages. Experimental and corpus-based approaches (2015), 129–151.

Loureda, Óscar, Laura Nadal and Inés Recio, 'El significado procedimental y las partículas discursivas del español: Una aproximación experimental', *Revista Signos. Estudios de Lingüística 49* (2016a), 52–77.

Loureda, Óscar, Laura Nadal and Inés Recio, 'Partículas discursivas y cognición: por tanto y la conexión argumentativa', *Romanistisches Jahrbuch, 67* (2016b), 240–254.

Loureda, Óscar, Giovanni Parodi, Martha Rudka and Shima Salameh (eds), *Marcadores del discurso y lingüística contrastiva en las lenguas románicas* (Iberoamericana/ Vervuert, forthcoming).

Loureda Óscar, Inés Recio, Laura Nadal and Adriana Cruz (eds), *Empirical Approaches to the Construction of Discourse: Information Structures, Argumentative Relations and Discourse Units*. Pragmatics & Beyond Series (Amsterdam: John Benjamins, forthcoming).

Martín Zorraquino, María Antonia, 'Los marcadores del discurso desde el punto de vista gramatical', in María Antonia Martín Zorraquino, and Estrella Montolío, eds, *Los marcadores del discurso. Teoría y análisis* (Madrid: Arco Libros, 1998), 19–53.

Maschler, Yael, 'What Can Bilingual Conversation Tell Us about Discourse Markers? Introduction', *International Journal of Bilingualism 4/4* (2000), 437–445.

Maschler, Yael, and Deborah Schiffrin, 'Discourse Markers Language, Meaning, and Context', in Tannen, Deborah, Heidi E. Hamilton and Deborah Schiffrin, eds, *The Handbook of Discourse Analysis* (Oxford, Blackwell, 2015), 189–221.

Matras, Yaron, 'Fusion and the Cognitive Basis for Bilingual Discourse Markers', *International Journal of Bilingualism 4/4* (2000), 505–528.

Meng, Katharina, and Sven Strömqvist, 'Discourse Markers in Language Acquisition', *Journal of Pragmatics 31/10* (1999), 1241–1244.

Müller, Stefan, *Discourse Markers in English Native and Non-Native Speakers* (Amsterdam: John Benjamins, 2006).

Nadal, Laura, Adriana Cruz, Inés Recio and Óscar Loureda, 'El significado procedimental y las partículas discursivas del español: Una aproximación experimental', *Revista signos 49* (2016), 52–77.

Nadal, Laura, Inés Recio Fernández, Martha Rudka and Óscar Loureda, 'Processing Additivity in Spanish: incluso vs además', in Anna María De Cesare, and Cecilia Andorno, eds, *Focus on Additivity: Adverbial modifiers in Romance, Germanic and Slavic languages* (Amsterdam/Philadelphia, PA: John Benjamins, 2017), 136–156.

Pander, Henk, and Ted Sanders, 'Connectives in Text', in Keith Brown, ed., *Encyclopedia of Language and Linguistics 3* (Amsterdam: Elsevier, 2006), 33–41.

Piedehierro, Carlota, 'La transferencia de instrucción: Estudio de interlengua sobre marcadores discursivos en producciones escritas de aprendices francófonos de E/LE', *Revista Nebrija de Lingüística Aplicada 5* (2009).

Pihler Ciglic, Barbara, 'Los marcadores verbales de modalidad epistémica y su papel en el desarrollo de las competencias comunicativas', *Lingüística 54* (2014), 381–395.
Polat, Brittany, 'Investigating Acquisition of Discourse Markers through a Developmental Learner Corpus', *Journal of Pragmatics 43/15* (2011), 3745–3756.
Poplack, Shana, 'Sometimes I'll start a Sentence in Spanish y termino en español: Toward a Typology of Code-Switching', *Linguistics 18* (1980), 581–618.
Rocchi, Lorenzo, 'Reti sociali e scelte linguistiche di emigrati italiani in ambiente anglofono', *Studi Linguistici e Filologici Online 6* (2008), 219–273.
Schiffrin, Deborah, *Discourse Markers* (Cambridge: Cambridge University Press, 1982/1987).
Schmidt, Richard W., 'The Role of Consciousness in Second Language Learning', *Applied Linguistics 11/2* (1990), 129–158.
Sharwood Smith, Michael, 'Comprehension versus Acquisition: Two Ways of Processing Input', *Applied Linguistics 7/3* (1986), 239–256.
Sperber, Dan, and Deirdre Wilson, *Relevance* (Oxford: Blackwell, 1995).
Sweetser, Eve, *From Etymology to Pragmatics: Metaphorical and Cultural Aspects of Semantic Structure* (Cambridge/New York: Cambridge University Press, 1990).
Thörle, Britta, and Margarita Borreguero, eds, Discourse Markers in Second Language Acquisition / Les marqueurs discursifs dans l'acquisition d'une langue étrangère. Studies on Italian and French as L2 / Études en Italien et en français langues étrangères. Special issue of *Language, Interaction and Acquisition 7/1* (2016).
Traugott, Elizabeth, 'The Semantic Development of Scalar Focus Modifiers', in van Kemenade, A., ed., *The Handbook of the History of English* (Oxford: Blackwell, 2006), 335–359.
Van Patten, Bill, 'Can Learners Attend to Form and Content while Processing Input?', *Hispania 72/1* (1984), 409–417.
Van Patten, Bill, 'Attending to Form and Content in Input. An Experiment in Consciousness', *Studies in Second Language Acquisition 12/3* (1990), 287–301.
Van Patten, Bill, and Teresa Cadierno, 'Explicit Instruction and Input Processing', *Studies in Second Language Acquisition 15/2* (1993), 225–243.
Van Silfhout, Gerdineke, Jacqueline Evers-Vermeul, and Ted J. M. Sanders, 'Connectives as Processing Signals: How Students Benefit in Processing Narrative and Expository Texts', *Discourse Processes: A Multidisciplinary Journal 52/1* (2015), 47–76.
Weydt, Harald (ed.), *Die Partikeln der deutschen Sprache* (Berlin/New York: de Gruyter, 1979).
Yule, George, 'Comprehensible Notions', *Applied Linguistics 7/3* (1986), 275–283.
Zufferey, Sandrine, and Liesbeth Degand, 'Annotating the Meaning of Discourse Connectives in Multilingual Corpora', *Corpus Linguistics and Linguistic Theory 13/2* (2013), DOI: <https://doi.org/10.1515/cllt-2013-0022>.

Zufferey, Sandrine, and Pascal M. Gygax, 'Processing Connectives with a Complex Form-Function Mapping in L2: The Case of French 'en effet.' *Frontiers in Psychology 8* (2017), 1198, DOI: doi: 10.3389/fpsyg.2017.01198.

Zufferey, Sandrine, Pim Mak, Liesbeth Degand and Ted Sanders, 'Advanced Learners' Comprehension of Discourse Connectives: The Role of L1 Transfer across On-line and Off-line tasks', *Second Language Research 31*/3 (2015), 389–411.

EUGENIA SAINZ

1 Evidentiality, intersubjectivity and ownership of the information: The evidential utterances with *así que* and *que* in Spanish

Introduction[1]

This paper focuses on utterances introduced by the conjunctions *así que* and *que*, when used at the opening of a conversation in absence of an explicit first member (Rodríguez Ramalle 2008, 2010, 2013, 2014a, 2014b, 2015, 2016). The research questions are as follows: How is the evidential meaning associated with the two utterances? Which semantic properties can be identified in each of them? What is their function in the interaction?

The paper is structured in six parts: In the second section, the theoretical background for the analysis is presented, closely following the results produced from research into evidentiality (among others, Lazard 1999, 2001; Ifantidou 2001; Plungian 2001; Nuyts 2001, 2006, 2012; Aikhenvald 2004; Bermúdez 2005; Cornillie 2009; Cuenca 2015). Then, attention is drawn to the utterance introduced by *así que*. Thirdly, in order to refine the analysis and better capture the semantic properties of the evidential meanings, a comparison is made with the evidential utterance introduced by *que* (Rodríguez Ramalle 2016). The fifth section addresses the pragmatic function of evidentials in interaction (Fox 2011; Nucholls and Michael 2014). Conclusions are offered in the last section. The language samples are drawn from the *Corpus de Referencia del Español Actual (CREA)*.

1 We would like to thank the reviewers for their valuable comments and suggestions, which have been very useful for revising and improving the final version of this paper.

Theoretical fundamentals for the analysis of the evidentiality

The concept of evidential modality

Evidential modality or evidentiality is understood to be the linguistic reference to the source of the information expressed in the utterance. Despite the clarity of the notion, the literature is divided concerning the way in which this must be understood, that is, the moment when it is acceptable to speak of evidential function in a language. Ifantidou (2001) clearly presents three theoretical positions that coexist now and which are only a reflection of the linguistic variation of a phenomenon that is very probably universal.

> In its broadest sense, an utterance has an evidential function if and only if it overtly communicates evidential information, whether this information is linguistically encoded or pragmatically inferred. More narrowly, we can regard a linguistic construction as being evidential if and only if this information is not only communicated but encoded. More narrowly still, we can regard a construction as being evidential if and only if it plays a highly restricted syntactic role, e.g., as a clitic, particle, 'discourse marker,' bound morpheme or some other minor syntactic category. (Ifantidou 2001: 161)

So in the most restricted sense, we can talk about evidentiality only in the event that the reference to the source is codified in the grammatical system. This is the case for several indigenous languages of the American and Asian continents, and it is the theoretical position supported by, for example, Aikhenvald (2004: 4–6): 'Linguistic evidentiality is a grammatical system (and often one morphological paradigm). In languages with grammatical evidentiality, marking how one knows something is a must. Leaving this out results in a grammatically awkward "incomplete" sentence.' Like other European languages, Spanish lacks an evidential grammatical system, and it is therefore impossible to talk about evidentiality in the strictest sense. It does, however, possess adverbs and constructions from a lexical base that have codified an evidential meaning, such as, for example, *como* (Brucart 2009), *evidentemente, aparentemente, al parecer, según parece, según dicen, por lo visto, desde luego* (Martín Zorraquino 2011a,

2011b, 2013; González Ramos 2016; Torner 2016). The evidential meanings bound to certain verbal tenses, such as the imperfect, the conditional and the future have been already studied (Reyes 1994; Leonetti and Escandell 2003; Bermúdez 2005; Escandell 2010; Rodríguez Rosique 2013; García Negroni 2016). There are also linguistic forms, such as the conjunction *que* and the illative conjunctions as *así que*, which, when interacting with particular forms of utterance, trigger an evidential meaning by default. Evidentiality can, then, be discussed in a broad sense.

Parameters for the analysis of the evidential domain

Research carried out up to now on languages which have grammaticalized the reference to the source has highlighted the relevance or significance of two parameters for the analysis of the evidential domain: firstly, how information is accessed (Willet 1988; Plungian 2001; Aikhenvald 2004; Cornillie 2009), and secondly, who can access it (Nuyts 2001, 2006, 2012; Bermúdez 2005). The aforementioned parameters are useful for shedding light on the evidential domain in languages like Spanish, where the reference to the source must in most cases be inferred in a non-conventional way.

From the point of view of the means of access to information, it is usual to distinguish between direct evidence and indirect evidence (Willet 1988; Cornillie 2009):

> *Direct evidentials* are used when the speaker has witnessed the action while *indirect evidentials* are used when the speaker has not witnessed the action personally but has either deduced the action or has heard about it from others. When the action is deduced, we are talking about inferentials; when information about the event is conveyed through others, they are called hearsay markers, reportatives or quotatives. (Cornillie 2009: 45)

Direct evidence takes place when the speaker accesses the information contained in the clause by means of his/her senses (sensory evidence, either visual or of a different kind) or by means of feelings (the endophoric evidence that Tournadre (1996) and Aikhenvald (2004) have documented in languages in Tibet and in some American languages such as Quechua). Indirect or mediative evidence (Lazard 1999, 2001) happens when the speaker accesses information by means of inference, deduction or reasoning based on clues (inferential evidence) or in the case of information reported by others (reported evidence, with different possibilities depending on the more or less determined nature of the reference: *hearsay*[2] *quotative* or popular tradition).[3]

The second parameter is the interactive dimension of the (inter) subjectivity: who has access to the information (Nuyts 2001, 2006, 2012; Bermúdez 2005: 15–17). From this point of view, there are four possibilities: the information contained in the clause a) is exclusive to the speaker, and consequently it is new to the listener; b) is shared by the speaker and by their interlocutor; c) is shared by the whole linguistic community, and d) is universal knowledge. We quote Nuyts (2001: 393–394):

> the dimension [of subjectivity] can be defined in terms of a difference in the status of the evidence and the epistemic evaluation based on that evidence from the perspective of the (knowledge of the) interaction partners in that situation. The alternatives within this dimension could then be phrased as follows: one pole involves the speaker's indication that (s)he alone knows (or has access to) the evidence and draws conclusions from it; the other pole involves his/her indication that the evidence is known to (or accessible by) a larger group of people who share the same conclusion based on it. In the former case the speaker assumes strictly personal responsibility for the epistemic qualification, in the latter case (s)he assumes a shared responsibility among those who have access to the evidence and accept the conclusions from it (including him/herself). (Nuyts 2001: 393–394)

2 Anscombre's *omni-locutor* (generic speaker) is of this type. As the author says, 'The origin of a knowledge can be given to a discourse character without further ado, that is to say, without any sensorial or testing process' (Anscombre 2014: 15).

3 See Plungian (2001: 351–352) and Bermúdez (2005: §2.1.1. 13–17). Whilst Willet's typology is the most frequent distinction, it is not the only one. Equally interesting is Plungian's (2001: 352–353) tripartite proposal, which distinguishes between direct evidence (that is, sensory or endophoric), deduced evidence (and within this, three types: synchronic inference, retrospective inference, and reasoning), and mediated evidence; a ternary system which is, in some languages, simplified to two: personal evidence (sensory or deduced) and mediated evidence.

The relationship between evidential modality and epistemic modality

Evidential modality and epistemic modality are two intimately related notions whose borders, as Cuenca (2015) points out, are blurred. The relationship between them is a controversial topic.[4] There are, at least, two ways of understanding the relationship established in the literature: a restricted approach and an unrestricted approach. From a restricted perspective, evidentiality and epistemic modality are two related but different categories.[5] From an unrestricted or broad perspective (Palmer 1986), evidentials are markers of epistemic attitude; that is, they are encompassed by a larger domain of epistemic modality and contribute to the expression of the degree of certainty or the degree of commitment of the speaker with respect to what is said.[6]

Nonetheless, even though evidentiality and epistemic modality work together in language, there are good reasons to keep the two categories separate. First, 'evidential' and 'epistemic' refer to two different things, and the fact that they are differentiated in the analysis allows certain things to be seen that would otherwise go unnoticed. The adjective *epistemic* refers to the degree of knowledge declared by the speaker, that is, a particular degree of certainty and of commitment regarding what was said and its truth value, and it is related to the notion of probability. By contrast, the term evidential refers to the source of knowledge, and it is related to the

4 For an overview of the different positions, see Dendale y Tasmowski (2001: 340–343); Nuyts (2006: 11–12); Nuyts (2006: 10–12) and González Ruiz, Izquierdo Alegría y Loureda Lamas (2016: 13–20).

5 This is the position supported, among others, by Lazard (1999, 2001); de Haan (1999), Plungian (2001); Aikhenvald (2004); Nuyts (2005); Cornillie (2009); Nucholls and Michael 2014 (13–14); Albelda (2016), González Vázquez 2016. It is also the position that we assume in this paper.

6 This is the theoretical position which the *Nueva gramática de la lengua española* appears to take, where the 'so-called evidentiality' is defined as a 'notion which describes the speaker's personal compromise with the truthfulness of the transmitted information or the source from which the information comes from' (*NGLE* 2009: I, §22.11h, p. 162–4).

notion of reliability: a source can be considered more or less reliable or accurate, that is, trustworthy.

A second reason is that the two categories are related, but they do not correlate. Reliability is not probability. As Cornillie (2009) argues, if evidentials were effectively at the exclusive service of the epistemic modality, it would be logical and expectable that a different evidential source (and, therefore, a different trustworthiness) would correspond to a differing degree of certainty. However, this is not the case.

> A source of information can be attributed to different degrees of reliability, but these should not automatically be translated into degrees of epistemic speaker commitment. The latter involves an evaluation of the likelihood, which is quite different from the evaluation of the reliability of the source of information. (Cornillie 2009: 44)

Thirdly, the assumption of the epistemic purpose of evidentials does not help us to understand the speakers' reasons to choose them. In fact, in the specific case of the utterances introduced by the conjunctions *así que* and *que*, the speaker's attitude is one of certainty; this means that the evidential utterance expresses the same epistemic commitment as the unmarked utterance, and it behaves in the same way. The argumentative orientation is identical and does not change even when a mark of epistemic doubt or uncertainty is present (Anscombre 1995):

(1a) ¿*Así que* María viene esta noche? Pon un plato más en la mesa. / #No pongas un plato más en la mesa.

[*So* Maria is coming tonight? Put an extra dish on the table. / #Don't put an extra dish on the table.]

(1b) ¿*Así que a lo mejor* María viene esta noche? Pon un plato más en la mesa. / #No pongas un plato más en la mesa.

[*So* Maria *may* come tonight. Put an extra dish on the table. / #Don't put an extra dish on the table.]

(2a) Oye, *que* María viene esta noche. Pon un plato más en la mesa. / #No pongas un plato más en la mesa.

[Listen, María is coming tonight. Put an extra dish on the table. / #Don't put an extra dish on the table.]

(2b) Oye, *que a lo mejor* María viene esta noche? Pon un plato más en la mesa. / #No pongas un plato más en la mesa.

[Listen, María *may* come tonight. Put an extra dish on the table. / #Don't put an extra dish on the table.]

Therefore, it follows that the reasons that lead speakers to prefer the marked utterance are not epistemic. When observed in the interaction, the purpose does not seem to codify the degree of commitment (although it may be an effect of meaning) but rather to introduce an argument authorizing the enunciation. It is something like an implicit argument from authority; an argumentative strategy similar to polyphonic authority (Ducrot 1999 [1984]: 158). This assumption is consistent with the notion of justification proposed by Anderson (1986: 274): 'Evidentials show the kind of justification for a factual claim which is available to the person making that claim' and 'Evidentials are normally used in assertions (realis clauses), not in irrealis clauses, nor in presuppositions' (277). The question is then why the speaker needs an argument from authority and why the speaker needs to justify his/her claim. In other words, in which contextual circumstances does the speaker prefer the marked form instead of the unmarked one? It is plausible to think that the answer lies in the interaction (Fox 2011; Nucholls and Michael 2014).

The evidential utterance introduced by *así que*: Form and meaning

We begin with the following assumption: the mere presence of *así que* is not sufficient to deduce the existence of a source for what is said. In a sentence like *Me trataban fatal. Así que me fui* [*I was treated badly, so I left*], there is nothing in either the codified meaning of the conjunction or in the sentence structure which leads to the conclusion that the speaker is invoking a source for the content expressed in the clause. From this, it can be deduced that the conjunction does not have evidential meaning in itself. In fact, if we take *así que* as an isolated word, we only know two things: firstly, that there is something before and something after, that is, connective meaning, a connection instruction, the property of anaphoric deixis; secondly, that what comes after (the second member or consequent) is the conclusion or consequence of what was previously said (the first member or antecedent). This marks the emergence of consecutive meaning.[7]

When it is used as a conjunction, the two members are explicit. However, *así que* is common in colloquial interactions, directly introducing a conversational turn, that is, in the absence of an explicit first member. Evidential meaning appears precisely in this type of cotext (see Rodríguez Ramalle 2014b: 134–135, and also 2010, 2013, 2014a, 2016). Hence, an utterance such as *¿Así que eres profesora?*[8] [*so you are a teacher?*] could be used by a speaker to start a conversation with someone showing only cordial interest. The situation could take place, for instance, at the departure lounge of an airport. The speaker has just heard two teenagers bid their farewells with the words 'Goodbye, teacher!'. This sensory clue serves as her basis for the deduction, and the shared situation that explains that the interlocutor is not surprised that a stranger should be in possession of the aforementioned information about her profession. The utterance would be equally suitable if the speaker formulated it upon seeing some exams to be corrected on a table at which their interlocutor is sitting (inference based on sensory evidence), after discovering it via others or from the interlocutor him- or herself in a previous moment of utterance (reported evidence). The means of access and also the source are indeterminate. Note that all these cases

7 As Álvarez points out (1999: §58.6.3, 3793), this meaning is compatible both with a cause-effect relationship: *Mañana es fiesta (causa), así que no habrá clase (consecuencia)* [*Tomorrow is a holiday (cause), therefore there will be no class (consequence)*], as well as with an explanation-deduction relationship: *Mañana no habrá clase, así que es fiesta* [*Tomorrow there will be no class, so it is a holiday*] according to how the clauses contained are ordered.

8 Although the tonal structure is interrogative, or nearly so, the utterance is assertive. Escandell Vidal 1999 speaks of 'esquema entonativo circunflejo' [circumflex intonational pattern] (§61.3.1.1) and of 'interrogativa atribuida' [attributed interrogative type] (§61.5.1). The information is not wholly claimed: the propositional function is left open, or is presented as such.

are concerned with some knowledge that is presented as mediated in the sense given by Lazard (1999, 2001),[9] that is, as indirectly acquired (hearsay or inference) from an indeterminate source. The features that the author ascribes to the mediative evidentials are also features that are possible to assign to the utterance introduced by *así que*:

- the speaker may choose between the unmarked register and the marked one;
- the marked register (the evidential forms) implies a reference to the acknowledgment of the event by the speaker;
- this reference is unspecified, consisting only of what may be paraphrased as 'as it appears';
- it creates a distance between the speaker and the speaker's own discourse;
- in itself, it expresses neither dubiety nor presumption. (Lazard 2001: 364).

It may also be noted that the absence of an explicit first member does not imply a vacuum in any way; on the contrary, there is an abundance of contextual information attained from indeterminate sources, which is incorporated in some way into the utterance. Anscombre (2011: 8) proposed the concept of the 'virtual utterance':

> an absence of a sign can be as significant as a physical presence: an absence of sign can be a real sign, and implicit is not the same as non-existent. [...] A theory that uses the concept of virtual utterance starts from the hypothesis that a part of what is commonly called context (ie, enunciative circumstances) is not really context, but cotext, and implicit cotext besides.
>
> [...] if we accept the notion of virtual utterance, we also accept that such utterances have a source (that is, an indicator of the origin of the information or the word) and

9 The term *mediativity* is used in different ways in the bibliography. For example, Anscombre (2011 and 2014) include under the concept the three main types of access to information: 'the inference (e.g. "I have proof"), the perception (e.g. "I saw you"), and the loan (e.g. "they told me that ...")' (Anscombre, 2011: 10). Lazard (1999, 2001) includes inference, loan and mirativity. Plungian (2001) distinguishes between direct, inferred, and mediated knowledge.

this allows us to relate phenomena such as negation, presupposition, etc. to other types of phenomena, namely, the mediative phenomena.

Ultimately, the hypothesis can be stated as follows: *así que* can introduce a conclusion in the absence of an explicit first member. In this specific type of cotext, the problem of the anaphora conventionally imposed by the linguistic meaning of *así que* (connective instruction) is resolved with the inference of the existence of a source for what is said, with the consequent leap from sentence anaphora (conjunction) to discourse deixis (marker). Thus, we believe that evidential meaning is an utterance-type-meaning which is obtained by default when the conjunction appears in this type of utterance (Levinson 2000) or discursive pattern (Taranilla 2015),[10] which is characterized by the presence of a virtual first member or implicit cotext that contains the information acquired indirectly from an indeterminate source.

From a semantic point of view, our hypothesis is that the utterance introduced by *así que* has two evidential properties: first, as we have argued before, it is a sign of indirect evidence or mediativity (Lazard 1999, 2001), and secondly, it is a sign of intersubjectivity (Nuyts 2001, 2006, 2012), as confirmed by the inadequacy of (3b) and (3c).

(3a) ¿*Así que* Sofía se ha comprado un coche? ¿Por qué no me lo has dicho?
[*So* Sofía has bought herself a car? Why didn't you tell me?]

(3b) ¿*Así que* Sofía se ha comprado un coche? #Me han dicho que tú no sabes nada.
[*So* Sofía has bought herself a car? #I have been told you don´t know anything.]

(3c) ¿*Así que* Sofía se ha comprado un coche? #Tú no lo sabías, supongo.
[*So* Sofía has bought herself a car? #I guess you didn't know anything.]

10 We share Taranilla's words (2015: 236–237): 'the discursive pattern contains procedural meaning that can be added to the basic meaning of a particle, so that its nuclear semantics is enriched with secondary values. [...] it is need to explore the discursive patterns in which a particle is traditionally embedded in order to systematize the updating of its secondary semantics'.

The evidential utterance-type with *así que* compared with the evidential utterance-type with *que*

In order to better understand the issue, it can be useful to compare the utterance-type with *así que* to the one introduced by the conjunction *que* when used in the same cotextual circumstances, that is to say, in the absence of the first member.[11] Our aim is to identify what joins and what separates the two utterances (4b) and (4c):

(4a) Oye, Sofía se ha caído.

[Listen, Sofía has fallen down.]

(4b) Oye, *que* Sofía se ha caído.

[Listen, [I have heard / I have seen] *that* Sofía has fallen down.]

(4c) Oye, *¿así que* Sofía se ha caído?

[Listen, *so* Sofía has fallen down?]

We follow the distinctions suggested by Nuyts (2006: 18):

> if one is talking about commitments, it is important to be able to make it very clear, in an immediate way, who is making them (performativity vs. descriptivity); and if one is concerned with attitudes, it is often essential to be able to make it clear whether one is alone in one's views, has backing for them (subjectivity vs. intersubjectivity), is neutral, or is subjectively biased in one's assessment (subjectivity vs. objectivity).

In both cases: a) the two utterances are typical of colloquial interaction: the interlocutors know each other, their relationship is non-hierarchical, and they speak about everyday topics; b) the two utterances can function

11 The conjunction *que* has been carefully studied and the bibliography is abundant: Reyes (1994), Porroche (2000, 2003), Pons Bordería (2003), Etxepare (2010), Demonte and Fernández-Soriano (2007, 2013), Gras (2012, 2016), Rodríguez Ramalle (2014b, 2016). Recently Rodríguez Ramalle (2016) has attributed the particle an evidential value in this type of utterance (see Anscrombre 2016, 2017 as well).

as the beginning of a speech event; c) they introduce an assertive speech act with its own illocutionary force, that is, they are not copies or echoes of a previous speech act, and they have assertive value; d) they legitimize the implicature of the existence of an indeterminate source of propositional content; and e) they legitimize the assumption that the source has been submitted to an evidential and epistemic evaluation by the speaker and that the speaker has deemed them to be trustworthy and the content to be truthful. Therefore, both of them are performative.

The differences are not less meaningful. First, an utterance such as *Juan, que Sofía se ha caído. Ven, por favor* [*Juan,* [*I have heard / I have seen*] *that Sofía has fallen down. Please, come!*] can be uttered by a speaker who has obtained the information via a third party (reported evidence) but also by one that was present during the subject's fall (direct evidence). Then, this could be a case of mediativity, in the sense described by Anscombre (2011): The speaker repeats the information acquired by the senses or by hearsay. By contrast, the utterance introduced by *así que* presents the propositional content as the result of the speaker's inference even in the event of sensorial perception.

Secondly, subjectivity should be taken into account. The information of the clause that is introduced by *que* (*que Sofía se ha caído*) is private to the speaker and unknown to the listener: a situation of non-shared evidence or solely subjective evidence. Consequently, from an informational perspective, rhematic content, that is new data, is presented into the common base. By contrast, the content of the clause introduced by *así que* (*¿Así que Sofía se ha caído?*) is, or is presented as being, shared by the speaker and the interlocutor (or even by the whole community): a situation of shared evidence or intersubjective evidence. Therefore, from an informational perspective, thematic content, that is, shared knowledge is introduced (the information is not new for the interlocutor).[12]

12 It is interesting to observe that the leap from conjunction to discourse connective entails a change in the informational nature of the consequent: rhematic content in the first instance; thematic content in the second. Compare:
(1a) Le trataron mal, *así que* se fue.
(1b) Oye *¿Así que* se fue?

Lastly, in the case of *que*, the responsibility for epistemic evaluation lies exclusively on the speaker because (s)he is the only one who has had access to the source and the knowledge. This means that the interlocutor may not share the same evaluation and the same conclusion that the speaker supports. In other words, (s)he should stop doing what (s)he was doing and help Sofia. By contrast, with *así que* the responsibility is presented as being shared and the content is presented as if it were true for both speaker and interlocutor since both have had access to the evidence. This means that they both share the same evaluation and support the same conclusion. The difference is important from an argumentative point of view and can explain the different use of the argument from authority in each case.

Approaching the evidential function: Subjectivization and strategic justification

As said above, our assumption is that the possession of a source, however indeterminate, functions as an argument from authority and the speaker uses it to justify his/her claim. It is plausible to hypothesize that the justification is strategic[13] because the evidential is not compulsory, and it is also plausible to hypothesize that it may be sensitive to the communicative circumstances and if so, deictic (de Haan 2005). We suppose that the choice is conditioned by at least two factors: the type of information regarding

13 Nuyts (2001) notices the importance of the active role of the speaker (how (s)he presents the facts) and the interaction partner (to what extent (s)he is willing to participate in the representation):

> An important (but maybe not a necessary) element in how this distinction actually works may then be whether the interaction partner belongs to those sharing the evidence and the conclusions, or not. In fact, it is important to realize that in any construal of the dimension, its reflection in actual expressions of epistemic modality is a matter of how the speaker presents the situation (rather than of how it 'really is'). In the present understanding of the dimension, then, the position of the interaction partner is likely to become critical. (Nuyts 2001: 394.)

the participants (that is, the participants' closeness to the information) and the speaker's communicative aim.

In fact, the first phenomenon that is observed is that the evidential formulation has a subjectivizing impact on the proposition.

(5a) Han cerrado el puente.
[They have closed the bridge.]

(5b) *Que* han cerrado el puente.
[[I have heard / I have seen] *that* they have closed the bridge.]

(5c) ¿*Así que* han cerrado el puente?
[*So* they have closed the bridge?]

(6a) Se ha caído una niña.
[Listen, a girl has fallen down.]

(6b) *Que* se ha caído una niña.
[Listen, [I have heard / I have seen] *that* a girl has fallen down.]

(6c) ¿*Así que* se ha caído una niña?
[Listen, *so* a girl has fallen down?]

The propositional content does not change but in the examples (b) and (c), the factual representation is intersubjectively biased towards the participants in the interaction. The information is presented as if it directly concerned the speaker and the interlocutor and as if they were personally affected to some extent. Hence, they also appear remarkably interested an even emotionally involved. The bridge that has been closed is not any bridge but the bridge that they cross every day to go to work. The girl is not any girl but one of the young girls enrolled in the summer camp supervised by them or by one of them. Our assumption is that it is the procedural form of the evidential utterance that projects the proposition in an intersubjective direction and transforms objective facts into (inter)subjective facts regarding the participants in the interaction. The bare objective information becomes intersubjective information belonging to a shared informative territory (Fox 2011).[14] And vice versa: the territory of information to which the proposition belongs (ordinary events in everyday life) determines the choice of the marked form instead of the unmarked one, thus creating a relationship of closeness and intimacy and specific expectations of relevance.

The utterance does not denote a bare state of affairs, but a state regarding the speaker and the interlocutor: a well-known bridge and young girl, which are (a bridge and a young girl) intersubjectively biased.[15] Similarly, the lexical items are intersubjectively biased because the hearer is asked to bring to memory only those lexical properties that agree with (that are consistent with) the purpose of the enunciation: the bridge is the bridge that the participants cross to go to the office; the girl is one of the young girls supervised by the speaker or/and the interlocutor. There is empathy, complicity and intimacy because the speaker presents himself as interested in the same information as the interlocutor.

If our hypotheses were correct and could be accepted, the notion of relevance might be understood not only with regard to the classic opposition new / old data for the listener but also with regard to the intersubjective bias of the information that is a deictic and social opposition: regarding / non regarding the participants in the interaction; close / far to them; belonging / not belonging to their informative territory. For the listener of (5b) *Que*

14 Fox (2011) focuses on the social notions of information ownership and territory of information. As Fox (2011: 174) explains, 'the territory of information model describes what information "belongs" to the speaker, the hearer, everyone or some people non present. For example, a speaker may know something to be true but he/she may not be entitled to say it as bare fact, because this piece of information "belongs" to someone else.' There seems to be 'an apparently cross-culturally held belief that some information is "closer" or "belongs" to some participants while being "more distant" or "not owned by" others' (175). 'From these prior studies, we have reason to believe that "ownership" of information, the power and rights to claim information, and the obligations incurred by doing so, are implicated in evidence giving generally, and in evidential uses more specifically' (176).

15 The evidential utterances introduced by *así que* and *que* constitute a good example of what Bermúdez (2005: 21) notes: 'The modal markers are expression of the subjectivity of the speaker while the evidential markers are related to the communicative situation as a whole (and especially to the listener and his capacity for evaluation) and therefore are inherently intersubjective.'

han cerrado el puente, the closure of the bridge is new information; for the listener of (5c) *¿Así que han cerrado el puente?*, the information is known. Nevertheless, in both cases, there are particular expectations of relevance because the evidential utterance presents the information as belonging to their territory and, therefore, as personally affecting them.

The communicative aims are not less important because they give us the key to understanding why the speaker considers it useful to justify his/her claim. In the first case, the speaker that chooses the evidential *que* (*Oye, que han cerrado el puente*) wants to do different things: to describe a state of affairs (assertive act); to express his/her concern (expressive act) and to convince him/her to do something (directive act). The evidential utterance is a very complex illocutive act, not merely assertive but also expressive, directive and argumentative. And we think it is again the evidential formulation that transforms the illocutive force. In this specific situation, it is plausible to suppose that having a source for what is said and allowing the inference of its existence seems to be strategically useful to achieve the goals. From a communicative and interactive point of view, the means of access to the knowledge (sensorial or reported evidence) or the specific reference of the source are not so central. What is really important is to have an argument from authority. The restricted access to knowledge (exclusive ownership) reinforces the utterance even more.

In the second case (*¿Así que han cerrado el puente?*), the evidential utterance allows a different strategy for a different communicative situation. The illocutive act is assertive and directive, although the proposition is unconfirmed information (Lazard 1999: 361–362). The speaker wants to approach the interlocutor and convince him to friendly talk about the bridge being closed or more precisely about his/her experience regarding the closure. Marking the utterance is strategically advantageous because it allows the speaker to appear as interested in a shared topic and, consequently, as interested in the interlocutor. But there is another important factor influencing the choice of the intersubjective evidential *así que*. The interlocutor has had access to the piece of knowledge before the speaker and consequently owns it 'more' than him, that is, the interlocutor has more entitlement and more authority to it (Fox 2011). By contrast, the speaker is a newcomer to this piece of knowledge. So in this particular situation, the evidential *así que* allows him/her to plan an interesting strategy pattern. The speaker assumes his/her condition of newcomer, reduces his/her authority claims (not needed because the epistemic evaluation is shared), grants the ownership to the interlocutor and leaves the proposition open (unconfirmed) to be closed by him/her. The following example works as a successful polite strategy for breaking the ice:

> (7) Durante una reunión familiar en la casa de los Yoma, se sentaron en un sofá de tres cuerpos de color celeste, cada uno en un extremo. '*¿Así que pintas?*', le preguntó Carlos Menem, mirando los cuadros que colgaban de la pared. Paisajes coloridos de pueblitos de la costa y retratos de la familia. (CREA: Wornat, Olga, *Menem-Bolocco*, 2001)
>
> [They sat down on a light-blue, three-seat sofa during a family gathering, each of them on an end. '*So you paint?*', Carlos Menem asked him, looking at the pictures that were hanging on the wall. Colourful landscapes of coastline villages and family portraits.]

Intersubjective informative bias may also be emotion or expressivity when the piece of information moves the speaker emotionally:

> (8) Olga estaba de pie junto al mesón, con un café humeante entre las manos.
>
> – ¿*Así que* te vas? – dijo sin mirarme, sorbiendo cautelosamente de su taza–. ¿Por un año entero?
>
> – Hasta el próximo verano –corroboré.
>
> Hizo una pausa, acariciando el borde de la taza con el dedo.
>
> – Te echaremos de menos – insistió, aún sin mirarme–. Eres parte ya de nosotros, Marcos. (CREA: Collyer, Jaime (2002): *El hablante del cielo*)
>
> [Olga was standing next to the tavern, holding a steaming coffee in her hands.
>
> 'so you are leaving?', she said without looking at me, carefully sipping her cup. 'for one whole year?'
>
> 'Until next summer', I confirmed.
>
> She paused for a moment, caressing the top of the cup with her finger.
>
> 'We will miss you', she insisted without looking at me yet. 'You are already part of us, Marcos.']

The pragmatic strategy allowed by the evidential is particularly useful in the colloquial interaction because of discursive functions, such as introducing a new discursive topic (*¿Así que han despedido a Jaime?* [*so they have sacked Jaime?*]) or resuming an interrupted one (*¿Así que conoces a María?* [*so you know María?*]). It presents them as shared and relevant information, interesting for both speaker and interlocutor. An utterance-type like *¿Así que ha dimitido el presidente?* [*so the president has resigned?*] invokes some knowledge that is shared by the entire linguistic community in terms of citizens of the same state. It can function to introduce a new topic into the discourse because it is based on the assumption that both parties are interested in the national politics, and it takes for granted the truth of the news reported in the press or on the television. The utterance allows the speaker to appear interested in the interlocutor (*¿Así que te vas a Alemania la próxima semana?* [*so you are going to Germany next week?*]) and even emotionally involved (*¿Así que te vas?* [*so you are going?*]). Intersubjectivity is also inter-responsibility and, because of that, the utterance-type can be used for requesting an explanation for something that has happened by expressing certainty and evidence. (*Por cierto, Pablo, ¿Así que no has enviado el informe?* [*By the way, Pablo, so you have not sent the file?*]). An utterance like *¿Así que me traicionas?* [*so you are betraying me?*] at the beginning of the speech event that is said to a friend, a colleague or a partner is the same as saying 'I know that it is true and you also know that it is true.' The force of the argumentation lies precisely in the possession of a source (authority) and the situation of shared evidence.

Sometimes the evidential utterance seems to approach reformulation[16] and *así que* can be commutable with a reformulation marker as *o sea que*. Note the following examples:

(9a) – Me obligaron a reconocer mi culpa y me comunicaron que en cuanto Lolita se fuera, yo también debía marcharme. Sin ella no van a necesitarme.

16 The *NGLE* states (§46.12l), 'Many illative conjunctions start the period and even the discourse turn-taking. When they start a question, usually a recapitulation is formulated, sometimes unexpectedly, or that we ask for an explanation of what has been said'. For the relationship between reformulation and conclusion, see Pons 2013 and Murillo (2016), with opposing positions.

– *Así que* Lolita se ha ido ... / *O sea que* Lolita se ha ido ...

Miss Francia asintió: Las lágrimas de la garganta apiñadas en los ojos.

(CREA corpus: Salisach, Mercedes 1975: *La gangrena*, Planeta, Barcelona, 1976)

[They forced me to acknowledge my blame and told me that as soon as Lola left, I had to leave, too. Without her, they are not going to need me.

'*So* Lolita has left .../ *You mean that* Lolita has left ...'

Miss France nodded: tears from her throat packed in her eyes.]

(9b) Un día nos habló de don Pablo. Nos confió el gran secreto. 'Nadie en el Banco lo sabe: únicamente don Alberto y mi pobre Jaume conocían la verdad.' Mi madre, al oírla, se quedó algo avergonzada. Le costaba creer lo que Angelina nos decía. Entonces aquellos casos eran muy raros y despertaban recelos. 'Es una buena persona ... Pero no se veía con ánimo para ejercer su ministerio. Colgó los hábitos y se echó a vivir.'

– *Así que* don Pablo es sacerdote. / *O sea que* don Pablo es sacerdote.

– De pies a cabeza.

– Pero ... ¿Cómo hizo eso?

(CREA corpus: Salisach, Mercedes 1975: *La gangrena*, Planeta, Barcelona, 1976)

[Once she told us about don Pablo. She told us the big secret. 'Nobody at the Bank knows it: only don Alberto and my poor Jaume knew the truth.' When she heard her, my mother got a bit ashamed. It was hard for her to believe what Angelina was telling us. Back then, those cases were very rare and used to arouse distrust. 'He is a good person ... But he didn't feel like performing his ministry. He left the priesthood and started to live.'

'So don Pablo is a priest. / You mean that don Pablo is a priest.'

'From head to toe.'

'But ... how did he do that?']

Nonetheless, it is very interesting to note that these are not equivalent discursive forms. The speaker's modal attitude with regard to the content is different. The evidential utterance is a signal that Lolita's leaving home and don Pablo's religious calling are two pieces of information that belong to the intersubjective territory, and, therefore, there is personal interest and emotional involvement. The speaker who chooses the evidential *así que* is (or wants to appear) personally interested in the information provided by the interlocutor (*¿Así que don Pablo es sacerdote?*) or even emotionally involved in the facts described (*¿Así que te vas? ¿Así que Lolita se ha ido?*). By contrast, the reformulation utterance containing *o sea que* expresses a more objective attitude with respect to a piece of information that falls outside the intersubjective territory. The commutation of the evidential *así que* by the reformulation particle causes a loss of subjective involvement. The speaker is not personally affected by this information. (S)he only wants to make sure that his/her conclusion is true. Hence, (s)he seems less interested or only interested in the objective data (*¿O sea que don Pablo es sacerdote?*) and less emotionally involved in the facts (*¿O sea que te vas? ¿O sea que Lolita se ha ido?*). Intersubjectivity does not seem to be only a matter of shared information, shared epistemic evaluation and shared conclusion, but also shared territory, shared informative interests, subjective attitude and emotional involvement. It is an interesting issue that deserves further investigation.

Conclusions

Our analysis yielded several conclusions. Firstly, the assumption that the function of evidentials is epistemic does not help us to understand the reasons that lead speakers to choose them. When observed in the interaction, their purpose does not seem to be epistemic, but rather to introduce an implicit argument that authorizes the enunciation and justifies the illocutive act. The question is then why the speaker needs to justify his/her claim.

Secondly, the evidential utterance introduced by the illative conjunction *así que* is considered. The assumption is made that the evidential interpretation is not linked to the conjunction, but rather to a specific type of utterance (Levinson 2000) or discursive pattern (Taranilla 2015) that is characterized by the presence of a virtual first member or implicit cotext which contains the information acquired indirectly from an indeterminate source. It is plausible to hypothesize two evidential properties: indirect evidence (inference and hearsay) from indeterminate sources (that is, mediativity in the sense of Lazard 2001) and intersubjectivity (Nuyts 2001, 2006, 2012); that is to say, thematic content, shared responsibility.

Thirdly, the evidential utterance introduced by *así que* has been compared with that introduced by the conjunction *que*. As a result, important differences have been noticed. In particular, the latter one is, first, a signal of reported evidence but also direct sensorial evidence (mediative in the sense of Anscombre 2011) and, secondly, a signal of solely subjective evidence (rhematic content, exclusive responsibility of the speaker).

Fourthly, the function of the two evidential utterances in the interaction have been analysed and an interesting feature has been highlighted. The evidential utterance is a signal of intersubjective information belonging to a shared informative territory. In both cases the evidential utterance projects the proposition in an intersubjective direction and transforms the objective facts into (inter)subjective ones regarding the participants in the interaction. The information is presented as if it directly concerned the speaker and the interlocutor and as if they were personally affected to some extent. Hence, they also appear very interested and even emotionally involved.

Finally, the analysis seems to confirm Anderson's hypothesis (1986). The evidential functions as an argument from authority to justify the claim. The justification is strategic. In the utterance introduced by *que*, the evidential contributes to reinforce the speaker's authority. The utterance introduced by *así que* allows a different strategy for a different communicative situation. The interlocutor has accessed knowledge before the speaker and consequently owns it 'more' than him, that is, (s)he has more entitlement and more authority to it. By contrast, the speaker is a newcomer to this knowledge. In this particular situation, the evidential *así que* allows him/her to plan an interesting strategy. The speaker assumes his/her condition of newcomer, reduces his/her authority claims, grants the ownership to the interlocutor and leaves the proposition open (unconfirmed) to be closed by him/her. This strategic pattern is particularly useful in the Spanish colloquial interaction. It is an interesting issue worthy of more careful study and investigation.

Bibliography

Aikhenvald, Alexandra Y., *Evidentiality* (Oxford: Oxford University Press, 2004).

Albelda Marco, Marta, 'Estableciendo límites entre la evidencialidad y la atenuación', in Ramón González Ruiz, Dámaso Izquierdo Alegría and Óscar Loureda Lamas, eds *La evidencialidad en español: teoría y descripción* (Frankfurt am Main: Iberoamericana Vervuert, 2016), 75–100.

Alvarez, Alfredo I., 'Las construcciones consecutivas', in Ignacio Bosque and Violeta Demonte, eds, *Gramática descriptiva de la lengua española*, vol. 3 (Madrid: Espasa Calpe, 1999), 3739–3804.

Anderson, Lloyd B., 'Evidentials, Path of Change, and Mental Maps: Typologically Regular Asymmetries', in Wallace Chafe and Johanna Nichols, eds, *Evidentiality: The Linguistic Coding of Epistemology* (Norwood NJ: Ablex Publishing Corporation, 1986), 273–312.

Anscombre, Jean-Claude, 'Semántica y léxico: topoi, estereotipos y frases genéricas', *Revista Española de Lingüística*, 25:2 (1995), 297–310.

Anscombre, Jean-Claude, 'Los marcadores del discurso: historia de un concepto, problemas y perspectivas', *Linred* (*Lingüística en la red*) 9 (2011), online.

Anscombre, Jean-Claude, 'Evidentiality, Generic Speakers, and Discourse Markers An account of Modern French: *on sait que, on dit que, on prétend que, on raconte que, on admet que*', *Archivum*, LXIV (2014), 7–26.

Anscombre, Jean-Claude, 'Les constructions en adverbe que p en français. Essai de caractérisation sémantique d'une matrice lexicale productive', *Cahiers de lexicologie*, 1: 108 (2016), 199–224.

Anscombre, Jean-Claude, 'Le QUE médiatif du français contemporain : perspectives diachronique et comparée', *Revue Romane* (2017), online, 12 December 2018.

Asociación de Academias de la Lengua Española, *Nueva gramática de la Lengua española* (Madrid: Espasa, 2009 vol. I y II).

Bermúdez, Fernando, *Evidencialidad: La codificación lingüística del punto de vista / Evidentiality: The Linguistic Coding of Point-of-View*. Doctoral dissertation (Department of Spanish, Portuguese and Latin American Studies, Stockholm University, 2005).

Brucart, Jos María, 'Sobre el valor evidencial de *como* en español, en la lingüística como reto epistémico y como acción social', in Montserrat Veyrat and Enrique Serra, eds, *La lingüística como reto epistemológico y como acción social. Estudios dedicados al profesor Ángel López García* (Madrid: Arco Libros, 2009), 583–593.

CREA = REAL ACADEMIA ESPAÑOLA: *Corpus de referencia del español actual.* <http://www.rae.es>

Cuenca, Maria José, 'Evidenciality (and Epistemicity) in Catalan Parliamentary Debate', *eHumanista IVITRA* 8 (2015), 362–382.

Cornillie, Bert, 'Evidentiality and Epistemic Modality: On the Close Relationship between Two Different Categories', *Functions of Language* 16/1 (2009), 44–62.

De Haan, Ferdinand, 'Evidentiality and Epistemic modality: Setting boundaries', *Southwest Journal of Linguistics* 18/1 (1999), 83–101.

De Haan, Ferdinand, 'Encoding Speaker Perspective: Evidentials', in F. ZYGMUNT, A. HODGES and D. R. ROOD, eds, *Linguistic Diversity and Language Theories* (Amsterdam: John Benjamins, 2005), 379–397.

Demonte, Violeta, and Olga Fernández-Soriano, 'La periferia izquierda oracional y los complementantes del español', in Juan Cuartero and Martine Emsel, eds, *Vernetzungen, Kognition, Bedeutung (kontrastive) Pragmatik* (Frankfurt: Peter Lang, 2007), 133–145.

Demonte, Violeta, and Olga Fernández-Soriano, 'El "que" citativo, otros "que" de la periferia izquierda oracional y la recomplementación', in Daniel Jacob and Katja Plooj, *eds, Autour de 'que'. El entorno de que* (Frankfurt: Peter Lang, 2013a), 47–69.

Dendale, Patrik, and Liliane Tasmowsky, 'Introduction: Evidentiality and Related Notions', *Journal of Pragmatics* 33 (2001), 339–348.

Ducrot, Oswald, 'Operateurs argumentatifs et visée argumentative', *Cahiers de Linguistique Française*, 5 (1983), 7–36.

Ducrot, Oswald, 'Esbozo de una teoría polifónica de la enunciación', in Oswald Ducrot, ed., *El decir y lo dicho* (Barcelona: Paidós Ibérica, 1999 [1984]), 175–239.

Ducrot, Oswald, *El decir y lo dicho* (Barcelona: Paidós, 1999 [1984]).

Escandell, Victoria, 'Los enunciados interrogativos. Aspectos semánticos y pragmáticos', in Ignacio Bosque and Violeta Demonte (eds), *Gramática descriptiva de la lengua española* III (Madrid: Espasa-Calpe, 1999), 3929–3992.

Escandell, Victoria, 'Futuro y evidencialidad', *Anuario de Lingüística Hispánica*, 26 (2010), 9–34.

Etxepare, Ricardo, 'From Hearsay Evidentiality to Samesaying Relations', *Lingua* 120 (2010), 604–627.

Fox, Barbara A., 'Evidentiality: Authority, Responsibility, and Entitlement in English Conversation', *Journal of Linguistic Anthropology* 11/2 (2011), 167–192.

García Negroni, María Marta, 'Polifonía, evidencialidad citativa y tiempos verbales. Acerca de los usos citativos del futuro morfológico y del futuro perifrástico', en Ramón González Ruiz, Dámaso Izquierdo Alegría y Óscar Loureda Lamas, eds, *La evidencialidad en español: teoría y descripción* (Frankfurt am Main: Iberoamericana Vervuert, 2016). 279–301.

González Ramos, Elisa, '*Por lo visto* y *al parecer*: evidencialidad y restricción del compromiso epistémico con la verdad del contenido enunciado', en Ramón González

Ruiz, Dámaso Izquierdo Alegría y Óscar Loureda Lamas eds, *La evidencialidad en español: teoría y descripción* (Frankfurt am Main: Iberoamericana Vervuert, 2016), 129–152.

González Ruiz, Ramón, Dámaso Izquierdo Alegría and Óscar Loureda Lamas, eds, *La evidencialidad en español: teoría y descripción* (Frankfurt am Main: Iberoamericana Vervuert, 2016)

González Vázquez, Mercedes, 'La naturaleza y función de la evidencialidad en español', en Ramón González Ruiz, Dámaso Izquierdo Alegría y Óscar Loureda Lamas eds, *La evidencialidad en español: teoría y descripción* (Frankfurt am Main: Iberoamericana Vervuert, 2016), 49–74.

Gras, Pedro, 'Entre la gramática y el discurso: valores conectivos de *que* inicial átono en español', in Daniel Jacob and Katja Plooj, eds, *Autour de 'que'. El entorno de* que (Frankfurt: Peter Lang, 2013), 89–112.

Gras, Pedro, 'Entre la codificación y la inferencia. Los valores citativos del que inicial átono en español', in Ramón González Ruiz, Dámaso Izquierdo Alegría and Óscar Loureda Lamas, eds, *La evidencialidad en español: teoría y descripción* (Madrid: Vervuert/Iberoamericana, 2016), 201–223.

Ifantidou, Elly, *Evidentials and Relevance* (Amsterdam/Philadelphia, PA: John Benjamins, 2001).

Lazard, Gilbert, 'Mirativity, Evidentiality, Mediativity, or Other?', *Linguistic Typology*, 3 (1999), 91–109.

Lazard, Gilbert, 'On the Grammaticalization of Evidentiality', *Journal of Pragmatics* 33 (2001), 359–367.

Leonetti, Manuel, and María Victoria Escandell, 'On the quotative reading of the Spanish Imperfecto', *Cuadernos de Lingüística*, 10 (2003), 135–154

Levinson, Stephen C., *Significados presumibles. La teoría de la implicatura conversacional generalizada* (Madrid: Gredos, 2004 [2000]).

Martín Zorraquino, María Antonia, 'Sobre la gramaticalización de *desde luego*', in A. Englebert et al., eds, *Les nouvelles ambitions de la linguistique diacronique. Actes du XXème Congrès International de Linguistique et Philologie Romanes III* (Tubinga: M. Niemeyer, 2011a), 307–317.

Martín Zorraquino, María Antonia, 'De nuevo sobre la gramaticalización de *desde luego*', in Ana María Cestero Mancera, Isabel Molina Martos, Florentino Paredes García, eds, *La lengua, lugar de encuentro: Proceedings of the XVI International Congress of the Asociación de Lingüística y Filología de América Latina* (2011b), 605–610.

Martín Zorraquino, María Antonia, 'La polifonía en algunos signos adverbiales disjuntos que matizan la aserción en español actual (*desde luego* y *sin duda; por lo visto* y *al parecer*)', in Paul Gévaudan, Vahram Atayan and Ulrich Detges, eds, *Modalität und Polyphonie / Modalité et polyphonie / Modalidad y polifonía* (Tubinga: Stauffenburg Verlag, 2013), 100–126.

Murillo, Silvia, 'Sobre la reformulación y sus marcadores. On reformulation and its markers', *AISPI (2016)*.

Nucholls, Janis, and Lev Michael, eds, *Evidentials in Interaction* (Amsterdam/Philadelphia, PA: John Benjamins, 2014).

Nuyts, Jan, 'Subjectivity as an Evidential Dimension in Epistemic Modal Expressions', *Journal of Pragmatics* 33 (2001), 383–400.

Nuyts, Jan, 'The Modal Confusion: On Terminology and the Concepts Behind it', in A. Klinge and H. Høeg Müller, eds, *Modality. Studies in Form and Function (*London/Oakville, CT: Equinox, 2005), 5–38.

Nuyts, Jan, 'Modality: Overview and Linguistic Issues', in Wolfgang Klein et al. eds, *The Expression of Modality* (Berlín: Walter de Gruyter, 2006), 1–26.

Palmer, Ferdinand, *Mood and Modality* (Cambridge: Cambridge University Press, 1986).

Plungian, Vladimir, 'The Place of Evidentiality within the Universal Gramatical Space', *Journal of Pragmatics* 33 (2001), 349–357.

Pons Bordería, Salvador, 'Que inicial átono como marca de modalidad', *ELUA* 17 (2003), 531–545.

Pons Bordería, Salvador, 'Un solo tipo de reformulación', *Cuadernos AISPI* 2 (2013), 151–170.

Porroche Ballesteros, Margarita, 'Algunos aspectos del uso de *que* en el español conversacional (*que* como introductor de oraciones "independientes")', *CLAC* 3(2000), 100–116.

Porroche Ballesteros, Margarita, 'Aspectos discursivos en el uso de algunas conjunciones españolas', *Oralia* 6 (2003), 259–282.

Reyes, Graciela, *Los procedimientos de cita: citas encubiertas y ecos* (Madrid: Arco/Libros, 1996 [1994]).

Rodríguez Ramalle, Teresa María, 'Estudio sintáctico y discursivo de algunas estructuras enunciativas y citativas del español', *RESLA* 21 (2008a), 269–288.

Rodríguez Ramalle, Teresa María, 'El valor de las marcas enunciativas en la configuración del discurso en el ámbito de las lenguas romances' (2008b).

Rodríguez Ramalle, Teresa María, '*Así que* y *así pues*: la función de la conjunción *que*, los rasgos de manera y la referencia anafórica', in Margarita Borreguero and Sonia Gómez-Jordana, eds, *Marqueurs du discours dans les langues romanes: une approche contrastive* (Limoges: Lambert Lucas, 2010), 210–224.

Rodríguez Ramalle, Teresa María, 'Notas para un estudio comparado de la evidencialidad', *Revista Española de Lingüística* 43/1 (2013), 171–196.

Rodríguez Ramalle, Teresa María, 'Sobre marcadores y su relación con la modalidad evidencial', in Marta García Negroni, ed., *Marcadores del discurso. Perspectivas y contrastes* (Buenos Aires/Santiago: Arcos Editor, 2014a), 233–250.

Rodríguez Ramalle, Teresa María, 'Una nueva reflexión en torno a los marcadores de reformulación con *que*', *Revista de Investigación Lingüística* 17 (2014b), 119–145.

Rodríguez Ramalle, Teresa María, 'Información contextual, estructura discursiva y modalidad evidencial en la selección de las locuciones consecutivas del español', *Spanish in Context* 12:1 (2015), 80–101.

Taranilla, Raquel, 'La noción de patrón discursivo y su utilidad en la descripción de los marcadores del verbo *parecer*', in Margarita Borreguero and Sonia Gómez-Jordana, eds, *Marqueurs du discours dans les langues romanes: une approche contrastive* (Limoges: Lambert Lucas, 2010), 233–248.

Torner, S., 'Los adverbios evidenciales en español', in Ramón González Ruiz, Dámaso Izquierdo Alegría and Óscar Loureda Lamas, eds, *La evidencialidad en español: teoría y descripción* (Madrid: Vervuert/Iberoamericana, 2016), 251–276.

Tournadre, Nicolas, 'Comparaison des systèmes médiatifs de quatre dialectes tibétains (tibétain central, ladakhi, dzonkha et amdo)', in Zlatka Guentchéva, ed., *L'énonciation médiatisée* (Paris: Peeters, 1996), 195–213.

Willett, Thomas, 'A Cross-Linguistic Survey of the Grammaticalization of Evidentiality', *Studies in Language* 12 (1988), 57–91.

ELISA NARVÁEZ GARCÍA AND LOURDES TORRES

2 Processing causality in Spanish-speaking L2 English: An experimental approach to the study of *therefore*

Introduction[1]

Causal relations have been recognized to be among the most significant relations in the world (Mackie 1974; Kamlah 1991). Wilson and Sperber considered these relations to be 'highly relevant' and, therefore, to be expected that the mere juxtaposition of propositions is sometimes sufficient to interpret them as causally related (2012: 183, see 1).

(1) Peter left. Mary got angry.

(Taken from Wilson and Sperber 2012: 169)

An utterance such as (1) will very likely be interpreted not only as an addition/temporal relation, that is, readers will not only conceive them as two isolated facts in a timeline: 1) Peter left and 2) Mary got angry. Most likely they will see in Peter's departure the reason behind Mary's anger; in other words, they will causally link the two facts. This interpretation is known as *implicit causality*. It can be explained by the *Causality-by-Default hypothesis* proposed by Sanders (2005). According to this hypothesis, aiming at building the most informative representation possible, readers assume by default that discourse coherence is causal, and only consider other kinds of coherence relations when a causal reading is not possible (Sanders 2005).

1 We would like to express our gratitude to Prof. Dr. Óscar Loureda Lamas, chief of our research group *Diskurspartikeln und Kognition*. His comments and suggestions on previous versions of this article have led to many improvements. Needless to say, any remaining shortcomings and errors are solely the authors' responsibility.

Besides simple juxtaposition, in which case the causal interpretation will rely exclusively on the nature of the uttered propositions in combination with the context and the receiver's world knowledge (Keenan et al. 1984; Myers et al. 1987; Foucart et al. 2016), speakers have at their disposal a wide range of linguistic means to explicitly express causal relations (Degand 1996), that is to causally link two propositions.

Among the linguistic devices available to explicitly express causation, natural languages offer connectives, prepositions, verbs, nouns, cue phrases and signalling phrases. The present study addresses causality expressed through connectives. The forward causal connective *therefore* was studied in order to determine its effect on language processing in Spanish-speaking L2 English. A self-paced reading experiment was designed for this study. Two independent variables were tested: explicitness and pragmatic plausibility of the causal relation. A total of 80 college students read the texts while their eyes were monitored by an eye-tracker. To analyse the data, three dependent variables were taken into consideration: i) total reading time, ii) first-pass reading time, and iii) second-pass reading time. In the case of plausible and implausible utterances, no remarkable difference was registered between explicit and implicit causality, explicit causality being slightly easier to process.

This paper is structured in five sections: the section after this introduction provides a brief overview of the studies on causal relations and the processing of these relations which served as theoretical background to this research. The following section is structured in five sub-sections dedicated to the description of the dependent variables, experimental design, participants, materials and procedure. Results are presented and discussed in the fourth section. Finally, the last section summarizes the main conclusions of this study.

Connectives and causal connectives

Language has fundamentally an argumentative function (Anscombre and Ducrot 1983). Connectives are one-word items or fixed-word combinations that embody a procedural meaning (Blakemore 1987, Pander Maat and Sanders 2006). They indicate how a segment is relevant to its context (Pander Maat and Sanders 2006: 130), and by doing so, they mark the argumentative orientation of discourse (Portolés 1993) and provide instructions on how information should be processed (inferential process, cf. Sperber 1994; Sperber and Wilson 1995, 2002; Wilson and Sperber 2002; Wilson 2003; Pons 2004; Portolés 2004).

An essential property of connectives is their rigidity (Escandell and Leonetti 2011:81). That is, they impose a particular reading of the concepts they connect (Loureda et al. 2016a:59). Unlike the conceptual words, connectives cannot be adjusted to fit their context. In this sense, their relation with the words they coerce is asymmetric (Escandell and Leonetti 2011).

Causal connectives express the linearity of the relation they point out. They indicate where in speech the cause and its effect, or the evidence and the conclusion extracted from it, are placed. *Therefore* is a forward direction connective. This means that it introduces the drawn conclusion and its premise in the same order they occur, so that the evidence precedes its conclusion (Canestrelli et al. 2012).

(2) It has rained. Therefore, fields are wet. (premise → conclusion)
(3) The fields are wet. Therefore, it has rained.
(Taken/adapted from Sanders and Spooren 2015: 54)

Therefore compels a forward causal relation. It introduces a conclusion derived from the speaker's reasoning. Having inversed the order of the segments linked through it, the interpretations of (2) and (3) are diametrically opposed. In (2), the speaker concludes that the fields must be wet because it has rained; while in (3), the observation of the wet state of the fields is an evidence for the speaker's conclusion that it has rained. In (2), the speaker knows that it has rained, in (3) that the fields are wet.

Causal connectives and the processing of causal discourse relations

Causal discourse relations are essential in language processing and comprehension (Noordman and de Blijzer 2000; Pander Maat and Sanders 2000). As functional words encoding an instruction, causal connectives trigger a causal reading of the utterances they link. However, they are neither sufficient (4) nor indispensable (5) for expressing causal discourse relations.

(4) John ate a banana. Therefore, the hair of the dog is a drink to counteract a hangover.
(5) Mr Smith was killed the other night. The steering on the car was faulty.
(Taken/adapted from Sanford 2006: 87)

The presence of the connective *therefore* does not guarantee a successful causal reading of the utterance (4). This is because, in order for a causal interpretation to be possible, the reader must be able to connect what is being said with his/her world knowledge (Sanford 2006). Needless to say, there is no way that the fact that John ate a banana might cause the hair of the dog to be a drink to counteract a hangover. The connective will indeed prompt a causal reading of the utterance, but it will have to be rejected when confronted with the reader's knowledge of the world. The causal reading might prevail, but the utterance will be considered implausible. The connectives' impossibility to adjust themselves to their context shows the rigidity of their procedural meaning (Escandell and Leonetti 2011). Another example of implicit causality is found in (5), as previously discussed. Any reader could easily infer that the faulty steering was to some extent the cause behind Mr Smith's death.

Causally related sentences are more easily processed than any other kind of coherence relation, as is demonstrated by the fact that they are read faster (Haberlandt 1982; Millis and Just 1994), more effectively remembered and better understood (Black and Bern 1981; Caron et al. 1988;). Numerous research efforts have been devoted to investigating the impact of causal connectives on processing. However, there seems to be no consensus on this matter (Degand and Sanders 2002: 740). While for some scholars (Haberlandt 1982; Millis and Just 1994; Mouchon et al. 1995; Sanford 2006; Cain and Nash 2011), clauses appear to be even more stable and better remembered when they are coherently linked by causal connectives, for others (Meyer 1975; Sanders and Noordman 2000), they have no impact, or rather a negative effect on the processing of information (Millis et al. 1993). These differences might be due to flaws in the experimental designs.

The nature of the causal relation is not the only factor in determining the processing cost of causal relations; the characteristics of the reader also seem to matter, although their actual impact on information processing is controversial. Some studies refute the importance of these characteristics, suggesting that causal connectives have an equal impact in skilled and unskilled readers (Irwin 1980; Degand and Sanders 2002); some others confirmed it, either postulating that their positive effect is more visible in less skilled readers (Irwin 1980; van Silfhout et al. 2014), or that only skilled readers benefit with the presence of these connectives (Goldman and Murray 1992; Cooper 1984).

Degand and Sanders' (2002) study with L2 failed to demonstrate that the impact of causal connectives was higher in L2 readers than in L1 readers, but they did assert that the presence of these devices is advantageous for both L1 and L2. They concluded that their results could be due to the level of proficiency of the subjects, which might have been 'high enough to understand the general functions of the signals and their usage conditions' (p. 753). In the same vein, Irwin (1980) compared the performances of fifth grade and college-level students when reading backward and forward, explicit and implicit causality. In the case of presence of the connectives, the first group benefited more than the second. By marking the coherence relation, connectives turn the segments they link into more comprehensible texts. Skilled readers are more able to infer these relations than unskilled readers, and, therefore, the positive effect of these devices is less evident in them (Irwin 1980; van Silfhout et al. 2014).

Low language proficiency reduces the impact of connectives in processing (Cooper 1984; Goldman and Murray 1992). It is natural that in order to exercise influence over the utterances' processing costs, the readers must be aware of the meaning of the connectives linking them. According to Goldman and Murray's (1992) and Cooper's (1984) results, this is not always the case. In this sense, they signalled that L2 low language proficiency prevents the readers from recognizing these devices and their functions in text coherence, and therefore do not benefit from their presence in texts. Skilled readers who are familiar with their meaning and functions do, as a result, benefit from explicit causality.

Studies on language production in English have pointed out that connectives constitute an 'area of difficulty' in language acquisition even for advanced learners (Crewe 1990; Granger and Tyson 1996; Narita et al. 2004). Some studies on online processing in different languages (Universiteit Utrecht 2012–2014), linguistic backgrounds (Degand and Sanders 2002; Zufferey, et al. 2015) and kinds of coherence relations (Zufferey et al. 2015) have detected, however, no substantial differences in the reading performances of advanced learners and native speakers. That is why we set out to study the performance of upper intermediate L2 English readers. Specifically, we have studied the Spanish-speaking English-learners' processing of forward causal relations. Our core goal is to contribute to the understanding of how learners process these relations by examining a group with a linguistic background that has not yet been studied. Accordingly, the main objective of our research is to verify experimentally in Spanish-speaking L2 English the procedural meaning of the connective *therefore* and its role as guide to understanding utterances by imposing a certain information structure.

Methodology

Outputs of the eye-tracking methodology include an online control of the ongoing cognitive processes that take place during complex information processing tasks such as reading, and measurement of the reader's cognitive effort (Irrazábal and Molinari 2005; Richardson et al. 2007).

Reading is not a straightforward linear movement. Our eyes move across the line in an alternating pattern of quick jumps called *saccades* and periods of relative stillness known as *fixations*. Only during fixations new information is acquired from text and it is widely assumed that fixation time reflects the load of cognitive processing (Rayner 1998).

In our eye-tracking reading experiment, fixations are taken as the principal metric of processing effort (Rayner 2009) and processing costs are analysed here in three dependent variables: total reading time, first-pass reading time and second-pass reading time. Total reading time (TRT) is the sum of all fixations made within a critical region or area of interest (AOI), including those fixations during the first reading and all re-readings. First-pass reading time is the summed fixation time on a region before leaving it, either to the left or to the right. Second-pass reading time is the sum of all fixations on a region or AOI after being already fixated during initial reading. The distinction between first and second reading correlates to the time required for the construction of an initial assumption derived from an utterance ostensively communicated and the processing effort needed for the reconstruction or confirmation of the initially constructed assumption, respectively (Nadal et al. 2017). All types of linguistic information are therefore processed according to a near-simultaneously processing model (Pulvermüller et al. 2009), under which access to lexical, semantic, syntactic and pragmatic information takes place in parallel (Escandell 2005; Egorova et al. 2013).

Participants

Eye movement behaviour was recorded for 80 participants with the same profile. All of them were Costa Rican native speakers of Spanish with an upper intermediate proficiency in English as a foreign language, had completed some form of higher education and were between 18 and 30 years old. An initial language test[2] was administered to all participants in order to assess their appropriate English knowledge.

2 Only participants who reached a score between 60 and 80% – evidence of an upper intermediate proficiency – proceeded to read the self-paced experiment. To assess their English proficiency, they were asked to take the online English test *LexTALE* (Lexical Test for Advanced Learners of English), a quick lexical recognition test of English as L2 which measures both vocabulary knowledge and language proficiency. In the study conducted by Zufferey et al. (2015) on English advanced learners, L2 proficiency was assessed with two different measures: LexTALE and the self-assessment questionnaire LEAP-Q2007, a reliable indicator of global language performance (Marian et al. 2007). As the results provided by each evaluation method yielded a

Materials and design

Sixteen experimental utterances were created specifically for the present study. Each one consists of two discourse members linked (or not) by the connective *therefore*, follows an affirmative SVO pattern with a plural subject and has a verb conjugated in the simple present tense. Words in the utterance have approximately the same number of letters and cover a variety of topics.[3] Following Clifton et al.'s recommendations (2007), the frequency and familiarity of the words in the experimental items have been controlled. Similarly, all words lack polysemy, have a simple morphology and belong to Standard English. As readers tend to fixate longer sentence-final words (Just and Carpenter 1980; Rayner et al. 1989; Rayner et al. 2000), a third segment was included after the critical utterance to avoid wrap-up effects.[4]

(6) Benjamin and Jacqueline take fast trains.[S1] T[herefore, t]hey save time.[S2] The university pays for the tickets.[S3]

All experimental items were divided into four counterbalanced lists using a Latin square design, so that each material list contained four critical items (each one in a different experimental condition and topic). Each stimulus was preceded by a contextualization consisted of a picture, a short presentation and a filler utterance. In addition, a fixation cross in a blank screen was set before each target utterance to avoid uncertainty about the eye location in first fixations. Stimuli were interspersed with filler items with a 1:2 ratio to control for order effects, such as fatigue or practice with the task. They were also alternated with distractors (critical items from other experiments) to prevent readers from becoming aware of the aim of the study. Each critical

very similar proficiency level for participants, LexTALE was the only tool to estimate the English level of our participants.

3 All the topics and stimuli used in the present study are presented in the Appendix at the end of the chapter.

4 The term of *wrap-up effects* was introduced by Just and Carpenter (1980) to describe an increase in reading times at the end of a clause due to semantic integration processes taking at this point.

item was wrapped up in short stories[5] that were presented pseudorandomly to ensure that target items from the same condition would not be presented sequentially within lists and that materials were counterbalanced (Cowart 1997; Gries 2013) across participants.[6]

The experiment is a 2×2 factorial design. Each level of one independent variable is paired with each level of the other variable to obtain all possible experimental conditions (2 x 2 = 4), which in turn determines the number of material lists required. The independent variables tested in the study are (1) explicitness in the conditions (a) explicit and (b) implicit, and (2) plausibility in the two conditions (a) plausible and (b) implausible. Critical items in the following experimental conditions were read by all the participants:

Table 2.1. Experimental conditions and example items from topic A

Experimental conditions	Stimuli in experiment
1. (1a2a) explicit/plausible causal relation	*Benjamin and Jacqueline take fast trains. Therefore, they save time.*
2. (1b2a) implicit/plausible causal relation	*Benjamin and Jacqueline take fast trains. They save time.*
3. (1a2b) explicit/implausible causal relation	*Benjamin and Jacqueline take slow trains. Therefore, they save time.*
4. (1b2b) implicit/implausible causal relation	*Benjamin and Jacqueline take slow trains. They save time.*

Reading time values per word for the whole utterance (U) and for each area of interest (AOI) were calculated from the total processing times. The

5 Stimuli were wrapped up in short stories made of five slides. The first one introduced the protagonists with a picture and a presentation (e.g. *Benjamin and Jacqueline are English professors in Berlin and Hamburg*). It was followed by a filler item (*They live in Hamburg. Their house is very close to the Central Train Station*). The third slide was a blank screen with a fixation cross; the fourth contained the critical item and the last slide presented a new filler sentence (*Hamburg is not that far from Berlin, but it takes them almost two hours to get there*).

6 To keep the participant's attention, questions about the stories were inserted after 25% of the trials. The possible answers were 'Yes', 'No' and 'I don't know' and were selected via eye gaze.

analysed AOIs were the connective (C), the first discourse segment (DS1), and the second discourse member (DS2). All AOIs are shown in (9).

(7) a. [Benjamin and Jacqueline take fast trains. Therefore, they save time.][U]
b. [Benjamin and Jacqueline take fast trains.][DS1] [Therefore,][C] [they save time.][DS2]
c. [Benjamin and Jacqueline take fast trains. They save time.][U]
d. [Benjamin and Jacqueline take fast trains.][DS1] [They save time.][DS2]

Data collection

Data was recorded by means of a RED 500 eye-tracking system by SMI (Sensomotoric Instruments). The eye-tracker device was mounted directly below a computer screen placed on a desktop. Participants were seated at a distance of approximately 65–70 cm away from it.

The present English self-paced reading experiment was combined with a similar Spanish study. Prior to any experiment, all participants were asked to take the online English test. Participants undertook the Spanish experiment first. They read the instructions displayed on the monitor and performed an initial calibration. Some trial utterances were also shown to familiarize them with the task. After finishing the first experiment, those participants with the required L2 knowledge performed the English one. They were notified by a message on screen about the new self-paced test. As they had already read the instructions, they were only presented with a few slides in their L2 to become familiarized with the new language. No time constraint was imposed for the self-pace reading, and participants completed it in less than 10 minutes.

Data treatment and analyses

Gathered data were analysed by linear mixed-effects models using the R software (R Core Team 2014) with *mgcv* package (Wood 2011). Linear mixed-effects models allow performing analyses that account for missing values and correlation structure using both fixed and random effects. In accordance with the recent statistical suggestions, p-value is not given in the present study, since it does not measure the magnitude of the difference found between two groups subject to comparison (Clark 2004). Instead, estimation was used to interpret our results in terms of size and relevance. When designing the study, we established the minimum magnitude of the difference that is considered relevant as > 5% (Argimon 2002, Gómez 2016).[7] The AOIs of each condition were considered fixed effects, while participants and lists were included as random effects. Three models were computed for every dependent variable: total reading time, first-pass reading time and second-pass reading time. Outliers and extreme values were identified and discarded if: a) the first-pass reading time was 0 for any AOI, except the connective itself (first skip); b) both the first and the second-pass reading times for the AOI average utterance word were lower than 80 ms per word (fast readers, cf. Pickering et al. 2000); and c) the total reading time for an average utterance word was higher than 800 ms per word (slow readers, cf. Recio, Nadal and Loureda forthcoming). In the experiment, 19 out of 344 observations were considered outliers and deleted.

Results and discussion

From the point of view of its meaning, the connective *therefore* does not generate a causal relation; it only makes it explicit. In order to produce a coherent utterance, the discursive members linked by this connective must be argumentatively co-oriented through the lexical content of the words that comprise them, so that the first segment leads to the consequence expressed in the second. Considering this, three hypotheses were set for this research and, accordingly, three models were designed to test them. This subsection deals with these models and includes a discussion, as well as an interpretation of the

7 The scale values used to quantify the magnitude of the differences found are given as follows: 20% (very large effects), 10–19.99% (large effects), 5–9.99% (medium effects), <5% (trivial effects). Designations are adapted from Cohen's classification for effect sizes (cf. Cohen 1988).

results for each model. The first two subsections will cover the explicitness of the causal relation in the case of pragmatically plausible and implausible sentences. Thereafter, the effect of the connective in utterances with different kinds of plausibility will be reviewed. A general discussion introduces a fourth model, in which all the conditions were contrasted.

Model 1: Explicit and implicit, plausible causal relations

As the causal interpretation of pragmatically plausible utterances does not derive from the procedural instruction of *therefore*, but from the words comprising the segments it links, it was expected that the processing costs of plausible utterances in which the distinctive property is the explicitness of the causal relation would not show substantial differences. If there were differences, in accordance with Haberlandt's (1982) and Millis and Just's (1994) results, the processing costs for the explicit relation should be lower. Table 2.2 shows exactly that: there are trivial differences between the total reading time values of the considered AOIs in the analysed conditions. Even so, a very large difference between the processing values for the whole utterances (26.77%) indicates that processing is harder when the discourse relation between the segments they constitute is not specified.

Table 2.2. Total reading time values[8]

(Explicit and implicit pragmatically plausible causal relations)

	DS1: cause	connective *therefore*	DS2: consequence	whole utterance	conceptual meaning
condition 1: explicit	234.92	**628.5**	403.22	135.61	162.29
condition 2: implicit	237.76		420.81	**171.91**	**171.91**
difference	1.21%		4.36%	26.77%	5.93%

8 Data correspond to average processing time values per word (considering its number of letters) so that it is possible to compare the different AOIs. Since the number of letters was controlled when calculating the models, some estimated parameters of the reference categories became negative values. This does not mean errors in the model, nor in the data.

Table 2.2 also shows how the connective requires the highest cognitive effort. It guides the processing paths of the other areas, redistributing their processing costs. A trivial difference (1.21%) is found in the reading time values of DS1 in both conditions. These values are considerably lower than those computed for DS2 as a result of the difficulties that, with or without the connective, linking two segments embodies. Although the effect of the connective in the second segment is also considered trivial (4.36%), it should be noted that integrating the consequence segment seems to be slightly more difficult in the absence of the connective, as is evidenced by the higher values of DS2 in the implicit condition (420.81 vs 403.22). In a nutshell, processing the first and second members of a plausible explicit or implicit causal relation requires similar efforts. However, this does not mean that the connective plays no role. On the contrary, the distribution of the processing costs seems to be determined by its presence. It redistributes the cognitive efforts, easing the processing of the segment it introduces: the consequence member. Tables 2.3 and 2.4 show the impact of *therefore* in the first and second-pass times.

Table 2.3. First reading time values

(Explicit and implicit pragmatically plausible causal relations)

	DS1: cause	connective *therefore*	DS2: consequence	whole utterance	conceptual meaning
condition 1: explicit	133.46	**340.26**	189.01	186.13	173.19
condition 2: implicit	**152.99**		**293.11**	**204.16**	**204.16**
difference	14.63%		55.08%	9.69%	17.88%

In both cases, the connective seizes the highest reading time values. It is immediately striking that *therefore* inverts the strategy of information processing. Without its guidance, the integration of the second segment and the construction of the first assumption rely on the lexical and syntactic material, demanding much more effort than the analogous processes for the explicit causality (55.08%). Nevertheless, once the first assumption has been established, the second reading, that is, the confirmation of the established assumption, is much easier (204.16 vs −84.43, a decrease of 141.35%, see Tables 2.3 and 2.4). Conversely, the presence

Table 2.4. Second reading time values

(Explicit and implicit pragmatically plausible causal relations)

	DS1: cause	connective *therefore*	DS2: consequence	whole utterance	conceptual meaning
condition 1: explicit	**70.6**	**361.53**	**212.21**	−101.95	−147.39
condition 2: implicit	54.74		160.79	**−84.43**	**−84.43**
difference	22.46%		24.23%	17.18%	42.72%

of the connective signals the coherence relation and, as a result, eases the integration of the second segment and the construction of the first assumption. Yet this assumption must be confronted with the context and the reader's world knowledge in the second pass, which leads to a greater cognitive effort (189.01 vs 212.21, an increase of 12.27%, Tables 2.3 and 2.4).

These findings are mirrored by the results of Loureda et al.'s (2016b) study on the Spanish causal connective *por tanto*. They concluded that *por tanto* 'regulates the access strategy to the conventional implicature [...] and reverses the strategy of extracting the information' (p. 250).

Model 2: Explicit and implicit, implausible causal relations

By default, discourse coherence is expected to be causal and other kinds of coherence relations are only considered when a causal reading is not possible (Sanders 2005). That is what we hypothesized would happen in the case of an implicit, implausible causal relation: after reading the whole utterance, the readers would discard a causal connection and try to find an appropriate coherence relation to link the two segments. This process should be even more complex in the case of explicit, implausible causal relations. The presence of *therefore* strongly confirms a causal reading of the utterance before the subject has finished reading it. Once (s)he is past it, however, (s)he will have to discard the assumption that the connective had already confirmed and try to come to a new one,[9] which results in longer processing times. Although the differences are not relevant, if we consider the analysed AOIs, this is apparent in Table 2.5.

Table 2.5. Total reading time values

(Explicit and implicit pragmatically implausible causal relations)

	DS1: cause	connective *therefore*	DS2: consequence	whole utterance	conceptual meaning
condition 3: explicit	227.80	**771.05**	480.19	121.36	**144.36**
condition 4: implicit	217.12		475.89	**130.03**	130.03
difference	4.69%		0.01%	7.22%	9.93%

The global processing path of this model shares some similarities with the one that has been previously reviewed: 1) the processing cost of the connective is notably higher than any other AOI, 2) the differences between the DS1 and DS2's processing values are trivial, 3) processing time values of the second segment are higher than those of the first, and 4) utterances are harder to process when the discourse relation between the segments they constitute is not specified (7.22%); however, in this case, the effects are not as large as they were in the first model (7.22% vs 26.77%, Tables 2.5 and 2.2). There is, nevertheless, one important difference between these two models: in the case of implausible relations, the processing value of the conceptual meaning is 9.93% lower for the implicit causality. The mismatch between the connective's instruction and the reader's world knowledge triggers longer processing times, which stands out as an evidence for the rigidity of the procedural meaning that these devices embody (Escandell and Leonetti 2011). Tables 2.6 and 2.7 display the distribution of the processing effort in

9 The reader could insist on the causal reading and try to find a less straightforward causality, a more subjective one. *Benjamin and Jacqueline take slow trains. Therefore, they save time*, for instance, could be interpreted this way: long hours in the train allow Benjamin and Jacqueline to work during their trip and therefore save time.

the first and second-pass, respectively, where the difference between this model and model 1 is more clearly appreciated.

Table 2.6. First reading time values

(Explicit and implicit pragmatically implausible causal relations)

	DS1: cause	connective *therefore*	DS2: consequence	whole utterance	conceptual meaning
condition 3: explicit	113.28	**561.79**	**376.02**	9.06	**52.76**
condition 4: implicit	109.36		310.80	**24.48**	24.48
difference	3.46%		17.34%	170.20%	53.60%

Table 2.7. Second reading time values

(Explicit and implicit pragmatically implausible causal relations)

	DS1: cause	connective *therefore*	DS2: consequence	whole utterance	conceptual meaning
condition 3: explicit	**111.51**	**231.93**	116.79	82.56	76.38
condition 4: implicit	104.41		**177.28**	85.01	**85.01**
difference	6.37%		51.79%	2.97%	11.30%

In both the first and second reading-pass, the connective constitutes the peak of difficulty in the processing of the utterance. That is because, as was explained for the previous model, *therefore* assumes the leading role in the processing, inversing the reader's strategy of information extraction. The reader's strategy in the case of implausible relations seems to be opposite to his/her strategy to process plausible relations. Integrating the second segment of an implausible causal relation is very difficult without a connective guiding the construction of the first assumption, but it is 17.34% faster than when the instruction given by the connective does not match its context. Such large effects on the processing cost of this segment in the first reading are due to the reader's impossibility to accommodate the second member to the instruction given by the connective. It also affects the values of the conceptual meaning, which is 53.60% more difficult to process than its implicit counterpart. The reader will then revisit the causal clause to try to adjust it to the consequence segment, what results in a rise of the reading times for the first segment in the second pass. After verifying the instruction of the connective, the rigidity of its meaning will persuade the reader to stop trying to make sense out of the utterance. Without the connective, the reader pursues his/her attempt to build a coherent relation until the end of the utterance, hence the very large effects found in the processing values of the second segment (51.79%) favouring the processes of the explicit, implausible relation. This attempt also affects the conceptual meaning value, which is 11.30% higher.

Model 3: Plausible and implausible, explicit causal relations

The connective *therefore* confirms the reader's expectations of causal discourse coherence very quickly. After reading it, (s)he knows that what follows is the consequence or conclusion of what has been previously uttered and is ready to interpret it that way. In the case of implausibility, unable to establish a coherent relation at the end of the second segment, the reader will have to discard the inference that the connective had already confirmed and reread the sentence in order to try to make sense out of it. The complexity of this process – we expected – would increase the reading times of the utterance. Thus, we have conjectured that processing explicit, implausible causality should require greater efforts than processing explicit, plausible relations. The expected reading behaviour can be observed in Table 2.8: not only is it harder to process all the analysed AOIs in case of implausible causal relations, but also large effects are registered in the whole utterance values, implausible relations being 19% costlier.

Again, processing the connectives requires bigger efforts than any other AOI; with a medium difference (7.15%), this effort is higher in the case of implausible relations. In fact, our outcomes show that processing

Table 2.8. Total reading time values
(plausible and implausible, explicit causal relations)

	DS1: cause	connective *therefore*	DS2: consequence	whole utterance	conceptual meaning
condition 1: plausible	243.73	588.54	398.27	182.38	197.73
condition 3: implausible	**275.52**	**630.61**	417.22	**217.03**	**231.68**
difference	13.04%	7.15%	4.76%	19.00%	17.17%

implausible relations is, in general, more difficult. In different degrees, the AOIs on the 3rd condition are harder to process and, consequently, the whole utterance and their conceptual meaning values are, with large differences, greater (19% and 17.17%, respectively). The effects are also large on the cause segment (13.04%). This matches with what should be expected from the way coherence relations are built. As argumentative relations are established forwards (Anscombre and Ducrot 1983; Portolés 1993), it is expected that the second segment follows the argumentative direction set by the first one. In case of discrepancy, the reader goes back to the first member to verify the course it had determined before moving forwards. This step backwards entails cost overruns.[10] Tables 2.9 and 2.10 show the processing time values for plausible and implausible causal relations in the first and second-pass readings.

The data show large effects on the processing cost of the first segment in the analysed conditions (18.92%). The connective cannot, however, be credited for this difference, since it takes place before its appearance. There is also a large difference in the processing cost of the connective (12.44%), signalling again the implausible condition as harder to process. The effect of the connective is first appreciated in the DS2. In the case

10 This can also explain the fact that in the second model the effect of the connective is bigger on consequence segment. Whereas, in the first model, its effect is larger on the cause member. Again, when an utterance is implausible, the reader will go backwards to try to make sense out of the first segment. Conversely, when the utterance is plausible, the highest effort will be dedicated to integrate the second segment.

Table 2.9. First reading time values

(plausible and implausible, explicit causal relations)

	DS1: cause	connective *therefore*	DS2: consequence	whole utterance	conceptual meaning
condition 1: plausible	119.44	382.95	313.04	126.03	130.79
condition 3: implausible	**142.03**	**430.59**	305.01	**161.75**	**165.20**
difference	18.92%	12.44%	2.57%	28.34%	26.31%

Table 2.10. Second reading time values

(plausible and implausible, explicit causal relations)

	DS1: cause	connective *therefore*	DS2: consequence	whole utterance	conceptual meaning
condition 1: plausible	83.95	304.65	127.58	−19.58	**3.19**
condition 3: implausible	**92.87**	299.79	**156.54**	−20.08	1.35
difference	10.62%	1.59%	22.70%	2.52%	57.65%

of plausibility, it is possible to successfully integrate this segment, but naturally this operation requires more time. As a result, it is marginally harder (2.57%) to process this segment in this condition that in the case of implausibility. In the latter case, the reader will have to go back to the first segment to try to adjust its conceptual meaning to the given instruction. That is why, in the second reading pass, it is harder to process the first segment in this condition with a large difference (10.62%). Before giving up his/her attempt to build a coherent relation, the reader will try to accommodate the consequence segment to the connective's direction once more; hence, the processing of this implausible segment also takes longer. Confirming the first assumption established in the case of plausibility does not require considerable efforts. In fact, there is a very large difference (22.70%) that indicates it is easier to process a coherent consequence than an incoherent one.

Conclusions

In the light of these results, some general conclusions can be drawn about the processing of causal relations and the effect of causal connectives: 1) the connective not only always demands the higher processing efforts, but also regulates the processing of the other areas (Tables 2.2–2.11); 2) explicit causality is read faster than implicit causality (Tables 2.2–2.7 and Figure 2.1); 3) plausible relations are easier to process than implausible relations (Tables 2.2–2.10 and Figure 2.1); and 4) the effect of the connective is bigger in case of implausibility (see the conceptual meaning values in Tables 2.2, 2.5 and 2.8).

With the sole exception of the last claim, these conclusions were also confirmed on a fourth model that was developed to compare the processing costs of all the analysed conditions simultaneously. These general results are shown in two tables and a figure below. Table 2.11 presents the media value of all the considered AOIs in all the conditions, while Figure 2.1 and Table 2.12 offer a general picture of the total reading time values for all the tested conditions.

Table 2.11. All the conditions' AOIs

	DS1: cause	connective *therefore*	DS2: consequence
first-pass	175.44	**375.80**	263.77
second-pass	84.31	**294.51**	137.11
total reading time	229.89	**779.00**	435.47

As has been shown, the connective leads the processing of the whole utterance and, therefore, constitutes its highest point of difficulty (Table 2.11). We also observe in the table above that integrating the second segment of an utterance is in general more effort demanding, which is in accordance with Portoles' (1993) claim that argumentative relations are established forwards. More eloquent are perhaps the figure and table below based on the total reading time values. They offer a panoramic view of the difficulty

(Figure 2.1) and the difference in the degree of difficulty (Table 2.12) of processing all the analysed conditions.

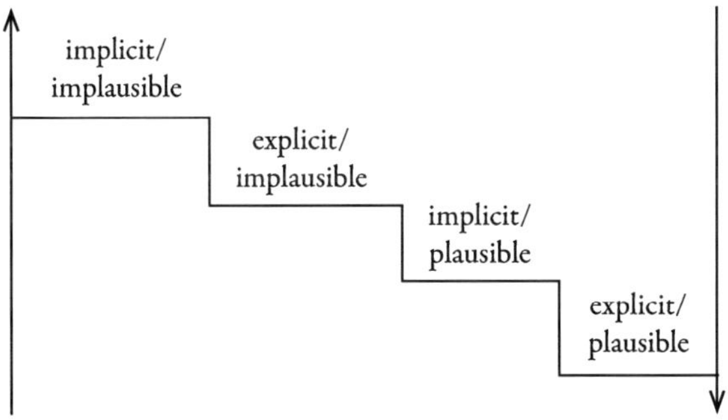

Figure 2.1. Scale of difficulty

Table 2.12. Differences in the total reading time values of the analysed conditions

implicit/ implausible	143.27			
explicit/ implausible	5.53%	135.76		
implicit/ plausible	11.07%	5.25%	128.99	
explicit/ plausible	42.47%	35.00%	28.27%	100.56
	implicit/ implausible	explicit/ implausible	implicit/ plausible	explicit/ plausible

Figure 2.1 is the graphic representation of conclusions 2 and 3 offered above. It shows that processing the explicit, plausible condition requires less effort than processing the implicit, plausible one. These relations, in turn, are more straightforwardly processed than implausible, explicit causality. The peak of difficulty is represented by the processing of implicit, implausible relations, where the reader is left with no guidance as to how to make sense out of an incoherent sentence. These utterances are in fact 42% more difficult to process than the explicit, plausible relations, the trough of difficulty in the scale. It is worth mentioning that the positive effect of the presence of the connective is very large in the case of plausibility (28.27%), while there is only a medium difference between the explicit and implicit implausible

conditions (5.53%). Implicit, plausible causality is only 5.25% and 11.07% easier to process than explicit and implicit, implausible relations. This brings it closer to implausibility than to the explicit plausible causality.

Bibliography

Anscombre, Jean-Claude, and Oswald Ducrot, *L'argumentation dans la langue* (Bruxelles: Pierre Mardaga, 1983).

Argimon, Josep M., 'El intervalo de confianza: algo más que un valor de significación estadística', *Med Clin* 118 (2002), 382–384.

Black, John B., and Hyman Bern, 'Causal Coherence and Memory for Events in Narratives', *Journal of Verbal Learning and Verbal Behavior* 20 (1981), 267–275.

Blakemore, Diane, *Semantic Constraints on Relevance* (Oxford: Blackwell, 1987).

Canestrelli, Anneloes R., Willem M. Mak and Ted Sanders, 'Causal Connectives in Discourse Processing: How Differences in Subjectivity are Reflected in Eye Movements', *Language and Cognitive Processes* 28/9 (2012), 1394–413.

Caron, Jean, Hans Christoph Micko and Manfred Thüring, 'Conjunctions and the Recall of Composite Sentences', *Journal of Memory and Language* 27 (1988), 309–323.

Clark, María Luisa, 'Los valores P y los intervalos de confianza: ¿en qué confiar?', *Revista Panamericana de Salud Pública* 15(5) (2004), 293–296.

Clifton, C., Adrian Staub and Rayner Keith, 'Eye movements in reading words and sentences', in Roger P. G. van Gompel, Martin H. Fischer, Wayne S. Murray and Robin L. Hill, eds, *Eye Movements: A Window on Mind and Brain* (Amsterdam: Elsevier, 2007), 341–371.

Cohen, Jacob, *Statistical Power Analysis for the Behavioural Sciences* (Hillsdale, NJ: Erlbaum Associates, 1988).

Cooper, Malcolm, 'Linguistic competence of practical and unpractical non-native readers in English', in J. Charles Alderson and A. H. Urquhart, eds, *Reading in a Foreign Language* (London: Longman Group Limited, 1984), 122–125.

Cowart, Wayne, *Experimental Syntax: Applying Objective Methods to Sentence Judgments* (London: Sage Publications, 1997).

Crewe, William, 'The Illogic of Logical Connectives', *ELT Journal* 44 (1990), 316–325.

Degand, Liesbeth, *A Situation-Based Approach to Causation in Dutch with Some Implications for Text Generation* (PhD thesis, Université Catholique de Louvain, 1996).

Degand, Liesbeth, and Ted Sanders, 'The Impact of Relational Markers on Expository Text Comprehension in L1 and L2', *Reading and Writing: An Interdisciplinary Journal* 15 (2002), 739–757.

Egorova, Natalia, Yury Shtyrov and Friedemann Pulvermüller, 'Early and Parallel Processing of Pragmatic and Semantic Information in Speech Acts: Neurophysiological Evidence', *Frontiers in Human Neuroscience* 7 (86) (2013), 1–13.

Escandell-Vidal, Victoria, *La comunicación* (Madrid: Gredos, 2005).

Escandell-Vidal, Victoria, and Manuel Leonetti, 'On the Rigidity of Procedural Meaning', in Victoria Escandell-Vidal, Manuel Leonetti and Aoife Ahern, eds, *Procedural Meaning: Problems and Perspectives* (Bingley: Emerald Group Publishing, 2011), 81–103.

Foucart, Alice, Carlos Romero-Rivas, Bernharda Lottie Gort, and Albert Costa, 'Discourse Comprehension in L2: Making Sense of What is Not Explicitly Said', *Brain and Language* 163/Supplement C (2016), 32–41.

Goldman, Susan R., and John D. Murray., 'Knowledge of Connectors as Cohesion Devices in Text: A Comparative Study of Native-English and English-as-a-Second Language Speakers', *Journal of Educational Psychology* 84 (4) (1992), 504–519.

Gómez, José, *Educational Research in Higher Education. Methods and Experiences* (Aalborg: River Publishers 2016).

Granger, Sylviane, and Stephanie Tyson, 'Connector Usage in the English Essay Writing of Native and Non-native EFL Speakers of English', *World Englishes* 15 (1996), 19–29.

Gries, Stefan Th., *Statistics for Linguistics with R. A Practical Introduction* (Berlin and Boston, MA: De Gruyter Mouton, 2013).

Haberlandt, Karl, 'Reader expectations in Text Comprehension', in Jean-François Le Ny and Walter Kintsch, eds, *Language and Comprehension* (Amsterdam: North-Holland Publishing, 1982), 239–249.

Irrazábal, Natalia, and Carlos Molinari Marotto, 'Técnicas experimentales en la investigación de la comprensión del lenguaje', *Revista Latinoamericana de Psicología* 37/3 (2005), 581–594.

Irwin, J. W., 'The Effects of Explicitness and Clause Order on the Comprehension of Reversible Causal Relationships', *Reading Research Quarterly* 15 (1980), 477–488.

Just, Marcel Adam, and Patricia A. Carpenter, 'A theory of Reading: From Eye Fixations to Comprehension', *Psychological Review* 87 (1980), 329–354.

Kamlah, Andreas, 'The Causal Relation as the most Fundamental Fact of the World. Comments on Hans Reichenbach's Paper: the Space Problem in the New Quantum Mechanics', *Erkenntnis* 35 (1991), 49–60.

Keenan, Janice, Susan Baillet and Polly Brown, 'The Effects of Causal Cohesion on Comprehension and Memory', *Journal of Verbal Learning & Verbal Behavior* 23 (1984), 115–126.

Loureda, Óscar, Laura Nadal and Inés Recio, 'El significado procedimental y las partículas discursivas del español: Una aproximación experimental', *Revista Signos. Estudios de Lingüística* 49 (2016a), 52–77.

Loureda, Óscar, Laura Nadal and Inés Recio, 'Partículas discursivas y cognición: *por tanto* y la conexión argumentativa', *Romanistisches Jahrbuch*, 67 (2016b), 240–254.

Recio, Inés, Laura Nadal and Óscar Loureda, 'On Argumentative Relations in Spanish: Experimental Evidence on the Grammaticalization of Cause-Consequence Discourse Markers', in Salvador Pons and Óscar Loureda, eds, *Beyond Grammaticalization and Discourse Markers: New Issues in the Study of Language Change* (Leiden: Brill, forthcoming).

Mackie, John Leslie, *The Cement of the Universe: A Study of Causation* (Oxford: Clarendon, 1974).

Marian, Viorica, Henrike K. Blumenfeld and Margarita Kaushanskaya, 'The Language Experience and Proficiency Questionnaire (LEAP-Q): Assessing Language Profiles in Bilinguals and Multilinguals', *Journal of Speech, Language and Hearing Research* 50 (2007), 940–67.

Meyer, Bonnie J. F., *The Organization of Prose and its Effect on Memory* (Amsterdam: North-Holland Publishing, 1975).

Millis, Keith K., Arthur C. Graesser and Karl Haberlandt, 'The Impact of Connectives on the Memory for Expository Texts', *Applied Cognitive Psychology* 7 (1993), 317–339.

Millis, Keith K., and Marcel Adam Just, 'The Influence of Connectives on Sentence Comprehension', *Journal of Memory and Language* 33/1 (1994), 128–147.

Mouchon, Segre, Michel Fayol and Daniel Gaonac'h, 'On-line Processing of Links between Events in Narratives: Study of Children and Adults', *Cahiers de Psychologie Cognitive/Current Psychology of Cognition* 14/2 (1995), 171–193.

Myers, Jerome L., Makiko Shinjo and Susan A. Duffy, 'Degree of Causal Relatedness and Memory', *Journal of Memory and Language* 26/4 (1987), 453–65.

Nadal, Laura, Inés Recio Fernández, Martha Rudka and Óscar Loureda, 'Processing Additivity in Spanish: *incluso* vs. *además*', in Anna-Maria De Cesare and Cecilia Andorno, eds, *Focus on Additivity. Adverbial modifiers in Romance, Germanic and Slavic languages* (Amsterdam/Philadelphia, PA: John Benjamins 2017), 137–154.

Narita, Masumi, Chieko Sato and Masatoshi Sugiura, 'Connector Usage in the English Essay Writing of Japanese EFL Learners', *Proceedings from 4th International Conference on Language Resources and Evaluation*. Lisbon, Portugal (2004), 1171–1174.

Noordman, Leo, and Femke de Blijzer, 'On the Processing of Causal Relations', in Elizabeth Couper-Kuhlen and Bernd Kortmann, eds, *Cause, Condition, Concession, Contrast. Cognitive and Discourse Perspectives* (Berlin: de Gruyter, 2000), 35–56.

Pander Maat, Henk, and Ted Sanders, 'Domains of Use or Subjectivity? The Distribution of Three Dutch Causal Connectives Explained', in Elizabeth Couper-Kuhlen and Bernd Kortmann, eds, *Cause, Condition, Concession, Contrast. Cognitive and Discourse Perspectives* (Berlin: de Gruyter, 2000), 57–82.

Pander Maat, Henk and Ted Sanders, 'Connectives in Text', in Keith Brown, ed., *Encyclopedia of Language and Linguistics* (Amsterdam, etc.: Elsevier (Volume 3), 2006), 33–41.

Pickering, Martin J., Matthew J. Traxler and Matthew W. Crocker, 'Ambiguity Resolution in Sentence Processing: Evidence against Frequency-Based Accounts', *Journal of Memory and Language* 43(3) (2000), 447–475.

Pons Bordería, Salvador, *Conceptos y aplicaciones de la Teoría de la Relevancia* (Madrid: Arco Libros, 2004).

Portolés, José, 'La distinción entre los conectores y otros marcadores del discurso en español', *Verba* 20 (1993), 141–170.

Portolés, José, *Marcadores del discurso* (Barcelona: Ariel, 1998).

Portolés, José, *Pragmática para hispanistas* (Madrid: Síntesis, 2004).

Pulvermüller, Friedemann, Yury Shtyrov and Olaf Hauk, 'Understanding in an Instant: Neurophysiological Evidence for Mechanistic Language Circuits in the Brain', *Brain and Language* 110, 2 (2009), 82–94.

R Core Team, *R: A Language and Environment for Statistical Computing* (Vienna, Austria: R Foundation for Statistical Computing, 2014). <http://www.R-project.org/>.

Rayner, Keith, 'Eye Movements in Reading and Information Processing: 20 Years of Research', *Psychological Bulletin* 124 (1998), 372–422.

Rayner, Keith, 'Eye Movements and Attention in Reading, Scene Perception, and Visual Search', *The Quarterly Journal of Experimental Psychology* 62:8 (2009), 1457–1506.

Rayner, Keith, Gretchen Kambe and Susan A. Duffy, 'The Effect of Clause Wrap-up on Eye Movements during Reading', *The Quarterly Journal of Experimental Psychology* 53A (4) (2000), 1061–1080.

Rayner, Keith, Sara C. Sereno, Robin K. Morris, A. Réne Schmauder and Charles Clifton Jr, 'Eye Movements and On-line Language Comprehension Processes', *Language & Cognitive Processes* 4 (1989), 21–49.

Richardson, Daniel, Rick Dale and Michael J. Spivey, 'Eye Movements in Language and Cognition: A Brief Introduction', in Monica Gonzalez-Marquez, Irene Mittelberg, Seana Coulson and Michael J. Spivey, eds, *Methods in Cognitive Linguistics* (Amsterdam: John Benjamins, 2007), 323–344.

Sanders, Ted, 'Coherence, causality and cognitive complexity in discourse', *Proceedings/Actes SEM-05, First International Symposium on the Exploration and Modelling of Meaning* (2005), 105–114.

Sanders, Ted, and Leo Noordman, 'The Role of Coherence Relations and Their Linguistic Markers in Text Processing', *Discourse Processes*, 29(1) (2000), 37–60.

Sanders, Ted J. M., and Wilbert P. M. Spooren, 'Causality and Subjectivity in Discourse: The Meaning and Use of Causal Connectives in Spontaneous Conversation, Chat Interactions and Written Text', *Linguistics* 53(1) (2015), 53–92.

Sanford, Anthony, 'Coherence: Psycholinguistic Approach', in Keith Brown, ed., *Encyclopaedia of Language and Linguistics* (Oxford: Elsevier Ltd, 2006), 585–591.

Silfhout, Gerdineke van, Jacqueline Evers-Vermeul and Ted J. M. Sanders, 'Establishing Coherence in Schoolbook Texts: How Connectives and Layout Affect Students' Text Comprehension', *Dutch Journal of Applied Linguistics* 3, 1 (2014), 1–29.

Sperber, Dan, 'Understanding Verbal Understanding', in Jean Khalfa, ed., *What is Intelligence?* (Cambridge: Cambridge University Press, 1994), 179–198.

Sperber, Dan, and Deirdre Wilson, *Relevance Theory: Communication and Cognition* (Oxford: Blackwell, 1995).

Sperber, Dan, and Deirdre Wilson, 'Pragmatics, Modularity and Mind-reading', *Mind & Language* 17 (2002), 3–23.

Universiteit Utrecht, *Final Report Summary – DISCOM (Discourse Connectives and the Mind: a Cross-Linguistic Analysis of Processing and Acquisition)* (2012–2014).

Wilson, Deirdre, 'New Directions for Research on Pragmatics and Modularity', *UCL Working Papers in Linguistics* 15 (2003), 303–324.

Wilson, Deirdre, and Dan Sperber, 'Relevance Theory', *UCL Working Papers in Linguistics* 14 (2002), 249–287.

Wood, Simon N., 'Fast Stable Restricted Maximum Likelihood and Marginal Likelihood Estimation of Semiparametric Generalized Linear Models', *Journal of the Royal Statistical Society* 73, 1 (2011), 3–36.

Zufferey, Sandrine, Pim Mak, Liesbeth Degand and Ted Sanders, 'Advanced Learners' Comprehension of Discourse Connectives: The Role of L1 Transfer across On-line and Off-line Tasks', *Second Language Research* 31(3) (2015), 389–411.

Appendix

Story 1, topic A. *Benjamin and Jacqueline are English professors in Berlin and Hamburg. They live in Hamburg. Their house is very close to the Central Train Station.* ***Benjamin and Jacqueline take fast/slow trains. Therefore, they save time****. The university pays for the tickets. Hamburg is not that far from Berlin, but it takes them almost two hours to get there.*

Story 2, topic B. *Elizabeth and Christian run a travel agency. Mutual friends thought they were a good match and introduced them to each other.* ***Elizabeth and Christopher provide poor/good services. Therefore, they receive complaints****. It is frustrating. They love to travel and do it often. Their friends suggested that they start a travel agency.*

Story 3, topic C. *Phillippe and François are two French pastry chefs. They are very good friends and run their own shop.* ***Phillippe and François bake delicious/disgusting cakes. Therefore, they please customers****. It motivates them to keep on working. They work a lot, but they enjoy it enormously.*

Story 4, topic D. *Sebastian and Alexandra are two kindergarten teachers. They work at a big nursery. It has a lot of benefits.* ***Sebastian and Alexandra tell funny/boring stories. Therefore, they entertain children****. It makes them happy. The children love them and sometimes cry when they have to leave.*

OLGA IVANOVA AND IRIA BELLO VIRUEGA

3 Pragmatic processing in second language: What can focus operators tell us about cognitive performance in L2?

Introduction

In cognitive psycholinguistics, there is no uniform position on whether non-native speakers are able to process second language (L2) in the same way as native speakers do. The debate resolves around the ability of non-native speakers, specifically those with high proficiency in L2, to develop native-like competence for processing a second language (Jackson and van Hell 2011: 195). In this respect, researchers have focused on language processing at different levels, including phonetics, morphology, semantics, syntax and pragmatics.

Some studies have proven that at certain levels of L2 language proficiency (normally, high proficiency or native-like proficiency), non-native speakers are similar to L1 speakers not only in expressive output, but also in cognitive performance and neuronal response (Rossi, Gugler, Friederici, and Hahne 2006; Sabourin and Stowe 2008; Dudschig, de la Vega, and Kaup 2015). However, many other studies have shown that L2 language processing is far from L1 language processing, even in nearly bilingual speakers, as L2 processing presupposes more complexity for the speaker than the same process in L1 (Foucart, Garcia, Ayguasanosa, Thierry, Martin and Costa 2015: 291). In this sense, the Critical Period Hypothesis argues that maturational changes in the brain, which occur after the biological time lapse open to language acquisition, convey discontinuity in neurocognitive structure for this ability (Hopp 2010: 901) and, hence, to variation in the cortical and mental background for L2. Reasons for this include the dissociation of activation areas underlying L1 and L2 processing and comprehension (see Abutalebi 2008), and, importantly, certain inconsistency in area activation across L2 speakers (Dehaene et al. 1997) and in cortical (sensory, motor and cognitive) response to language stimuli (Hahne 2001: 264).

The analysis of processing dissociation for L1 and L2 also draws on the need to consider the linguistic level one refers to, that is, the nature of the task the non-native speaker is to perform in the L2. The opposition may be established between structural linguistic knowledge, which is based on set language elements of form (like *phonemes, morphemes, words*, and *sentences*) (Payne 2006: 3), and non-structural linguistic knowledge, which mostly refers to meaning and interpretation (*pragmatics*) (Lambrecht 1998: 4). Processing of different structural components, which affects word recognition, semantic decoding, syntagmatic processing and integration, syntactic association and parsing, as well as syntactic-semantic integration, is known as low-level processing (Stemmer 2010: 232; Loureda, Cruz, Recio, and Villalba 2014). Its underlying formula is based on the assumption that the difficulty of understanding the structural unit (*word, utterance* or *sentence*) is proportional to the time lapse the speaker spends on its assimilation (Rayner and Pollatsek 2006: 621), and that this kind of operations mainly activates specific areas of the left hemisphere (Stemmer 2010: 231). By comparison, high-level processes normally refer to non-structural components, like pragmatics itself, semantic pragmatics (Castaño 2003: 784) and executive functions of language (Golestani 2014: 26). They do not imply individual fixation on structure units but rather a general involvement into meaning reflection, which would engage several areas from the right hemisphere (Stemmer 2010: 231) and, hence, involve a more complex neural network (Stemmer 2017: 577). This perspective suggests that L2 processing is a neurocognitively variable parameter, whose performance largely depends on the nature of language knowledge.

In the present paper it is argued that, against structural language levels, which are processes susceptible to full acquisition, culturally and mentally dependent levels like L2 pragmatics are difficult to achieve nativeness in. As a result, the formulation of pragmatic inferences in L2 may not correlate with L2 structural proficiency and, thus, may not necessarily coincide in terms of command. This idea is core to the present research, which focuses on confirming the hypothesis that different types of linguistic information display different processing success, with pragmatics as the most susceptible L2 knowledge to not be achieved natively. The formulation of this hypothesis is consistent with the results reported by other studies (Sabourin and Stowe 2008), which argue for the implication of structural similarity between L1 and L2 in the nativeness of L2 processing.

To test the stated hypothesis, the present study will draw on the results of an eye-tracking experiment with L1 and L2 English speakers processing pragmatically marked utterances with similar semantic constraints. Pragmatic marking is given by the focus operator *even*, which belongs to a subgroup of adverbs that associate to a grammatical constituent known as focus in order to evoke a series of pragmatic computations (Ferrari, Giammateo and Albano 2011: 30–31, 36) from apparently simple semantic constructions. Grammarians place *even* and its equivalents in other languages at the positive pole, and suggest that this operator triggers a pragmatic scale, on which the element introduced by *even* is put on an extreme (Fuentes 1987: 164). As Fauconnier (1975: 364) points out after Horn, *even* does not only introduce the presupposition that all other elements besides the introduced focus are included in the predicated action; it also implies that the focus is the least likely element to be included in the predicated action. As for its informational function, *even* (like other focus operators) precedes a *focus* that presents non-presupposed information as new (Ferrari, Giammarco and Albano 2011: 32). When using this operator, the speaker throws off from a series of elements that she considers important, and presupposes the hearer not to know them and to be able to be surprised by them; as for the hearer, this element will be the most informative within the context (Fuentes 1987: 172). As a result, the focus operator *even* may be considered, in terms of a rhematic procedure, an element that re-makes presuppositions and emphasizes the given element (Fuentes 1987: 173). So, if one analyses the example from Schwarz (2005: 126): Hans even knows ITALIAN, *even* may suggest that Hans knows a set of different things, among which Italian stands out as a surprising element (either because it is hard to learn or any other possible reason).

In the present paper, we aim to experimentally test whether native and L2 speakers show the same semantic processing track and dissimilar pragmatic processing track in understanding pragmatic scales with *even*, as suggested by the main research hypothesis.

Pragmatic processing in L2

Pragmatic skills are essential for correct comprehension of non-literal meaning (Tesink et al. 2009: 1942) and, together with lexical and compositional semantic skills, they constitute a compulsory source of meaning understanding (Politzer-Ahles, Fiorentino, Jiang, and Zhou 2013: 135). However, it is precisely pragmatic knowledge, which is traditionally described as the most challenging aspect of L2 acquisition. Unlike structural knowledge, pragmatic skills cannot be normally learnt prescriptively (Fernández Amaya 2001: 172; Ivanova 2013: 60) and, actually, will not necessarily approach native-like pragmatic competence if acquired formally (Kasper and Rose 1999: 96). It has been consistently shown that not even high proficiency in all structural domains of L2 will presuppose concomitant development of L2 pragmatic skills (Kecskés 2000: 618).

Indeed, pragmatic failures may be considered to be the main reason of non-native-like pragmatic performance in L2 (Thomas 2006: 27). Pragmatic failures, which are defined after Thomas' classical work as 'the inability to understand "what is meant by what is said"' (1983: 91), arise from transfer between L1 and L2 systems and associated sociocultural background (Escandell 1996: 108; Fernández Amaya 2008: 14) and, broadly, are due to the dominance of L1 conceptual base, which rules the cognitive mechanisms responsible for pragmatic behaviour in L2 (Kecskés 2000: 618).

As a result, the two aspects of pragmatic skills, *production* and *processing*, may exhibit different degrees of acquisition in L2 learners. While language production may adjust to pragmatic native-likelihood thanks to fixed routinized and formulaic strategies, which are based on memory (Kecskés 2000: 606), pragmatic processing may not be influenced by any explicit approach, but, as Pouscoulous, Noveck, Politzer, and Bastide (2007: 348) suggest, they will rather depend on semantic or inferential strategies. This is probably one of the most challenging questions in relation to the assessment of learners' cognitive performance in L2 pragmatics, since their ability to apply either literal language interpretation, which is more common for L2 speakers (Kecskés 2000: 621), or functional (non-literal) language interpretation may be indicative of their L2 pragmatic competence.

One of the best ways to test the disposition of L2 speakers to either literal or functional interpretation of pragmatically constrained language stimuli is to analyse their inclination towards semantic or inferential interpretation of pragmatically loose and pragmatically marked utterances. Pragmatically loose or vague utterances are those, whose interpretation may vary from context to context (Zhang 2015: 15), as in (1):

(1) George adores cats.

and are normally semantically strict (in (1) there is no room for ambiguous or imprecise understanding for *George*, *adores* and *cats*).

Conversely, pragmatically marked or precise utterances leave no room to more than one interpretation of the statement and, curiously, are usually semantically vague (Marmor 2014: 99), as in (2):

(2) Of course he does.

(here, *he* and *does* require knowing explicit reference in order to semantically understand who is *he* and what action *he does*. *Of course*, however, marks clearly the pragmatic intention to reinforce the truth of the unknown action). Words and units like *of course* are usually grouped under *pragmatic markers*, that is, a class of language items with little semantic load and specificity, but with high contextual sensitivity and important pragmatic functions in meaning interpretation (Andersen 2001: 39–40).

Processing pragmatic scales

There are different subgroups of pragmatic markers – adpositions, interjections, conjunctions, modal particles, discourse markers, etc. (Mosegaard Hansen 1998: 37) – which may bear different discourse functions. One of the least studied subgroup from these are *focus operators*, which are distinguished from other markers because of their specific function: to emphasize (or focus; hence the name) elements of informational importance in the utterances (Kay 1990: 66; Fischer and Alm 2013: 62). Focus operators are usually adverbs (*only, also, still, even, either*, etc.) and are considered function words that establish a specific relation between a focus and a set of possible alternatives (König 2005, Rooth 1992). As Gotzner, Wartenburger and Spalek (2016) and Gotzner (2017) pointed out, focus structures have direct consequences on sentence processing and facilitate the encoding of information in memory. They contribute to the distribution of information within a context by imposing restrictions to a set of alternatives and selecting the most relevant element (Huddleston and Pullum, 2002: 594, Gast and Van der Auwera, 2011, Schwenter 2013). For example, in (3)

(3) George eats only apples.

the exclusive *only* places *apples* as a member of a group (potentially of fruits or things that can be eaten) and selects it as the most informative element. The focus *apples* will lead to a true assertion, but the alternatives will not (Gotzner, Spalek, and Wartenburger 2016). The operator triggers a search for alternatives and leads to a competition between alternatives, either explicit or implicit, and the focus operator (Gotzner 2017). In other words, in (3) (*only)* is helping the receiver to better infer implicatures by marking a pragmatic restriction.

The functional performance of focus operators is normally related to pragmatic scales, which, in Fauconnier's (1975) conception, are orders of possibilities that reflect pragmatic assumptions shared by speakers. They move from the most expected to the least expected constituent (Fuentes 1987: 165) and are ordered by conversationally implied entailment (Schwenter 2013: 185). For example, in (4)

(4) Baby George can even climb.

the focus (*climb*) is introduced by a focus operator (*even*). This leads to the inclusion of more expected constituents by conversational implicature, in this case, easier actions a baby can do, like standing, crawling and walking, among others, which appear explicitly in (5):

(5) Baby George can stand, crawl, walk and even climb.

In this way, focus operators do not only emphasize the focus but also elicit a series of alternatives (Sainz 2012: 41) which, depending on whether they are explicitly included in the utterance, the receiver may have to reconstruct with an element of the same semantic value than the focused element (Rooth 1992). Consequently, focus operators do pragmatically mark utterances by limiting the potential ambiguity of given information, although, at the same time, they call for additional elaboration effort in order to correctly infer the implied information (Loureda, Cruz, and DPKog 2013: 78). To sum up, focus operators fulfil three functions: emphasize the focalized constituent (*emphasis*); contrast the focus with other elements of the pragmatic scale (*alternativity*); and include the focus among the implied pragmatic scale elements (*exhaustiveness*) (Ferrari, Giammateo and Albano 2011: 36).

Focus-sensitive operators like *also, only and even* establish different relationships among the constituents of the scale they create. In the case of *even*, the element it introduces is put on an extreme (Fuentes 1987: 164). This process of argumentative marking turns the last member of the scale into the most informative and the least likely element to be included in the predicated action (Fauconnier 1975; Jacobs, 1983; König, 1991; Andorno, 2000; Gast and Rzymski, 2011). As a result, in (5), only the most complicated activity of the set, in this case *climbing*, can appear as focus after *even*.

From an informational perspective, *even* as well as other non-culminative focalizers like *also* or *as well (as)* precedes the *focus*, where new information is provided (Ferrari, Giammarco, and Albano 2011: 32). As for the hearer, this element will be the most informative within the context (Fuentes 1987: 172). Consequently, the operator *even* may be considered in terms of a rhematic procedure, which re-makes presuppositions and emphasizes the given element (Fuentes 1987: 173).

Different experimental studies on scalar utterances with focus operators have shown a specific cognitive processing pattern for native speakers. It has been observed that operators help restrict inferential calculations by assuming the role of information manager (Loureda, Cruz, and DPKog 2013, 2014; Loureda et al. 2015; Nadal et al. 2017) and are directly involved into retrieval of contextual alternatives (Gotzner, Spalek, and Wartenburger 2013: 2438; Gotzner 2017). These studies show that in adults the processing of the operator is linked to an increase in the processing effort. In the case of native acquisition in children, however, there seems to be less unanimity (see contrastive results in Paterson, Liversedge, Rowland, and Filik (2003) vs Höhle et al. (2009)).

Less is known about how L2 speakers would process focus operators in scalar utterances. It remains underexplored whether L2 speakers, even at native-like proficiency level, would make expected inferences from scalar marked utterances and, most importantly, whether such inferences would cognitively parallel native performance. In this respect, predictions may be controversial, since while from the point of view of neurolinguistics, L2 and L1 pragmatic processing would not depend on the same cognitive mechanisms, experimental research with different approaches has demonstrated the capacity of L2 speakers to correctly comprehend and interpret pragmatic information in L2.

Methodology

Experiment and stimuli

Following the methodological suggestions from Noveck and Sperber (2012: 318), a set of independent utterances with and without the focus operator *even* was designed in seeking to ensure that the 'enriched interpretation is not imposed by extra-pragmatic considerations'. Therefore, a story about Mike and Lucy, great music lovers, who cannot imagine their life without listening to melodies, gigs, tunes, jingles or songs, was invented and given as contextual reference to experiment participants. In the presentation of these characters, it was stressed that Mike and Lucy definitely prefer black and traditional music (like *folk, soul* or *jazz*), with the intention to direct participants towards the semantic retrieval of related concepts. So, it was assumed that, after being introduced into the experiment, participants would initially infer that Mike and Lucy like genres like folk, soul and jazz, the most popular genres of traditional and African-American music.

These three terms were included either explicitly or implicitly as target pragmatic scale into all critical utterances. However, each utterance also included a pragmatic distractor, which could not be expected following the introductory story: *punk*.

The aim of this scalar element was to observe how participants would process the introduction of rhematic information as a pragmatically marked unexpected member of the conventionally implied scale in utterances like (6) and (7):

(6) Mike and Lucy love folk, soul, jazz and punk.
(7) Mike and Lucy love folk, soul, jazz, even punk.

Utterance (6) is a contextual statement with a set of complex, explicit alternatives (*folk, soul, jazz*) and an unmarked focus (*punk*). In (7), the structure is modified by the introduction of the operator, which turns the focus into a marked element. The presence of *even* in (7) points out that there is a pragmatic scale of probability with regard to the context of the utterance (Ferrari, Giammarco, and Albano 2011: 36), in which the syntagma *punk*, the pragmatically unexpected information, is the scale extreme modified by *even*. The main objective is to contrast how L1 and L2 speakers process the restriction of this unexpected element by the focus operator *even*, against its unmarked presentation within the rest of the scale. The design of the utterances followed the principle of number of letters (n°=4) in order to reject the bias of word length into the measurement of the cognitive efforts required from participants during the reading task.

Technique

The experimental aim of this research is to find out whether the introduction of the focus operator *even* in the pragmatic scale reorders the cognitive processing and understanding of the scalar utterances by English native speakers and English L2 speakers in the same way. In other words, considering the theory of the semantic and pragmatic charge of focus operators discussed in the previous section, the objective is to experimentally test whether *even* is characterized by the pragmatic enrichment of 'inclusiveness' (*A even B*) against other type of additive relations (*A and B*), and whether such enrichment is processed and interpreted in the same way by L1 and L2 speakers.

The eye-tracking method was chosen as the most appropriate case technique because it is a sensitive online assessment method (Gillon Dowens and Carreiras 2014: 65), which makes 'one of the best ways to study the processes of language comprehension' (Rayner and Pollatsek 2006: 613). This is due to the fact that eye movements reflect the focus of attention during language processing. While eye fixation, contrary to eye movements, represents the sending of information to the brain (Fernández et al. 2013: 8345), eye movements themselves are linguistically mediated and reflect both the increasing linguistic interpretation and the output of composite language computations (Sedivy 2010: 116–117). In an experiment, the sensitivity of eye movement behaviour to the most 'subtle changes in the information uptake from the speech stream' (Sedivy 2010: 117) allows for detecting which linguistic stimulus conditions the increase of the cognitive effort. In general terms, language-mediated eye movements permit to observe how the mental world and the external visual world interplay (Altmann and Kamide 2007: 502).

The registered part of the experiment was designed as a reading activity, which generally allows for an *ad hoc* observation of language processing. In the theoretical consideration on reading, the experimental design follows its functional conception as a brain activity, which 'involves linking semantic and syntactic information contained in written words and sentences to information stored in semantic memory to derive meaning' (Golestani 2014: 23). It was also considered that during reading, sentences dynamically unfold representations of events, with a beginning and an end, towards which the readers would develop expectations of what might follow (Altmann and Kamide 2007: 203 et seq.). These assumptions laid the foundation of the reading experiment, during which eye movements were tracked in order to trace the processing costs of different elements of target pragmatic scales.

Participants and procedure

A total of 30 English native speakers and 28 German native speakers with self-reported advanced proficiency in English participated in the reading experiment. There were nine women and 21 men with an average age of 42±17.2 in the control (English) group, and 15 women and 13 men with an average age of 33±8.7 in the critical (German) group. All participants had a university degree or were involved in university studies when they participated in the experiment. Data was recorded with a RED 500 eye-tracking system by SMI (Sensomotoric Instruments) mounted below a screen placed on a desk.

Each participant was subject to the reading of the full experiment, which included utterances (6) and (7), eight critical utterances that are not analysed here and 24 distractors, all appearing randomly and individually on the screen.

Before starting, participants were informed about the technical procedure and asked not to move during the experiment and not to turn their eyes away from the screen. Before recording, participants had their eyes calibrated in order to ensure the quality of the data. After that, they were asked to proceed with the self-paced reading experiment, during which after key pressing they were randomly shown, one per screen, the experimental stimuli.

Data analysis

After data collection, it was opted for analysing the effect of the independent variables (stimuli (6) and (7)) according to three dependent variables: (i) *total reading time*; (ii) *first-pass reading time* and (iii) *second-pass reading time.*[11] In choosing these three dependent variables, Rayner and Sereno's

11 This procedure follows the methodological suggestion by Noveck and Sperber (2012: 309), who define the measurement of the influence of an independent variable on a dependent variable, being the effect of other uncontrolled variables dismissed, as desirable methodological criteria.

(1994: 65) observation on that both first-term (early) and second-term (late) processes should be examined in order to obtain as much information as possible on the processing of a word, was taken into account.

Total reading time is the sum of all durations or fixations in a region (Traxler and Pickering 1996: 460) or an area of interest (AOI, hereafter). In this experiment, this variable was chosen in order to see whether the introduction of *even* into the utterances modifies speakers' total cognitive effort and whether the operator *even* is responsible for it. *First-pass reading time* makes the time that the eyes remain on an AOI when confronting it for the first time (Gillon Dowens and Carreiras 2014: 69). Therefore, it is the sum of durations of all consecutive fixations on an AOI, from the first entering until leaving that AOI (Rayner and Sereno 1994: 64; Clifton, Staub and Rayner 2007: 348; Loureda, Cruz, Recio and Villalba 2014: 13–14). Finally, *second-pass reading time* makes the sum of all fixations in an AOI after first-pass reading time, including zero times, when the area is not re-fixated (Clifton, Staub, and Rayner 2007: 349). According to Trueswell and Tanenhaus (1992: 495), *second-pass reading* time shows the re-analysis 'caused by arriving at an incorrect initial interpretation'.

The three dependent variables will be analysed for three internal AOIs of each stimulus: the alternative (*folk, soul, jazz*), the focus operator/conjunction (*even/and*) and the focus (*punk*). The *alternative* is the part of the pragmatic scale preceding the focus operator *even* and in this study will be taken as the total of alternative AOIs (*folk, soul, jazz*). All analyses are based on statistical calculations of descriptive parameters (in milliseconds, ms hereafter) and to Student's T-Test for significance.

Results

Processing unmarked pragmatic scales with complex, explicit alternatives

The processing of unmarked pragmatic scales with several explicit alternatives triggers similar cognitive behaviour in native and L2 English speakers. Both groups show a downward trend in cognitive processing as the utterance unfolds. The alternative triggers the maximum processing costs against the conjunction and the focus, which require less integration effort.

There are, however, two important differences between native and non-native speakers in understanding an unmarked scale. First, native speakers spend less time on processing separate AOIs (–165.41 ms for the alternative; –32.83 ms for the conjunction; –218.35 ms for the focus). This observation is predictable, since semantic integration is streamlined in L1: while L2 speakers rely mostly on shallow parsing focused on individual lexical-semantic representation, native speakers rely on shallow and full parsing at a time (Clahsen and Felser 2006). This gives native speakers a considerable advantage in language processing.

Second, natives and non-natives differ in terms of cognitive involvement when processing different AOIs. Native speakers spend significantly less time on processing the conjunction (–152.54 ms) and the focus (–301.39 ms) than on processing the alternative. Furthermore, the marked difference in processing the conjunction and the focus (–148.85 ms) is also statistically significant ($p < 0.05$) in native speakers.

In non-native speakers, a significant difference exists only between processing the conjunction and the alternative (–285.12 ms) and the focus and the alternative (–218.15 ms). No difference is observed between processing the conjunction and the focus, which retrieve similar cognitive costs in non-native speakers. Again, this observation may imply that semantic integration is highly dependent on shallow parsing in non-native speakers, for whom each new AOI is less predictable semantically than for native speakers.

When processing a scale with four explicit members, the set of the alternatives has to be identified as complementary to the focus and put in relation with it. The lexical information contained in the alternative might act as a guide to interpret the scalarity of the enumeration. This explains the sharp decrease in the cognitive effort needed by both L1 (–211.77%) and L2 (–38.96%) readers to process the alternative and the focus, as shown in Figure 3.1. Even if the focus is the AOI with the lowest reading times, this identification of the most informative element without any procedural guide indicating scalarity requires a higher cognitive effort (+58.96%) for the group of non-native readers. This group also spends more time (+7.93%) processing the alternatives but it is less sensitive (−7.10%) to the additive procedural guide contained in the conjunction.

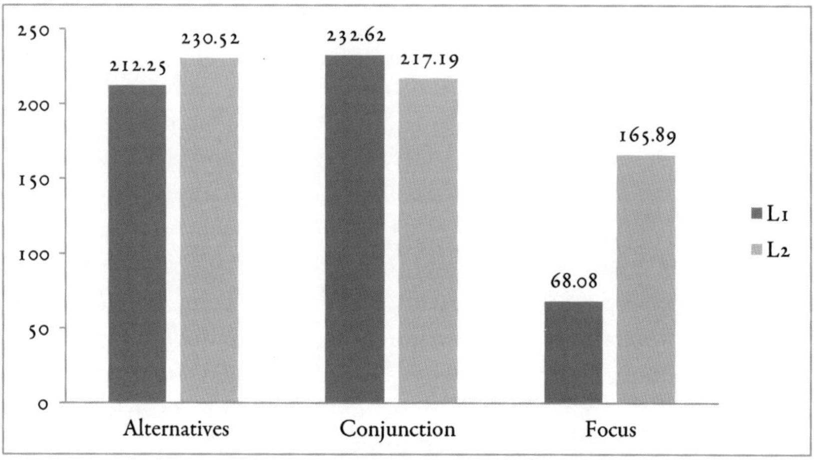

Figure 3.1. First-pass reading time (unmarked scale)

Re-reading times inform about the time readers spend reconsidering, that is, confirming, rejecting or modifying, the assumption made during the first reading. In Figure 3.2, it is shown that the alternatives are again the area with the highest processing costs. The cognitive effort needed to process this area and the focus remain stable during *first-* and *second-pass reading times*. The processing of the conjunction, however, decreases drastically (−396.95% in the L1 group and −128.45% in the L2 group), which might suggest different sensitivity to elements with conceptual and procedural content.

Data show that non-native readers require more time, especially when it comes to reconsidering the first assumption created in their minds. Processing times in the L2 group are higher in the AOI of the alternative (+40.11%), the conjunction (+50.76%) and the focus (+65.85%).

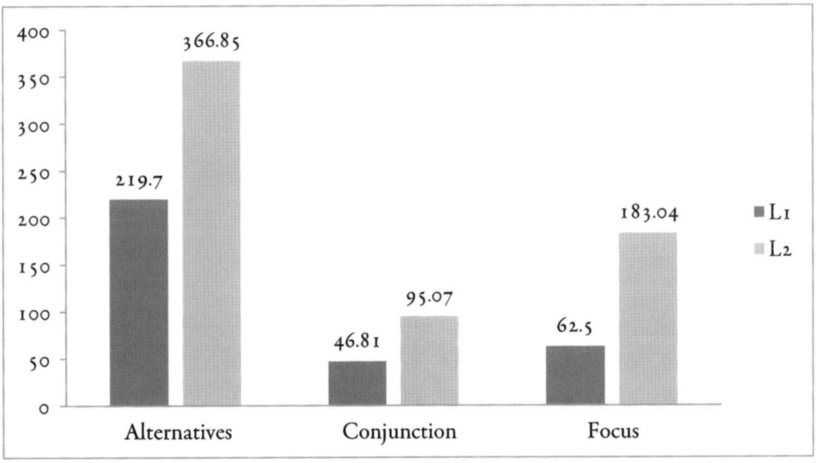

Figure 3.2. Second-pass reading time (unmarked scale)

If we consider the *total reading time* (Figure 3.3), the set of explicit, complex, alternatives require the highest cognitive effort of all the AOIs analysed and controls the information retrieval of the scale in both groups. In the L1 group, the processing costs of the alternatives are increased by 54.59% and 230.83% with regard to the conjunction and the focus, respectively. In the case of non-native speakers, the alternatives require an extra 91.31% processing costs than the conjunction and 71.21% than the focus.

Differences between the two groups indicate that whereas native readers seem to rely more on the semantic guide contained in the set of alternatives, L2 readers are less sensitive to semantic integration processes. Thus, the focus is 62.58% easier to process for native speakers. This difference is reduced to 27.69% in the AOI of the alternatives and to 10.51% in that of the conjunction.

Processing marked pragmatic scales with complex, explicit alternatives

Introducing the focus operator *even* changes the processing pattern for different AOIs in the utterance. These changes are important for describing

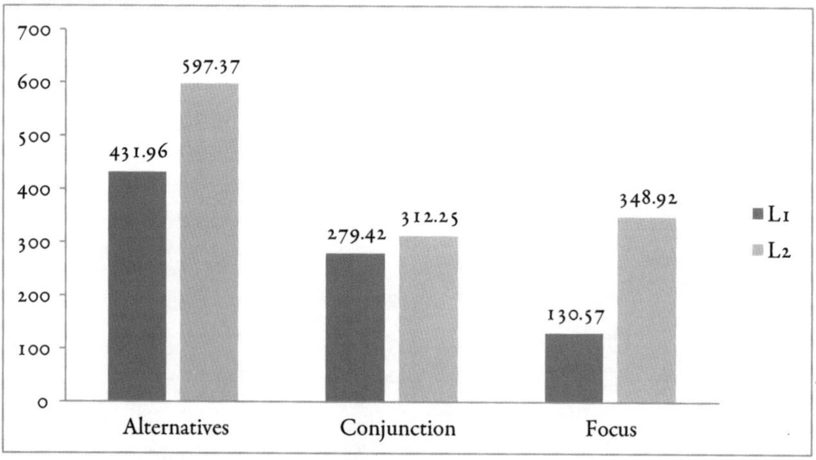

Figure 3.3. Total reading time (unmarked scale)

cognitive processing in natives and non-natives, whose behaviour diverges in markedness when the utterance becomes pragmatically restricted. In both groups, the operator is the AOI with the highest processing costs during the construction of the first assumption (Figure 3.4). The results of our experiment do replicate the results from other studies, which have shown that the inclusion of the focus operator significantly reduces the cognitive effort implied in processing the focus. Both native and non-native speakers spend significantly less time on decoding and integrating the pragmatic implication of *punk* in the utterance than on conveying the same processes for *even* (in natives –488.83% and in non-natives, 52.62%). The main difference in natives and non-natives, however, is found on the distribution of cognitive effort in the processing of the focus, which is 59.13% easier to process for native speakers. As it happened in the processing of utterances without the scalar operator, native speakers spend more time (+13.61%) processing elements with procedural meaning. As indicated by Bello Viruega and Bernales in the following chapter, this might be an indicator of a different processing pattern in the minds of non-native speakers, who seem to rely more on lexical information.

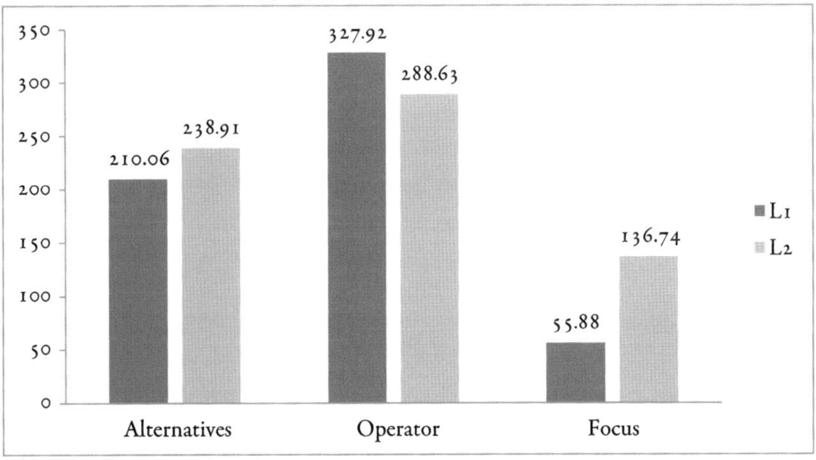

Figure 3.4. First-pass reading time (marked scale)

The inclusion of the operator reveals a completely different picture as far as the reanalysis of the first assumption is concerned (see Figure 3.5). The alternatives are the AOI with the highest processing costs and their values are similar to those registered for utterances without the operator. The length of the alternative, which includes three lexical items (*folk, soul, jazz*), may serve as an explanation for it, as readers need time to relate the elements of the set to each other and to the focus. The processing costs of the operator, however, are very different in both groups to that of the conjunction. Whereas in utterances containing *and* the conjunction was easier to process than the alternatives (369.34% in the L1 and 74.08% in the L2 groups, respectively), the processing costs of the operator are almost the same than those of the alternatives (–1.09%) in the L1 group as they are only 34.64% lower for non-native speakers. The length of the scale and the procedural guide contained in the operator result in a decrease in the processing costs of the focus (–374.99% for natives and –63.07% for non-natives), which is the AOI with the lowest processing costs despite being informatively marked. Such a 'lateral effect' (Loureda et al. 2015) was already found in the L1 group in those utterances containing the conjunction. This might indicate, again, that L2 speakers access information structure in a non-target like form and require stronger evidence to interpret pragmatic information.

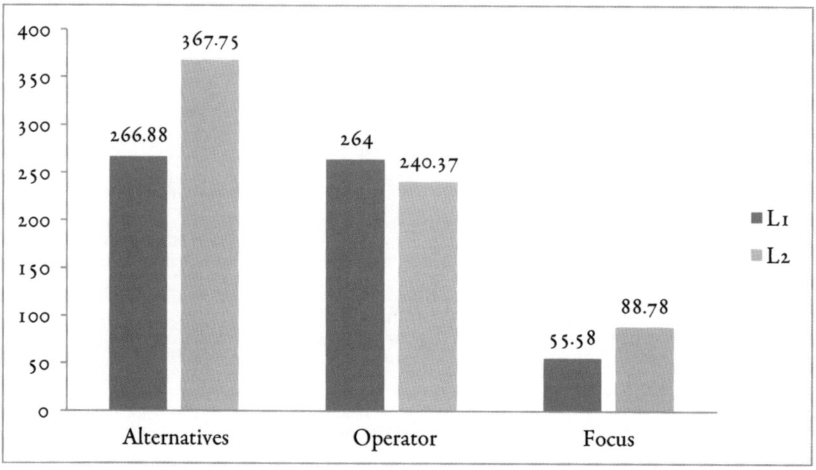

Figure 3.5. Second-pass reading time (marked scale)

For *total reading time*, *even* is significantly the most difficult AOI for natives (+24.11% and +431.06% compared with the alternative and the focus, respectively), which pulls the maximum processing cost in the whole utterance. The operator, however, is not the most difficult area for processing in non-natives, though it is the second most difficult area for processing after the alternative (−77.66 ms, $p > 0.05$). But, in the same way as native speakers, non-natives spend more time (57.37%) processing *even* than the focus. This observation is in line with other similar results, which explain that the triggering of the cognitive efforts by the focus operator is due to its role of inferential restrictor and information manager (Loureda, Cruz and DPKog 2013; Loureda, Cruz, Rudka, Nadal, Recio and Borreguero 2015). As a result, cognitive efforts on processing the focus significantly decrease in comparison with the whole utterance ($p < 0.01$), giving rise to a top-down curve for the operator-focus sequence. As it has been previously mentioned, the processing of *even* is more fleeting than the processing of the alternative, while the decrease in processing costs of the focus is not as notable as in natives. This tendency might indicate that even though non-natives use similar patterns to process pragmatically restricted scalar utterances, their cognitive implication is less marked than that of natives. Data for *total reading time* are provided in Figure 3.6.

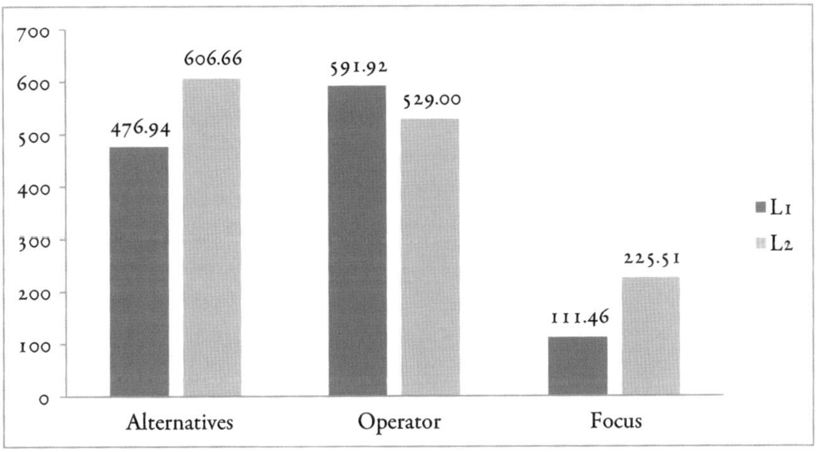

Figure 3.6. Total reading time (marked scale)

Conclusion

The aim of the present research was to find out whether proficient non-native speakers of English build the same pragmatic inferences from scaled utterances marked by *even*, and whether these inferences follow the same cognitive patterns. The results of the experiment have consistently proven that although non-natives generally exhibit similar cognitive processing distribution in pragmatically marked utterances, they do not show the same sensitivity towards processing elements with different pragmatic charges as native speakers. While native speakers clearly require more effort in processing pragmatic operators, non-native speakers are less sensitive to procedural instructions. Based on it, this paper suggests that non-native speakers must rely on memory and semantic processes, which do not interfere in native speakers, and thus confirms the idea that cognitive processing of pragmatic scales is not subject to native-like acquisition in L2.

These results are in line with previous observations in that non-native speakers spend more time on solving ambiguous propositions (Foucart et al. 2015: 292). In this respect, it has been suggested that differences in L1 and L2 processing correspond to differences in processing different types of information (semantic and pragmatic) rather than to differences in native and non-native language systems: whilst semantic processing primarily relies on proficiency, pragmatic processing relies on extra-linguistic cues, which are commonly employed by L2 speakers for comprehension (Foucart et al. 2015: 297, 298). This idea has been discussed throughout this chapter in order to highlight the necessity to distinguish between structural knowledge (like semantics) and non-structural knowledge (like pragmatics) for correct assessment of processing ability in non-native speakers.

In general, the results of the present research coincide with other studies that point to incomplete, or non-native-like pragmatic performance in L2. In this sense, they are consistent with previous observations on particular L2 learners' difficulties to acquire pragmatic functions (Rose 2005: 396). These difficulties might go back to mnesic procedures involved in language learning. Whereas L1 learning is based on implicit acquisition and is mediated by inborn learning mechanisms, L2 learning is explicit and declarative, that is, expressively taught (Perani and Abutalebi 2005: 202; Abutalebi 2008: 467), and thus is not as automated as L1. In this respect, major overlapping of neurocognitive substrate for L1 and L2 semantics may be an enabling factor for native-like performance on this level, against minor neurocognitive overlapping for L1 and L2 pragmatics. Kuperberg et al. (2000: 334) observed that pragmatically difficult sentences activate brain areas responsible for extralexical pragmatic meaning of the utterances and, at the same time, for the correct processing of individual words. In other words, L2 pragmatics requires a greater demand than any other L2 structural knowledge, for example, semantics. Importantly, this double activation of lexical processing for understanding pragmatic meaning in L2 might be the key to our understanding of why semantic processing can show native-likeness and why pragmatic processing cannot.

To sum up, it seems clear that L2 proficient speakers are definitely able to make correct inferences from pragmatically marked utterances, which confirms the suggestion of general non-impaired pragmatic comprehension in second language (Tesink et al. 2009: 1942). This study showed that non-natives quantitatively reconstruct the same implicatures from utterances like (6) *Mike and Lucy love folk, soul, jazz and punk*, coinciding with natives in that this proposition might not clearly derive in inferring that, despite *punk, Mike and Lucy love other musical genres* (natives: 54%; non-natives: 63%), but is rather a pragmatically loose utterance. Similar consistent implicature reconstruction was also observed for (7) *Mike and Lucy love folk, soul, jazz, even punk*, with both natives and non-natives understanding that *punk* is less prone to be loved than other musical genres (natives: 61%; non-natives: 74%).

The difference in cognitive processing between non-native and L1 speakers, however, shows that pragmatic processing in L2, albeit native-like in comprehension, is not as sensitive to subtle inferential contrasts. Here, the explanation may rely on Felser, Roberts, Marinis and Gross's (2003: 479) observation on that L2 processing is not based on universal parsing principles like in L1, but rather on more direct mapping from surface semantics.

Bibliography

Abutalebi, Jubin, 'Neural Aspects of Second Language Representation and Language Control', *Acta Psychologica* 128 (2008), 466–478.

Altmann, Gerry T. M., and Yuki Kamide, 'The Real-Time Mediation of Visual Attention by Language and World Knowledge: Linking Anticipatory (and Other) Eye Movements to Linguistic Processing', *Journal of Memory and Language* 57 (2007), 502–518.

Andersen, Gisle, *Pragmatic Markers and Sociolinguistic Variation: a Relevance-Theoretic Approach to the Language of Adolescents* (Amsterdam/Philadelphia, PA: John Benjamins, 2001).

Castaño, Julio, 'Bases neurobiológicas del lenguaje y sus alteraciones', *Revista de Neurología* 36(9) (2003), 781–785.

Clahsen, Harald, and Claudia Felser, 'How Native-Like is Non-Native Language Processing?', *Trends in Cognitive Sciences* 10 (2006), 564–570.

Clifton, Charles Jr, Adrian Staub, and Keith Rayner, 'Eye Movements in Reading Words and Sentences', in Roger P. G. van Gompel, Martin H. Fischer, Wayne S. Murray, and Robin L. Hill, eds, *Eye Movements: A Window on Mind and Brain* (Oxford: Elsevier, 2007), 341–372.

Dehaene, Stanislas, Emmanuel Dupoux, Jacques Mehler, Laurent Cohen, Eraldo Paulesu, Daniela Perani, Pierre-Francois van de Moortele, Stéphane Lehéricy, and Denis Le Bihan, 'Anatomical Variability in the Cortical Representation of First and Second Language', *NeuroReport* 8 (1997), 3809–3815.

Dudschig, Carolin, Irmgard de la Vega, and Barbara Kaup, 'Embodiment and Second-Language: Automatic Activation of Motor Responses during Processing Spatially Associated L2 Words and Emotion L2 Words in a Vertical Stroop Paradigm', *Brain and Language* 132 (2014), 14–21.

Escandell Vidal, María Victoria, 'Los fenómenos de interferencia pragmática', in *Didáctica del Español como Lengua Extranjera. Cuadernos del Tiempo Libre* (Madrid: Actilibre, 1996), 95–109.

Fauconnier, Gilles, 'Pragmatic Scales and Logical Structure', *Linguistic Inquiry* 6(3) (1975), 353–375.

Felser, Claudia, Leah Roberts, Theodore Marinis, and Rebecca Gross, 'The Processing of Ambiguous Sentences by First and Second Language Learners of English', *Applied Psycholinguistics* 24 (2003), 453–489.

Fernández, Gerardo, Pablo Mandolesi, Nora P. Rotstein, Oscar Colombo, Osvaldo Agamennoni, and Luis E. Politi, 'Eye Movement Alterations during Reading in Patients with Early Alzheimer Disease', *Investigative Ophthalmology & Visual Science* 54 (2013), 8345–8352.

Fernández Amaya, Lucía, 'El fallo pragmático en la traducción al español de Time and the Conways y Look Back in Anger', *ELIA* 2 (2001), 171–179.

Fernández Amaya, Lucía, 'Teaching Culture: Is It Possible to Avoid Pragmatic Failure?', *Revista Alicantina de Estudios Ingleses* 21 (2008), 11–24.

Ferrari, Laura, Mabel Giammatteo, and Hilda Albano, 'Operadores de foco: el caso de *incluso, hasta, solo* y *aun*', *Cuadernos de la ALFAL* 3 (2001), 30–41.

Fischer, Kerstin, and Maria Alm, 'A Radical Construction Grammar Perspective on the Modal Particle-Discourse Particle Distinction', in Liesbeth Degand, Bert

Cornillie, and Paola Pietrandrea, eds, *Discourse Markers and Modal Particles* (Amsterdam/Philadelphia, PA: John Benjamins, 2013), 47–88.

Foucart, Alice, Xavier Garcia, Meritxell Ayguasanosa, Guillaume Thierry, Clara Martin, and Albert Costa, 'Does the Speaker Matter? Online Processing of Semantic and Pragmatic Information in L2 Speech Comprehension', *Neuropsychologia* 75 (2015), 291–303.

Fuentes, Catalina, 'Pragmática y Relación Intratextual: El Caso de *hasta*, *incluso* y *ni siquiera*', *ELUA* 4 (1987), 159–176.

Gast, Volker, and J. van der Auwera, 'Scalar Additive Operators in the Languages of Europe'. *Language, 87*/1 (2011), 2–54.

Gillon Dowens, Margaret, and Manuel Carreiras, 'Psycholinguistic Approaches to Second Language Spanish', in Kimberly L. Geeslin, ed., *The Handbook of Spanish Second Language Acquisition* (Malden/Oxford/Chichester: Wiley Blackwell, 2014), 64–79.

Golestani, Narly, 'Brain Structural Correlates of Individual Differences at Low- to High-Levels of the Language Processing Hierarchy: A Review of New Approaches to Imaging Research', *International Journal of Bilingualism* 18(1) (2014), 6–34.

Gotzner, Nicole (2017). *Alternative Sets in Language Processing: How Focus Alternatives are Represented in the Mind.* Palgrave studies in Pragmatics, Language and Cognition, Palgrave Macmillan.

Gotzner, Nicole, Katharina Spalek, and Isabell Wartenburger, 'How Pitch Accents and Focus Particles affect the Recognition of Contextual Alternatives', in M. Knauff, M. Pauen, N. Sebanz, and I. Wachsmuth, eds, *Proceedings of the 35th Annual Conference of the Cognitive Science Society* (Austin, TX: CogSci, 2013), 2434–2439.

Gotzner, Nicole, Katharina Spalek, and Isabell Wartenburger. 'The Impact of Focus Operators on the Recognition and Rejection of Contrastive Alternatives.' *Language and Cognition* 8, no. 1 (2016), 59–95.

Hahne, Anja, 'What's Different in Second-Language Processing? Evidence from Event-Related Brain Potentials', *Journal of Psycholinguistic Research* 30(3) (2001), 251–266.

Höhle, Barbara, Frauke Berger, Anja Müller, Michaela Schmitz, and Jürgen Weissenborn, 'Focus Particles in Children's Language: Production and Comprehension of *auch* "also" in German Learners from 1 year to 4 years of age', *Language Acquisition* 16(1) (2009), 36–66.

Hopp, Holger, 'Ultimate Attainment in L2 Inflection: Performance Similarities between Non-Native and Native Speakers', *Lingua* 120 (2010), 901–931.

Horn, Laurence R., 'A Presuppositional Analysis of *only* and *even*', *CLS* 5 (1969), 97–108.

Huddleston, Rodney, and Geoffrey Pullum (2002). *The Cambridge Grammar of English Language* (Cambridge: Cambridge University Press).

Ivanova, Olga, 'La Competencia Pragmática en Español L2: Un Caso de Inmigrantes Rusohablantes en Inmersión Lingüística Continua', *Lengua y Migración* 5(1) (2013), 57–81.

Jackson, Carrie N., and Janet, G. van Hell, 'The Effects of L2 Proficiency Level on the Processing of Wh-Questions among Dutch Second Language Speakers of English', *International Review of Applied Linguistics in Language Teaching* 49(3) (2011), 195–219.

Kasper, Gabriele, and Kenneth R. Rose, 'Pragmatics and SLA', *Annual Review of Applied Linguistics* 19 (1999), 81–104.

Kay, P. (1990). 'Even'. *Linguistics and Philosophy*, *13*, 59–111.

Kecskés, Istvan, 'A Cognitive-Pragmatic Approach to Situation-Bound Utterance', *Journal of Pragmatics* 32 (2000), 605–625.

König, Ekkehard, *The Meaning of Focus Particles: A Comparative Perspective* (London: Routledge, 2005).

Kuperberg, G. R., P. K. McGuire, E. T. Bullmore, M. J. Brammer, S. Rabe-Hesketh, I. C. Wright, D. J. Lythgoe, S. C. R. Williams, and A. D. David, 'Common and Distinct Neural Substrates for Pragmatic, Semantic, and Syntactic Processing of Spoken Sentences: an fMRI Study', *Journal of Cognitive Neuroscience* 12(2) (2000), 321–341.

Lambrecht, Knud, *Information Structure and Sentence Form. Topic, Focus, and the Mental Representations of Discourse Referents* (Cambridge: Cambridge University Press, 1998).

Loureda, Óscar, Adriana Cruz, and DPKog research group, 'Aproximación experimental sobre los costes de procesamiento de las partículas focales del español *también* e *incluso*', *Cuadernos AISPI* 2 (2013), 75–98.

Loureda, Óscar, Adriana Cruz, and DPKog research group. 'En los márgenes del léxico: las partículas focales del español (incluso, también) y el análisis experimental.' In Luque Toro, Luis and Rocío Luque eds, *Léxico Español Actual*, Vol. IV (Venice: Cafoscarina, 2014), 85–104.

Loureda, Óscar, Adriana Cruz, Inés Recio, and Cristina Villalba, '*Incluso* en posición pre- y postfocal: un análisis experimental de los costes de procesamiento de escalas pragmáticas', *Revista de la Sociedad Española de Lingüística* 44(2) (2014), 95–129.

Loureda, Óscar, Adriana Cruz, Martha Rudka, Laura Nadal, Inés Recio, and Margarita Borreguero, 'Focus Particles in Information Processing: An Experimental Study on Pragmatic Scales with Spanish *incluso*', *Focus Particles in the Romance and Germanic Languages. Experimental and Corpus-Based Approaches* 71(2) (2015), 129–151.

Luzondo-Oyón, Alba, and Rocío Jiménez-Briones, 'FrameNet and FunGramKB: A Comparison of two Computational Resources for Semantic Knowledge Representation', in Brian Nolan and Carlos Periñán-Pascual, eds, *Language Processing and Grammars. The Role of Functionally Oriented Computational Models* (Amsterdam/Philadelphia, PA: John Benjamins, 2014), 197–232.

Marmor, Andrei, *The Language of Law* (Oxford: Oxford University Press, 2014).

Mosegaard Hansen, Maj-Britt, *The Function of discourse Particles* (Amsterdam: John Benjamins, 1998).

Nadal, Laura, Inés Recio Fernández, Martha Rudka, and Óscar Loureda. 'Processing Additivity in Spanish: *incluso* vs *además*'. In Anna Maria De Cesare and Cecilia Andorno, eds, *Focus on Additivity: Adverbial Modifiers in Romance, Germanic and Slavic languages* (Amsterdam: John Benjamins, 2017), 136–156.

Noveck, Ira, and Dan Sperber, 'The Why and How of Experimental Pragmatics: The Case of "Scalar Inferences"', in Deirdre Wilson, and Dan Sperber, eds, *Meaning and Relevance* (Cambridge: Cambridge University Press, 2012), 307–330.

Paterson, Kevin B., Simon Liversedge, Caroline Rowland, and Ruth Filik, 'Children's Comprehension of Sentences with Focus Particles', *Cognition* 89(3) (2003), 263–294.

Payne, Thomas E., *Exploring Language Structure* (Cambridge: Cambridge University Press, 2006).

Perani, Daniela, and Jubin Abutalebi, 'The Neural Basis of First and Second Language Processing', *Current Opinion in Neurobiology* 15 (2005), 202–206.

Politzer-Ahles, Stephen, Robert Fiorentino, Xiaoming Jiang, and Xiaolin Zhou, 'Distinct Neural Correlates for Pragmatic and Semantic Meaning Processing: An Event-Related Potential Investigation of Scalar Implicature Processing Using Picture-Sentence Verification', *Brain Research* 1490 (2013), 134–152.

Pouscoulous, Nausicaa, Ira A. Noveck, Guy Politzer, and Anne Bastide, 'A Developmental Investigation of Processing Costs in Implicature Production', *Language Acquisition* 14(4) (2007), 347–375.

Rayner, Keith, and Alexander Pollatsek, 'Eye-Movement Control in Reading', Matthew J. Traxler, and Morton A. Gernsbacher, eds, *Handbook of Psycholinguistics* (Oxford: Elsevier, 2006), 613–658.

Rayner, Keith, and Sara C. Sereno, 'Eye Movements in Reading: Psycholinguistic Studies', in Morton A. Gernsbacher, ed., *Handbook of Psycholinguistics* (San Diego: Academic Press, 1994), 57–81.

Rooth, Mats. 'A Theory of Focus Interpretation.' *Natural Language Semantics* 1(1992), 75–116.

Rose, Kenneth R., 'On the Effects of Instruction in Second Language Pragmatics', *System* 33 (2005), 385–399.

Rossi, Sonja, Manfred F. Gugler, Angela D. Friederici, and Anja Hahne, 'The Impact of Proficiency on Syntactic Second-Language Processing of German and Italian: Evidence from Event-Related Potentials', *Journal of Cognitive Neuroscience* 18 (12) (2006), 2030–2048.

Sabourin, Laura, and Laurie A. Stowe, 'Second Language Processing: When are First and Second Languages Processed Similarly?', *Second Language Research* 24(3) (2008), 397–430.

Sainz, Eugenia, '*Tra l'altro*: conexión y focalización. Análisis contrastivo con el español', *Cuadernos de Filología Italiana* 19 (2012), 41–68.

Schwarz, Bernhard, 'Scalar Additive Particles in Negative Contexts', *Natural Language Semantics* 13 (2005), 125–168.

Schwenter, Scott, *Pragmatics of Conditional Marking. Implicature, Scalarity, and Exclusivity* (London: Routledge, 2013).

Sedivy, Julie C., 'Using Eyetracking in Language Acquisition research', in Elma Blom, and Sharon Unsworth, eds, *Experimental Methods in Language Acquisition Research* (Amsterdam: John Benjamins, 2010), 115–138.

Stemmer, Brigitte, 'Imaging Brain Lateralization', in Harry A. Whitaker, ed., *Concise Encyclopedia of Brain and Language* (Oxford: Elsevier, 2010), 231–234.

Stemmer, Brigitte, 'Neural Aspects of Pragmatic Disorders', in Louise Cummings, ed., *Research in Clinical Pragmatics* (Cham: Springer, 2017), 561–586.

Tesink, C. M. J., J. K. Buitelaar, K. M. Petersson, R. J. van der Gaag, C. C. Kan, I. Tendolkar, and P. Hagoort, 'Neural Correlates of Pragmatic Language Comprehension in Autism Spectrum Disorders', *Brain: A Journal of Neurology* 132 (2009), 1941–1952.

Thomas, Jenny, 'Cross-Cultural Pragmatic Failure', *Applied Linguistics* 4 (1983), 91–112.

Thomas, Jenny, 'Cross-Cultural Pragmatic Failure', in Kingsley Bolton, and Braj B. Kachru, eds, *World Englishes: Critical Concepts in Linguistics* (London: Routledge, 2006), 22–48.

Traxler, Matthew J., and Martin J. Pickering, 'Plausibility and the Processing of Unbounded Dependencies: An Eye-Tracking Study', *Journal of Memory and Language* 35 (1996), 454–475.

Trueswell, John C., and Michael K. Tanenhaus, 'Consulting Temporal Context during Sentence Comprehension: Evidence from the Monitoring of Eye Movements in Reading', in *Proceedings of the Fourteenth Annual Conference of the Cognitive Science Society* (Mahwah, NJ: Lawrence Erlbaum, 1992), 492–497.

Zhang, Grace Q., *Elastic Language: How and Why We Stretch Our Words* (Cambridge: Cambridge University Press, 2015).

IRIA BELLO VIRUEGA AND CAROLINA BERNALES

4 Processing focus operators and pragmatic scales: An eye-tracking study on information processing in English L2

Introduction[1] [2]

One of the basic principles in pragmatics and psycholinguistics states that communication takes place with the help of a series of inferential processes in which speakers blend together external input – the linguistic code in the form of graphic or acoustic stimuli – and internal input – linguistic information, word knowledge, and their own experience – to create a mental representation of the text and recover the communicated assumption (Van Dijk and Kintsch 1983). But these processes are neither automatic nor perfect. Languages have specific devices to help minimize these cognitive efforts. Focus operators are one of those devices. They are invariable linguistic units that guide the inferences made in communication according to their different semantic, morphosyntactic and pragmatic properties thus leading the reader (or hearer) to expected effects and saving processing effort (Blakemore 1987; Sperber and Wilson 1995, 2002; Levinson 2000; Wilson and Sperber 2002). This is possible because not all linguistic units contribute in the same way to information processing. Hence, in (1)

(1) Cynthia and Antoine learn Spanish, English, even Chinese.

1 The research presented in this chapter has been conducted within the project CONICYT International co-operation No. 201150058.
2 We would like to thank Prof. Dr. Óscar Loureda Lamas for the time and patience he has invested in discussing earlier versions of this chapter.

nouns and verbs provide lexical information with propositional content that enable the creation of mental representations and affect the truth conditions of the utterances in which they occur. They include conceptual information that is intuitively related to people and systems that (may) exist in real life. On the other side, the adverb *even* cannot make any difference to the truth condition of the utterance, and as a result cannot be considered as encoding concepts. It contains information on how to constrain the inferential computations undergone (conceptual vs procedural meaning, cf. Blakemore 1987; Carston 2002, 2004).[3]

Focus operators are procedural units that guide comprehension processes and impose certain information patterns on other elements of the utterance. They work at the textual level by delimiting the informative structure of discourse. More specifically, they provide instructions on how to connect segments both by cohesion and coherence relations. According to Halliday and Hassan (1976: 4), cohesion takes place 'when the interpretation of some element in the discourse is dependent on that of another'. Based on this definition, Sanders and Maat (2006) defined coherence as a type of connectedness that is not only based on textual signals but takes into account connectedness between discourse segments, which create mental representations based on inferences.[4] However, information is not always homogeneously distributed in discourse. Speakers make use of thematic structures, focalization, topicalization, dislocation, passivization and nominalization, among other strategies, to adjust their message according to their intention, receivers' knowledge or discourse dynamics (Halliday 1985, 2004; Martin 1993; Halliday and Matthiessen 2004).

The processing of dicourse markers has been extensively studied in L1 (for an example, see Chapter 1 by Sainz in this volume). Relatively speaking, a smaller number of second language acquisition studies have looked at how non-native speakers (henceforth NNs) process discourse

3 The procedural meaning of discourse markers has been described by Aijmer (2006) and experimentally tested by Nadal et al. (2016) (see also Loureda et al. 2014, 2015, 2016 and Nadal et al. 2017).

4 For Sanders, Spooren and Noordman (1992) and Spooren and Sanders (2008), coherence relations may be referential – present in smaller linguistic units with the same mental referent – or relational – established among discourse segments of varying length.

markers in comparison to the processing of the operators in different target languages (for Italian, see Andorno 2000, 2005; Dimroth 1998; Benazzo and Andorno 2010; Borreguero 2012; for German, see Becker and Rainer 1996; Bonvin and Dimroth 2016; see Benazzo et al. 2004 for a contrastive approach using Italian, German, Polish). In general terms, with respect to non-native discourse processing, these studies have concluded that although NNSs at different levels of proficiency can process and produce discourse markers in a target-like form, it is less possible for them to master these devices in a native-like manner (Flecken, Stutterheim and Carroll, 2013; Andorno and Turco 2015; Bonvin and Dimroth 2016). However, most of the abovementioned studies have focused on the production of discourse markers or the use of these markers as a way to organize discourse for comprehension but have not investigated L2 learners' online processing of focus operators using the eye-tracking technique. The study that we present in this edited volume is original in that it presents a L2 processing approach to the focus operator *even*, whose processing guiding properties in L2 acquisition have so far remained underexplored. More explicitly, the aim of this study was to investigate the focus operator *even* as a unit with procedural meaning to determine its role in aiding the processing of pragmatic scales by NNs of English at an intermediate proficiency level.

The chapter is organized in six parts. After the introduction, we present a review of relevant literature on the focus operator *even* and include previous studies that have explored the processing of discourse markers, with an emphasis on studies that have employed eye tracking. Then, we present the study and describe the methodology used. In the following sections, data analysis is explained and results are revealed. A discussion on the significance of the findings follows. The chapter ends with concluding remarks and suggestions for future research.

The focus operator *even*

Focalization is a key process in the structuring of information in discourse (Halliday 1967). Focus structures have direct consequences on sentence processing and receivers' perception (Gotzner, Wartenburger and Spalek

2016: 60). Focused elements are perceived as elements of informational importance and this has an impact on readers' attention (Birch and Garnsey 1995) and memory representations of discourse (Sandorf, Price and Sandorf 2009). Unmarked foci are common elements within thematic and information structures (Trager and Smith 1951; Jackendoff 1972; Gundel 1999; Loureda et al. 2015). Prototypically, they convey new information and are located in the rheme. The speaker may also choose to highlight the focus either prosodically or morphosyntactically by means of a focus operator, which usually reflects the intention of the speaker by directly signaling an element, the focus, as the most informative in an utterance (Kay 1990: 66), as in (1):

(1) Cynthia and Antoine learn Spanish, English, even Chinese.

Focus operators determine interpretation of focused elements in relation to their background (Nølke 1983; Rooth 1985, 1992). Therefore, they are context-dependent. They indicate the presence of alternatives that are relevant for interpretation (Rooth 1992; Gotzner, Wartenburger, and Spalek 2016) and impose paradigmatic restrictions by selecting the most relevant element in a specific context (Kay 1990; König 1991; Schwenter 1999; Gast and Van der Auwera 2011; Gast and Rzymski 2015). Focus operators may establish a focus by eliminating possible alternatives, or by combining alternatives and a focus. In (2),

(2) Cynthia and Antoine learn only Chinese.
(3) Cynthia and Antoine learn Spanish, English, and also Chinese.

the exclusive focus operator *only* eliminates possible alternatives to the focus. In (1) and (3) *even* and *also* add alternatives to the focus. In (1), alternatives are ordered within a scale of likelihood, from which the focus emerges as the most unexpected value (Kartunnen 1977; König 1991). The type of semantic value of the elements in the scale evoked by the focus operator *even* may differ in the source of coherence established between the focus and the alternatives. Thus, the scale can be semantic 'if the discourse segments are related because of their propositional content' (Sanders, Spooren and Noordman 1992: 7), as in (4):

(4) It is certainly not the only type, and maybe not even the best type.

If 'the discourse segments are related because of the illocutionary meaning of one or both of the segments' (Sanders, Spooren and Noordman 1992: 8), the scale would be pragmatic, as in (1) above. In an utterance like this, the listener/reader will infer that some languages are more difficult than others based on the scalar instruction triggered by *even*. However, pragmatic scales also reflect pragmatic assumptions shared by speakers (Fauconnier 1975). Hence, the mental representation that will emerge from the interaction of the alternatives, the operator and the focus will also need to include part of the encyclopedic knowledge stored in our long-term memory. Consequently, the listener/reader may interpret that the two names (Cynthia and Antoine) indicate a French origin and that, due to typological distance, it is easier for native French speakers to learn English than Chinese.

Pragmatic scales have an additive function. Additive scales may be culminative or non-culminative (Portolés 2007). In (1), the focus operator *even* establishes a culminative scale among all the members in the enumeration ('English, Spanish, Chinese'), the last of which ('Chinese') becomes the focus and also the more informative element in the scale (English, Spanish / Chinese) (König 1991; Gast and Rzymski 2015). This is the main difference with *also*, which establishes an egalitarian, non-culminative relationship between all the coordinated elements. In (5),

(5) Cynthia and Antoine learn Spanish, English and also Chinese.

the scale established by *also* arranges the elements so that the higher value is achieved by the sum of all values (studying English, Spanish and Chinese is more informative than studying English and Spanish). This feature is exclusive of non-culminative additive scales, and it allows for the rearrangement of the elements without altering the meaning as in (6) below. In contrast, when *even* is used, the rigidity of the procedural meaning contained in the operator (cf. Escandell-Vidal and Leonetti 2011) makes it harder to integrate the alternatives and the focus into their context, resulting in pragmatically awkward statements, as is the case in (7):

(6) Cynthia and Antoine learn Chinese, English and also Spanish.
(7) #Cynthia and Antoine learn Chinese, English even Spanish.

Eye-tracking experiments in Second Language Acquisition

A few of the studies discussed above have used psycholinguistic techniques such as eye-tracking to tap into readers' online language processing of discourse markers. As explained in preceding chapters, eye-tracking is a technique used to record eye-movement behaviour and track the readers' eyes as they read on a computer screen; more specifically, an eye-tracker provides temporal and spatial measurements of the cornea when the eyes visit a given stimulus (Keating and Jegerski 2015; for a more in-depth description, see Holmqvist et al. 2011). Based on the *Eye-Mind Hypothesis* (Just and Carpenter 1980), which assumes that eye movements and cognitive processes are inextricably linked, the eye-tracking technique has been said to give researchers a window into the reader's mind and provide crucial information about language processing.

In second language acquisition research in particular, online methods, such as eye-tracking, have been used to investigate issues concerning the learner's current knowledge of the second language and the way in which learners process the L2 in real time (see Roberts and Siyanova-Chanturia 2013; Godfroid and Gass 2013; Keating and Jegerski 2015; Winke, Conklin and Pellicer-Sanchez 2016; Ferreira and Bernales forthcoming). These studies emphasize that the importance of using L2 learners' processing data from eye-tracking lies in the information that can be accessed to advance our understanding of the type of knowledge that NNSs have of the target language and better capture the processes of language learning.

In recent years, an increasing number of L2 studies have used eye-tracking to explore the processing of discourse markers. Zufferey, Mak, Degand and Sanders (2015) tested L2 learner's explicit and implicit knowledge of discourse connectives using a grammaticality judgement task and eye movement recordings. The comparison of these two measures provided insights into the role of L1 transfer in the processing of discourse connectives. Eye-tracking data revealed a differential effect in L2 learners' sensitivity to the meaning conveyed by connectives in comparison to the offline task. Thus, evidence from eye-tracking showed that L2 learners were able to process connectives in a native-like manner whereas the grammaticality judgement task showed L1 transfer effects. Studies like Zufferey et al. (2015) are two-fold. They have advanced our understanding of L2 processing of discourse markers, while at the same time they have provided robust evidence for the benefits of using eye-tracking data to investigate L2 discourse processing.

In a similar vein, Degand and Sanders (2002) and Zufferey and Gygax (2017) also studied the processing of connectives in NNSs. However, focus operators, like *even*, have received more attention in L1 than in L2 studies. In Spanish, the operator *incluso* [*even*] has been analysed by Loureda, Cruz, and DPKog (2013, 2014), Loureda et al. (2015) and Nadal et al. (2017). In German, Rudka and Gerwien (2015; see also Gerwien and Rudka 2016) used the visual world paradigm to study the processing of the German *sogar* [*even*] and Gotzner (2017; see also Gotzner and Spalek 2016 and Gotzner, Wartenburger, and Spalek 2016) analysed the exclusive operator *nur* [*only*]. An exception to that would be Ivanova and Bello's exploratory study (this volume), which used an L1/L2 contrastive approach to the study of *even* and, thus, set the ground for an in-depth analysis of the focus operator *even* in L2.

Methodology

On the basis of previous L1 sentence processing research on discourse markers discussed in the previous section, in this study it was hypothesized that given its comprehension guiding properties (procedural meaning), the inclusion of a focus operator would trigger different paths in the processing of pragmatic scales. To test our hypothesis, an eye-tracking reading experiment was designed. This technique was used because it allows the tracking of the real-time cognitive effort that takes place when performing a complex activity like reading (Reinhart 1981; Rayner 1998, 2009; Papafragou and Musolino 2003; Pouscoulous et al. 2007; Richardson et al. 2007; Holmqvist 2011). Based on the assumption that gaze is a reliable indicator of visual attention, cognitive effort and linguistic processing, eye movement recordings were used to analyse the information processing of the focalization process triggered by the operator *even*.

Dependent variables

In order to measure processing effort, fixations[5] were taken as the basic measure. We analysed data according to three dependent variables: 1) the *total reading time*, which is the sum of all fixations in the interest area for the duration of the entire trial; 2) the *first-pass reading time*, which is the sum of the duration of all fixations on a word (or area of interest, AOI) before the reader fixates another word or area of interest; this measure reflects how low-level cognitive processes are carried out (Duchowski 2007: 3) and indicates initial stages of sentence processing; and 3) the *second-pass reading* time, equivalent to the time needed to re-read an AOI, which is an indicator of high-level processing in information retrieval (Hyönä, Lorch and Rinck 2003), when the initial assumption created during the first reading is confirmed, rejected or modified.

5 Fixations are periods of time in which the eyes remain still and new information is processed. They are combined with saccadic movements in which the eyes change the point of foveal fixation. Fixation durations normally range from 100 ms to over 500 ms, with a mean of approximately 250 ms (Rayner and Pollatsek 1989). However, eye fixation patterns and fixation duration are highly variable. They may depend on low level variables like word length (Rayner and McConkie 1976), word frequency (Just and Carpenter 1980; Inhoff and Rayner 1986), word familiarity (Rayner 1998) and polysemy (Sereno, O'Donnell, and Rayner 2006). High level parameters like readers' skills may also play a role (Ashby, Rayner, and Clifton 2005). Differences between NSs and NNSs concerning fixation duration and word recognition and predictability have been reported (Gottardo and Mueller 2009, Shakkour 2014).

Design and independent variables

The morphosyntax of critical experimental utterances was controlled following Clifton, Staub and Rayner's recommendations (2007). All words had simple morphology and they belonged to standard English. Polysemy was avoided, and word frequency and familiarity were controlled.[6] Word length effects were addressed by using words with approximately a similar number of letters (five to six characters long for all the words in the stimulus). Sentences had a simple syntax following an affirmative SVO pattern; verbs had a plural subject and were conjugated in the present tense. Reference words were avoided. A second sentence after the critical utterance aimed at avoiding the effect of increased processing associated with intra- and inter-clause integration (wrap-up effect, cf. Just and Carpenter 1980; Rayner, Kambe and Duffy 2000).

Critical experimental items were inserted in short stories presented in several slides, which consisted of a multimodal context (i.e. pictures), the critical items and several filler items (ratio 1:2). In each short story, the first slide contained the picture of the two protagonists of the story and a short introductory text. The alternatives of the pragmatic scale tested were explicitly mentioned so as to provide a context for the information presented in the critical items and enable the subsequent assemblage of background and new information. The function of the filler items, on the other side, was to prevent awareness about the linguistic variables addressed in the experiment and therefore prevent participants from altering their reading routine. Before slides containing critical and filler items, a fixation cross was introduced to secure that participants' visual target lied out of any of the AOIs when they gained access into slides with text. An example of one of the short stories contained in the experiment and its distribution in slides (marked with square brackets) is offered in (8).

6 All words were within *OED*'s Band 6, that is, those with occurrences 'between 10 and 100 times per million words in typical modern English usage' (*OED online*).

(8) [Cynthia and Antoine are two French students. They are interested in foreign cultures and have studied English, German, and Spanish for years.][Context/Filler1] [Their parents are very proud of them.][Filler 2] [Cynthia and Antoine learn English, German, Spanish, and even Chinese.] [Critical item] [They would like to travel around the world.][wrap up effect inhibitor]

To test how the focus operator was processed, two linguistic independent variables were tested in this experiment, namely a) the presence/absence of the focus operator and b) the use of a pragmatically informative/non-informative focus in the scale.

(9) a. Cynthia and Antoine learn English, Spanish, even Chinese.
b. Cynthia and Antoine learn English, Spanish and Chinese.
(10) a. Cynthia and Antoine learn English, Spanish, even Chinese.
b. Cynthia and Antoine learn Chinese, Spanish, even English.

The two conditions tested in variable a (presence/absence of the operator) studied the processing costs of the focus operator *even*. Both in (9a) and in (9b) a topic containing new information ('Chinese') was integrated into a scale whose context was already given in the general context of the story. In statements containing *even* (9a), the operator offers a procedural instruction and eliminates the need to contextualize information because it already includes information about the interpretation of focused elements in relation to their background. In variable b (informative/non-informative focus), the relationship among the focus, the focus operator and other alternatives in the utterance was analysed. Statements containing a pragmatically informative focus ('Chinese' in 10a) are structures where the operator reinforces the information provided in the pragmatic scale and agrees with our knowledge of the world. In statements with a less informative focus ('English' 10b) the premise introduced by the operator (that 'learning English and Spanish is more informative than learning Chinese') collides with our knowledge of the world ('learning Chinese is more informative than learning English, Spanish and German for French speakers').

Critical items were divided into several AOIs reflecting key regions in the focalization process: alternatives, operator and focus. The segmentation of critical items is shown in (11) and (12). In (11) the operator is present whereas in (12) it has been replaced by the conjunction *and*.

(11) Cynthia and Antoine learn [English, Spanish,]^Alternatives [even Chinese.]^Operators + Focus
(12) Cynthia and Antoine learn [English, Spanish]^Alternatives [and Chinese.]^Conjunction + Focus

All participants read all conditions in different topics following a pseudo-counterbalanced measure design that ensured the lack of order effects (Cowart 1997).

Experiment procedure

The reading experiments were recorded with an eye-tracker TOBII TX300 at a sampling rate of 300 Hz. Following the manufacturer's specifications, participants were seated at approximately 65 cm distance from the computer screen into which the eye-tracker was integrated, and a chin rest was used to ensure data quality. After reading the instructions and calibrating the gaze (a 5-point calibration grid was used), participants read the short stories. Reading was silent and self-paced as participants had to press the spacebar in the keyboard in front of them to change slides. Only after the experiment was completed, was the specific object of study disclosed to participants.

Data collection

This eye-tracking experiment was conducted with a convenience sample of 62 Spanish native speakers who were students in an English as a Foreign Language (henceforth EFL) teaching program in Chile. The selection criterion focused primarily on English proficiency. All the undergraduate students who volunteered to participate were in an intermediate English course at their institution, and they took the online version of the Vocabulary Size Test (Nation and Beglar 2007). On average, participants scored in the 6,000-word families range. Ages ranged from 19 to 26 years old. Gender was not deemed relevant for this study, but it can be reported that about 60% of the participants were female, and they had normal to corrected vision. Exclusion criteria included self-reported history of mental illness or learning disability. Ten participants were also excluded due to unsuccessful calibration. The final sample for data analysis was 52.

Results and discussion

From a semantic point of view, focus operators select an element belonging to a set or paradigm as the most relevant in a specific context (Nølke 1983; Rooth 1985; Gotzner 2017). More specifically, *even* has a scalar meaning, that is, it establishes some kind of scale among all the elements of the paradigm and presents the focused element as culminative. It triggers and guides the inferences needed to reconstruct the implicit meaning of the utterance, thus facilitating its processing. This facilitating effect has been proved in L1 readers but there is less certainty as to whether L2 readers would react in a similar way. In this study, two variables were developed to test the effect of the focus operator in the processing of pragmatic scales.

Variable a: Presence/absence of the operator

The presence of the focus operator *even* imposes a certain information pattern in the utterance and makes explicit a non-homogeneous informative structure in which the focus stands out as the most informative element in the scale in which it appears. As focus operators are linguistic units with procedural meaning, it is expected that their processing costs should be higher than those of words with conceptual content, as was demonstrated experimentally by Loureda et al. (2015) and Nadal et al. (2016, 2017) in their studies with L1 speakers on Sp. *incluso* [*even*]. Our data correspond broadly to their results and show that focalized structures with an explicit focus operator trigger different processing paths. Figure 4.1 shows that the focalization process demands higher processing costs during the first reading of the utterance. Both in (9a) and (9b) the cognitive effort required to process the operator (or conjunction) and the focus is higher than that needed to process the alternatives (39.97% and 38.94%, respectively). If we compare across conditions, there is an increase of 22.42% in the processing costs of the last part of the utterance when the operator is present.

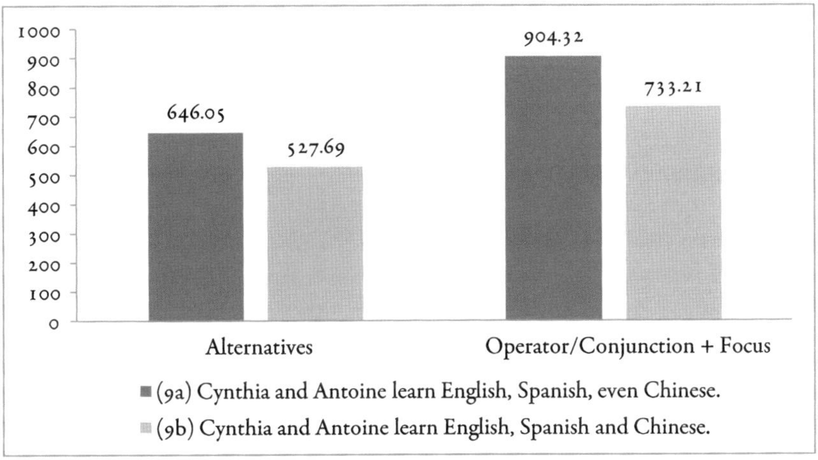

Figure 4.1. First-pass reading time, variable a (presence/absence of the operator)

In accordance with Loureda et al.'s (2015) results, it was expected that the syntactic integration of a marked focus in a SVO structure (the one co-occurring with *even*, as in (9a)) would not present higher processing costs in the AOI of the focus. Our data, however, reflect that unmarked foci are 58.53% easier to process (p >.01). Processing costs for the second alternative and the operator/conjunction stay relatively similar in both conditions (p =.13 and p =.06, respectively). This shows that the focalization process has suffered a process of internal redistribution. Unlike results reported by Loureda et al. (2015) and Nadal et al. (2016, 2017) that showed that native Spanish speakers required a higher processing effort in the AOI of the operator, in the case of English L2 speakers, this increase in effort associated with the focalization process is scattered across a wider area that concerns also the focus.

First-pass reading time informs about the decodification of semantic and morphosyntactic structures, as well as the creation of the first construction of the general assumption. After the first reading is complete, the reader may read specific areas again to extract the necessary information to reanalyse the communicated assumption and complete the process of information retrieval. In (9a), the focus operator enables and determines the reconstruction of the communicated assumption. Considering that the access to the procedural instruction offered by the operator implies a higher processing effort, more and longer fixations (and therefore higher values in Figure 4.2) were recorded in the AOI of the operator and the focus during second-pass (see Figure 4.2). Indeed, the introduction of the focus operator increases the processing costs of the last part of the utterance in 129.45%.

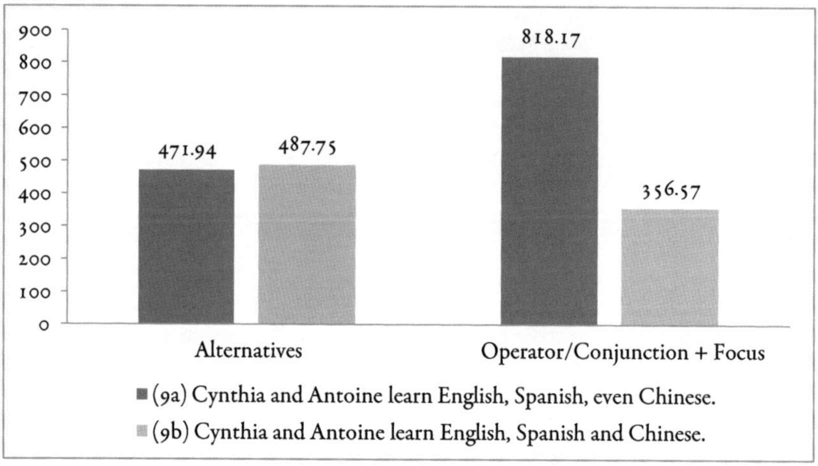

Figure 4.2. Second-pass reading time, variable a (presence/absence of the operator)

A further effect was expected during second-pass reading time. In comparison with what happens in the re-reading of the operator, which requires more effort, the processing costs of the focus should not increase during the successive re-readings and the reprocessing of an unmarked focus should not require higher processing costs than those of a marked one. This would be caused by a 'lateral effect' of the operator over the focus (Loureda et al. 2015), as the first constrains the effort needed to reprocess the latter. This results in the elicitation of the focus as the most informative element in the scale without causing an increase of its processing costs, which should be similar to those of the alternatives. Our data cannot confirm this lateral effect, as foci in utterances containing *even* have significantly higher processing costs than those in utterances containing *and* (p = >.01). On the contrary, the high processing costs of marked foci may be an indication that L2 speakers tend to disregard the procedural instruction provided by the operator and attempt to interpret the scalarity of the set of conceptual words from the last of its members.

There are also differences in the cognitive effort needed to process utterances with *even* and *and*. In data from Spanish L1 speakers, the presence of the operator leads to a redistribution of the processing costs within the utterance highlighting some areas and backgrounding others (Nadal et al. 2016: 62). However, instead of acknowledging the access strategy to the scalar implicature provided by the operator, L2 speakers seem to process utterances with *even* in a non-target like form. Thus, the instruction of scalarity introduced by the operator does not result in an increase of its processing costs, but is scattered among the alternatives, the operator and the focus. This progressive augmentation of processing costs is not paralleled in utterances without *even*, where cognitive effort seems similar in all areas of interest.

This internal redistribution of the processing of the focalization process can also be perceived in Figure 4.3. The total reading times in the last part of the utterance increase by 70% when the operator is present whereas the processing of the alternatives in the two conditions analysed is not significantly different.

Variable b: Informative/non-informative focus

The effect of focus operators on discourse processing depends on their specific semantic and syntactic properties, as well as on the interaction between such properties and the other elements in the utterance. The focus operator *even* establishes a scalar relationship among the members of the enumeration in which it is inserted highlighting the last as the most informative

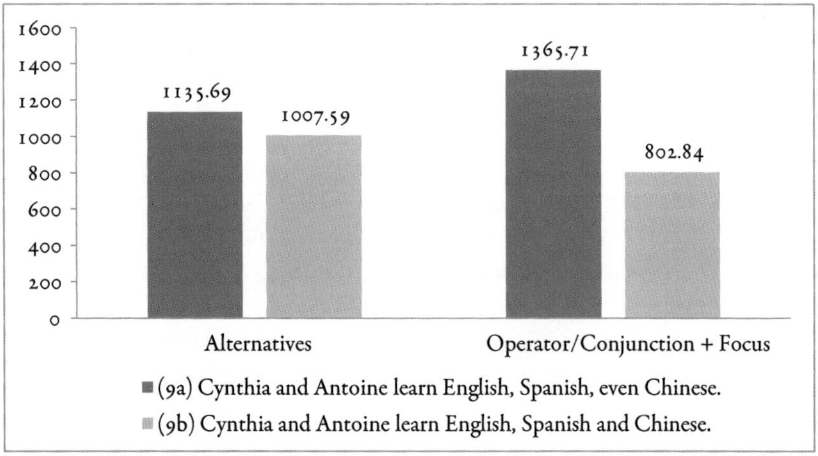

Figure 4.3. Total reading time, variable a (presence/absence of the operator)

(König 1991, Gast and Rzymski 2015). The linguistic input has yet to be blended with the reader's knowledge and own experience stored in their memory. Consequently, the co-occurrence of *even* with a non-informative focus (as in (10b)) can be expected to demand a higher cognitive effort, whereas informative foci (as in (10a)) should be easier to process when combined with the operator. However, this is not the situation depicted in Figures 4.4–4.6. L2 speakers show scarce sensitivity to the scalar instruction of the operator and the properties of foci in pragmatic scales. Data in Figure 4.4 show that focus operators combined with informative foci require an increase of 66.27% in processing costs.

Both during first-pass and second-pass (see Figures 4.4 and 4.5), the AOIs containing the operator and an informative focus require higher processing costs ($p=>.01$ in both cases). This contradicts the expectation that operators should be integrated in well-formed pragmatic scales in which the ordering of the elements coincides with our shared world knowledge whose last of element stands out as the least expected element in the set of alternatives.

Data in Figure 4.6 show that the processing of scales containing a non-informative focus (as in (10b)) follows a flat path in which none of the elements seems to stand out. The use of an informative focus (as in (10a))

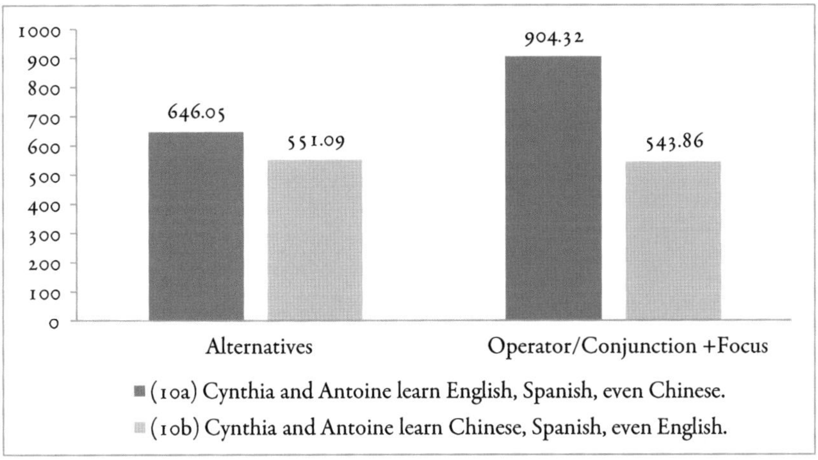

Figure 4.4. First-pass reading time, variable b (informative/non-informative focus)

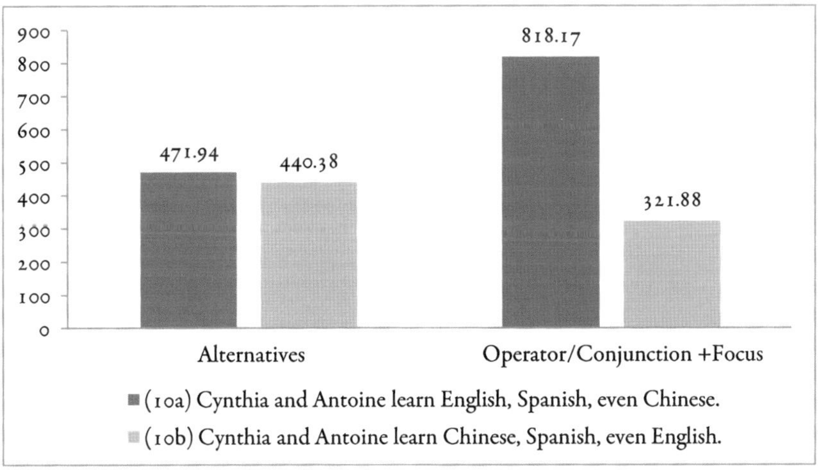

Figure 4.5. Second-pass reading time, variable b (informative/non-informative focus)

results in an increase of 154.18% in the processing costs of the last part of the utterances. The internal redistribution of the processing of the focalization process that was considered in the last section is in this case added to the pragmatically abnormal rearranging of the elements in the scale and it results in a change in the processing path, which becomes flat. Thus, when participants read a pragmatically awkward scale, they cease to integrate given and new information and concentrate their effort on the lexical element. Attention is then scattered over all AOIs and no longer maintained in the focalization region. The use of a (non-)informative focus can therefore be seen as a relevant element in the decodification of the information contained in pragmatic scales.

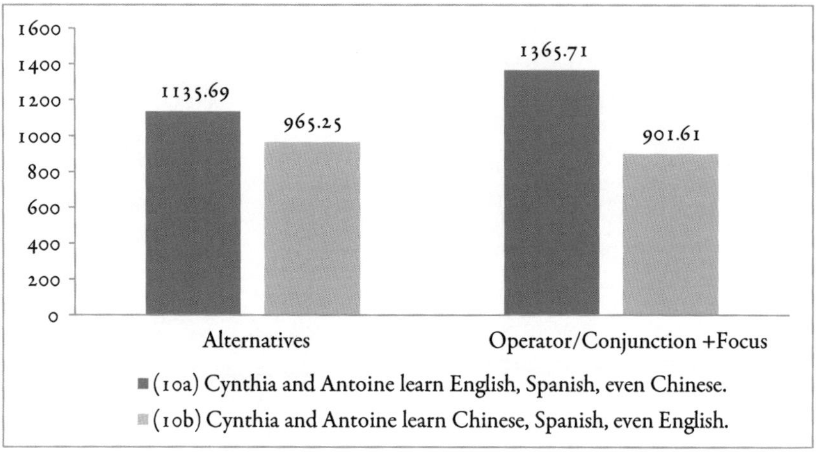

Figure 4.6. Total reading time, variable b (informative/non-informative focus)

Conclusions

The study presented in this chapter aimed to investigate second language learners' sensitivity to the procedural meaning of the focus operator *even* in processing pragmatic scales. Results showed different processing paths for additive (i.e. *and*) and scalar relations (i.e. *even*). However, L2 readers do not assign a facilitative role to the focus operator when reading pragmatic scales. Instead, we found a processing pattern that suggests learners' transition towards the acquisition of the procedural meaning of the scales based on lexical elements with conceptual meaning. This transition was revealed after a descriptive examination of the data and was evidenced in progressively higher early fixation measures (i.e. *first-pass*) and in higher late fixation measures (i.e. *total reading time* and *second-pass*) of the elements in the scale. Statistical analysis supported a significant higher processing cost of the focused element in the scale, which can be explained, as results show, by learners' inability to use the focus operator to aid the processing of the scale and by their tendency, instead, to rely more on other lexical elements in the utterances. Similarly, when presented with different levels of informativity in the scales, NNSs did not show a significantly different amount of attention to the focus operator, and selected the focus as the most relevant element to access the decodification of the scale. To some extent, the results of this study are supported by those obtained by Ivanova and Bello Viruega (this volume), which provide further evidence for a difference between native and non-native speakers in accessing procedural instructions displayed by the operator.

Interestingly, the findings discussed here seem to differ from the results for the connective *therefore* presented by Narváez García and Torres in this volume but are indeed complementary. As a matter of fact, certain discourse markers receive more attention and are explicitly taught in most EFL and English for academic purposes courses while others, like *even*, are neglected (which is also the case in other Foreign Language courses; see for example, Koch and Thörle in Chapter 5). The reason might be that *even* has different meanings (i.e. adjective and adverb), and thus, its scalar properties are rarely emphasized, if at all. Other connectives, like *therefore* (or *however*, *nevertheless*, etc.) are frequently explicitly learned, and consequently, they are much more familiar to second language learners. The pedagogical implication that can be derived from these findings is straightforward: focus operators need to be noticed to display their facilitative processing effects in L2 processing. Explicit attention to the operator and subsequent instruction on how to interpret scales might then become implicit knowledge and aid with processing costs in the long run. We believe that our findings represent an important attempt to understand and describe the processing of focus operators and, more generally, contribute to the characterization of discourse markers from a L2 processing perspective.

Bibliography

Andorno, Cecilia, *Focalizzatori e messa a fuoco. Il punto di vista delle varietà di apprendimento* (Milano: Franco Angeli, 2000).

Andorno, Cecilia, 'Additive and Restrictive Particles in Italian as a Second Language. Embedding in the Verbal Utterance Structure' in Henriette Hendricks, ed., *The Structure of Learner Varieties* (Berlin: Mouton de Gruyter, 2005), 405–460.

Andorno, Cecilia, and Giuseppina Turco, 'Embedding Additive Particles in the Sentence Information Structure. How L2 Learners Find Their Way through Positional and Prosodic Patterns' in Anna-María De Cesare, and Cecilia Maria Andorno, eds, *Focus Particles in the Romance and Germanic Languages. Corpus-based and Experimental Approaches. Linguistik Online 71/2* (2015), 57–79. DOI: <http://dx.doi.org/10.13092/lo.71.1778>.

Ashby, Jane, Keith Rayner, and Charles Clifton. 'Eye Movements of Highly Skilled and Average Readers: Differential Effects of Frequency and Predictability'. *The Quarterly Journal of Experimental Psychology Section A* 58, no. 6 (2005): 1065–1086.

Becker, Angelika, and Rainer Dietrich, 'The Acquisition of Scope in German'. *Zeitschrift für Literaturwissenschaft und Linguistik 104* (1996), 115–141.

Benazzo, Sandra, and Cecilia Andorno, 'Discourse Cohesion and Topic Discontinuity in Native and Learner Production: Changing Topic Entities on Maintained Predicates' in Leah Roberts, Martin Howard and David Singleton, eds, *EuroSLA Yearbook 10* (Amsterdam: Benjamins, 2010), 92–118.

Benazzo, Sandra, Christine Dimroth, Clive Perdue, and Marzena Watorek, 'Le rôle des particules additives dans la construction de la cohésion discursive en langue maternelle et en langue étrangère'. *Langages*, 3 (2004), 76–105.

Birch, Stacy L., and Susan M. Garnsey, 'The Effect of Focus on Memory for Words in Sentences'. *Journal of Memory and Language* 34, no. 2 (1995): 232–267.

Blakemore, Diane, *Semantic Constraints on Relevance* (Oxford: Blackwell, 1987)

Bonvin, Audrey, and Christine Dimroth, 'Additive Linking in Second Language Discourse: Lexical, Syntactic and Discourse Organizational Choices in Intermediate and Advanced Learners of L2 German with L1 French'. *A Journal of Linguistics, Psycholinguistics and Computational Linguistics* 18 (2016).

Borreguero Zuloaga, Margarita, 'Focalizzatori nelle varietà di apprendimento: il caso di anche.' In Patricia Bianchi, Nicola De Blasi, Chiara De Caprio, Francesco Montuori, eds, *La variazione nell'italiano e nella sua storia. Varietà e varianti linguistiche e testuali. Atti dell'XI Convegno della Società Internazionale di Linguistica e Filologia Italiana.* Firenze, Franco Cesati (2012), vol. 2, 219–230.

Carston, Robyn, *Thoughts and Utterances: The Pragmatics of Explicit Communication* (Oxford: Blackwell, 2002)

Carston, Robyn, 'Relevance Theory and the Saying & Implicating Distinction'. In Laurence Horn and Gregory Ward, eds, *The Handbook of Pragmatics* (Oxford, Blackwell, 2004), 633– 656.

Cowart, Wayne, *Experimental Syntax: Applying Objective Methods to Sentence Judgments* (Thousand Oaks, CA: Sage Publications Inc., 1997)

Clifton, Charles, Adrian Staub, and Keith Rayner, 'Eye Movements in Reading Words and Sentences.' In R. V. Gompel, M. Fisher, W. Murray, R. L. Hill, eds *Eye Movements: A Window on Mind and Brain* (Amsterdam: Elsevier, 2007)

Conklin, Kathy, and Ana Pellicer-Sánchez, 'Using Eye-Tracking in Applied Linguistics and Second Language Research.' *Second Language Research* 32, no. 3 (2016): 453–467.

Degand, Liesbeth, and Ted Sanders, 'The Impact of Relational Markers on Expository Text Comprehension in L1 and L2.' *Reading and Writing* 15, no. 7 (2002): 739–757.

Van Dijk, Teun Adrianus, and Walter Kintsch, *Strategies of Discourse Comprehension* (New York: Academic Press, 1983).

Dimroth, Christine, 'Indiquer la portée en allemand L2: une étude longitudinale de l'acquisition des particules de portée.' *Acquisition et interaction en langue étrangère* 11 (1998): 11–34.

Duchowski, Andrew T., 'Eye Tracking Methodology.' *Theory and Practice* 328 (2007).

Escandell-Vidal, Victoria, and Manuel Leonetti. 'On the Rigidity of Procedural Meaning', in Maria Victoria Escandell-Vidal, Manuel Leonetti, and Aoife Ahern, eds, *Procedural Meaning: Problems and Perspectives* (Bingley: Emerald, 2011), 81–102.

Ferreira, Roberto, and Carolina Bernales, 'Exploring Foreign Language Learning with Eye-Tracking & Electroencephalography (EEG). What Can Online Tools Add to the Story?', in Anastassiou Fontini and Georgia Andreou, eds, *English as a Foreign Language: Investigating Innovative Theories of Acquisition, Teaching and Development of Communication and Intercultural Skills* (Cambridge Scholars Publishing, forthcoming).

Flecken, Monique, Christiane von Stutterheim, and Mary Carroll, 'Principles of Information Organization in L2 Use: Complex Patterns of Conceptual Transfer.' *International Review of Applied Linguistics in Language Teaching* 51, no. 2 (2013): 229–242.

Gast, Volker, and Christoph Rzymski, 'Towards a Corpus-Based Analysis of Evaluative Scales Associated with *even*.' *Linguistik online* 71, no. 2 (2015).

Gast, Volker, and Jan van der Auwera, 'Scalar Additive Operators in the Languages of Europe', *Language 87*, 1, 2–54.

Gerwien, Johannes, and Martha Rudka (poster presentation), 'Using the Visual World Paradigm to Study the Online Processing of the German Scalar Focus Particle 'sogar'.' *3rd AttLis workshop*, 10–11 March 2016, Potsdam, Germany. Poster

Godfroid, Aline, and Paula Winke, 'Investigating Implicit and Explicit Processing using L2 Learners' Eye-Movement Data.' In Patrick Rebuschat, ed. *Implicit and Explicit Learning of Languages* (Amsterdam: Benjamins, 2015), 73–90.

Gottardo, Alexandra, and Julie Mueller, 'Are First-and Second-Language Factors Related in Predicting Second-Language Reading Comprehension? A Study of Spanish-speaking Children Acquiring English as a Second Language from First to Second Grade.' *Journal of Educational Psychology* 101, no. 2 (2009): 330–344.

Gotzner, Nicole, 'Alternative Sets in Language Processing: How Focus Alternatives are Represented in the Mind.' *Language and Cognition, Palgrave Macmillan* (2017).

Gotzner, Nicole, Isabell Wartenburger, and Katharina Spalek. 'The Impact of Focus Particles on the Recognition and Rejection of Contrastive Alternatives.' *Language and Cognition* 8, no. 1 (2016), 59–95.

Gundel, Jeanette K., 'On Different Kinds of Focus'. In Peter Bosch, ed. *Focus: Linguistic, Cognitive, and Computational Perspectives* (Cambridge: Cambridge University Press, 1999), 293–305.

Halliday, Michael A. K., *An Introduction to Functional Grammar* (London: Continuum, 1965).

Halliday, Michael A. K., 'Notes on Transitivity and Theme in English: Part 2.' *Journal of Linguistics* 3, no. 2 (1967): 199–244.

Halliday, Michael A. K., 'On the Language of Physical Science'. In Jonathan Webster, ed., *The Language of Physical Science* (London: Continuum, 2004), 162–178.

Halliday, Michael Alexander Kirkwood, and Ruqaiya Hasan, *Cohesion in English* (Harlow: Longman, 1976)

Halliday, Michael, and Christian Matthiessen, *An Introduction to Functional Grammar 3rd edition* (London: Arnold, 2004)

Holmqvist, Kenneth, Marcus Nyström, Richard Andersson, Richard Dewhurst, Halszka Jarodzka, and Joost Van de Weijer, *Eye Tracking: A Comprehensive Guide to Methods and Measures* (Oxford: Oxford University Press, 2011)

Horn, Laurence, 'A Presuppositional Analysis of *only* and *even*', *Chicago Linguistic Society* 5 (1969), 97–108.

Hyönä, Jukka, R. F. Lorch, and Mike Rinck, 'Eye Movement Measures to Study Global Text Processing.' In J. Hyönä, R. Radach and H. Deubel, eds, *The Mind's Eye: Cognitive and Applied Aspects of Eye Movement Research* (Amsterdam: Elsevier, 2003), 313–334.

Inhoff, Albrecht Werner, and Keith Rayner, 'Parafoveal Word Processing during Eye Fixations in Reading: Effects of Word Frequency.' *Perception & Psychophysics* 40 (1986), 431–439.

Jackendoff, Ray S., 'Semantic Interpretation in Generative Grammar' (Cambridge, MA: MIT Press, 1972).

Just, Marcel A., and Patricia A. Carpenter. 'A Theory of Reading: From Eye Fixations to Comprehension.' *Psychological Review* 87, no. 4 (1980), 329–354.

Kay, Paul. 'Even', *Linguistics and Philosophy*, 13 (1990), 59–111.
König, Ekkehard, *The Meaning of Focus Particles: A Comparative Perspective* (London: Routledge, 2002).
Levinson, Stephen, *Presumptive Meanings: The Theory of Generalized Conversational Implicature* (Cambridge, MA: MIT Press, 2000)
Loureda, Óscar, Adriana Cruz, and DPKog research group, 'Aproximación experimental sobre los costes de procesamiento de las partículas focales del español *también* e *incluso*.' *Cuadernos AISPI. Estudios de lenguas y literaturas ibéricas e iberoamericanas, 2 – Nuevas tendencias en la lingüística del discurso* (2013), 75–98.
Loureda, Óscar, Adriana Cruz, and DPKog research group, 'En los márgenes del léxico: las partículas focales del español (*incluso*, *también*) y el análisis experimental.' In Luque Toro, Luis and Rocío Luque, eds, *Léxico Español Actual*, Vol. IV (Venedig: Cafoscarina, 2014), 85–104.
Loureda, Óscar, Adriana Cruz, Martha Rudka, Laura Nadal, Inés Recio, and Margarita Borreguero Zuloaga, 'Focus Particles in Information Processing: An Experimental Study on Pragmatic Scales with Spanish *incluso*.' In Anna Maria De Cesare and Cecilia Andorno, eds, *Linguistik online 71, 2/15 Focus Particles in the Romance and Germanic Languages. Experimental and Corpus-Based Approaches* (2015), 129–151.
Martin, James R., 'Literacy in Science: Learning to Handle Text as Technology'. In Michael A. K. Halliday and James R. Martin, eds, *Writing Science: Literacy and Discursive Power* (Pittsburgh, PA: University of Pittsburgh Press, 1993), 166–202.
Nadal, Laura, Adriana Cruz, Inés Recio, and Oscar Loureda, 'El significado procedimental y las partículas discursivas del español: Una aproximación experimental.' *Revista Signos* 49 (2016), 52–77.
Nadal, Laura, Inés Recio Fernández, Martha Rudka, and Óscar Loureda, 'Processing Additivity in Spanish: *incluso* vs *además*'. In Anna Maria De Cesare and Cecilia Andorno, eds, *Focus on Additivity: Adverbial Modifiers in Romance, Germanic and Slavic languages* (Amsterdam/Philadelphia, PA: John Benjamins, 2017), 136–156.
Nation, I. S. P., and David Beglar, 'A Vocabulary Size Test.' *The Language Teacher* 31, no. 7 (2007): 9–13.
Nølke, Henning, *Les adverbes paradigmatisants: fonction et analyse* (Copenhagen: Akademisk Forlag, 1983).
Papafragou, Anna, and Julien Musolino, 'Scalar Implicatures: Experiments at the Semantics–Pragmatics Interface.' *Cognition* 86/3 (2003), 253–282.
Portolés, José, 'Escalas informativas aditivas: pruebas del español'. *Spanish in Context* 4/2 (2007), 135–157.
Pouscoulous, Nausicaa, Ira A. Noveck, Guy Politzer, and Anne Bastide, 'A Developmental Investigation of Processing Costs in Implicature Production.' *Language Acquisition* 14/4 (2007): 347–375.
Rayner, Keith, 'Eye Movements in Reading and Information Processing: 20 Years of Research.' *Psychological Bulletin* 124/3 (1998) 372–422.

Rayner, Keith, 'Eye Movements and Attention in Reading, Scene Perception, and Visual Search.' *The Quarterly Journal of Experimental Psychology* 62/8 (2009), 1457–1506.

Rayner, Keith, Gretchen Kambe, and Susan A. Duffy, 'The Effect of Clause Wrap-up on Eye Movements during Reading.' *The Quarterly Journal of Experimental Psychology: Section A* 53/4 (2000), 1061–1080.

Rayner, Keith, and George W. McConkie, 'What Guides a Reader's Eye Movements?' *Vision Research* 16/8 (1976), 829–837.

Rayner, Keith, and Alexander Pollatsek, *The Psychology of Reading* (Englewood Cliffs, NJ: Prentice Hall,1989)

Richardson, Daniel C., Rick Dale, and Michael J. Spivey, 'Eye Movements in Language and Cognition.' *Methods in Cognitive Linguistics* 18 (2007): 323–356.

Roberts, Leah, and Anna Siyanova-Chanturia, 'Using Eye-Tracking to Investigate Topics in L2 Acquisition and L2 Processing.' *Studies in Second Language Acquisition* 35/2 (2013), 213–235.

Rooth, Mats, *Association with Focus. Doctoral Thesis* (University of Massachusetts at Amherst, 1985)

Rooth, Mats, 'A Theory of Focus Interpretation.' *Natural Language Semantics* 1(1992), 75–116.

Rudka, Martha, and Gerwien, Johannes (oral presentation), 'The Focus Sensitive Element German "sogar" – Does the Procedural Meaning of *sogar* Help Speakers to Accelerate the Comprehension of a Semantic Scale?' (14th Conference of the International Pragmatics Association, Antwerp, Belgium, 2015).

Sanders, Ted J. M., and H. Pander Maat, 'Cohesion and Coherence: Linguistic Approaches'. In Keith Brown, ed., *Encyclopedia of Language and Linguistics*, Volume 2 (Amsterdam: Elsevier, 2006), 591–595.

Sanders, Ted J. M., Wilbert P. M. Spooren, and Leo G. M. Noordman, 'Toward a Taxonomy of Coherence Relations.' *Discourse Processes* 15, no. 1 (1992), 1–35.

Schwenter, Scott, *Pragmatics of Conditional Marking: Implicature, Scalarity and Exclusivity* (New York: Garland, 1999)

Sperber, Dan, and Deirdre Wilson, *Relevance* (Oxford: Blackwell, 1995)

Sperber, Dan, and Deirdre Wilson, 'Pragmatics, Modularity and Mind-reading.' *Mind & Language* 17/1–2 (2002), 3–23.

Trager, George L., and Henry Lee Smith, *An Outline of English Structure* (Norman: Buttenburg Press, 1951)

Sperber, Dan, and Deirdre Wilson, 'Relevance Theory.' *Working Papers in Linguistics* 14 (2002), 249–287

Winke, Paula M., Aline Godfroid, and Susan M. Gass, 'Eye-Movement Recordings in Second Language Research.' *Studies in Second Language Acquisition* 35/2 (2013): 205–212.

Zufferey, Sandrine, Willem Mak, Liesbeth Degand, and Ted Sanders, 'Advanced Learners' Comprehension of Dscourse Connectives: The Role of L1 Transfer across On-line and Off-line tasks.' *Second Language Research* 31, no. 3 (2015), 389–411.
Zufferey, Sandrine, and Pascal M. Gygax, 'Processing Connectives with a Complex Form-Function Mapping in L2: The Case of French "En Effet"'. *Frontiers in Psychology* 8 (2017), 1198.

CHRISTIAN KOCH AND BRITTA THÖRLE

5 The discourse markers *sí, claro* and *vale* in Spanish as a Foreign Language

Introduction

One step in acquiring communicative competence in a foreign language (henceforth FL) includes that learners become able to actively take part in conversational interaction by organizing their own speech in accordance with the requirements of the communicative context and by contributing to the organization of turns and topics of the conversation. Although adult learners have already acquired a general discursive competence in their L1, they still lack the linguistic means that are necessary to completely deploy this competence in the FL. Our interest in the acquisition of Discourse Markers (henceforth DMs) in Spanish as a FL is due to the fact that DMs are very efficient means by which speakers contribute to the organization of speech and interaction. Unlike other pragmatic resources, DMs are often not systematically taught in classes of ELE (*Español Lengua Extranjera* [Spanish as a Foreign Language]) (which is also the case in EFL courses as discussed previously in Chapter 4 in this volume). In addition, the relation between forms and functions of DMs clearly differs from one language to another so that they cannot be easily transferred from L1 to FL. DMs can thus be considered a central part of communicative competence and a quite difficult one to acquire. With this in mind, the research aim of this chapter is to describe the formal and functional characteristics of DMs in the interlanguage of German learners of ELE in order to advance hypotheses concerning general principles in the acquisition of DMs in FL.

Previous research in this field has shown that the use of lexical DMs in FL is not less frequent than in L1 (cf. Feldmann 1984: 180), and that it is even much higher if we take into consideration nonverbal markers like laughing or gestures (cf. Iñigo Mora and Álvarez Benito 2006). However, the repertoire of forms is extremely limited, especially on the initial levels of competence. Learners of these levels have at their disposal a small set of DMs that are mostly phonetically uncomplex and formally and/or functionally close to DMs in the L1. It is only at higher levels of proficiency that learners show a wider variety of markers, although the progress in the domain of DMs is slower than other (lexical or morpho-syntactic) domains of competence. Even if a greater variety of markers can be observed, learners at these levels still have difficulties to exactly grasp the function of more complex DMs or those that have no similar counterparts in L1 (for an overview of the state of the research see Borreguero Zuloaga and Thörle 2016).

In this paper, we will relate to these findings and reconsider them in the light of the use of DMs by German learners of Spanish as a FL.[1] We will concentrate on the forms *sí*, *claro* and *vale* that prototypically function as affirmation particles. These markers have been chosen because of a) their high-level frequency in our corpus, and b) the observation that they are not only employed in affirmative contexts, but in other conversational situations. In order to determine the role and the dynamics of these elements in the interlanguage of German learners, our approach combines formal and functional and comparative analyses. From a formal point of view, repertoires on different proficiency levels will be compared in order to gain insight into the (quantitative) development of DMs during the process of acquisition. As we start from the assumption that DMs are often not systematically taught in classroom contexts and, therefore, not predominantly learnt by instruction but mainly acquired in spontaneous interaction, we pay special attention to the changes in the interlanguage that can be observed after a period of immersion in the target language. The comparison of repertoires of students with different proficiency levels will therefore be complimented by the comparison of the repertoires of

1 Further publications based on this corpus are Diao-Klaeger and Thörle (2013), Thörle (2015, 2016) for French FL, and Koch (2016, forthcoming) and Thörle (2017) for Spanish FL.

individual students before and after a stay abroad. From a functional point of view, we will take a closer look at the way *sí, claro* and *vale* are used in learner interaction. This will help us to better understand the quantitative findings and to formulate hypotheses regarding the acquisition process.

To summarize, the following questions will be addressed in this chapter:

- What kinds of DMs form part of the repertoire of German students of Spanish as a FL, and what is the relevance of *sí, claro* and *vale* within the repertoire?
- How do the repertoire and the use of the markers differ a) in different proficiency levels and b) before and after a semester or year in a Spanish speaking country?
- What kind of functions do the markers *sí, claro* and *vale* fulfil in the Spanish interlanguage of the students tested?

In the following paragraphs, we will discuss the theoretical background of our study and show how our methodological approach of qualitative and quantitative conversational analyses reveals evidence for DM acquisition approaching native-like speech habits.

Sí, claro and *vale*: Affirmation particles and discourse markers

In the linguistic literature, the term 'discourse marker' is used in quite a heterogeneous way (also see the Introduction to this edited volume). What is considered a DM depends on the theoretical background in which the term is used. Therefore, it seems necessary to us to briefly outline our understanding of the term as well as to describe on this basis the different functions that the forms *sí, claro* and *vale* fulfil in verbal interaction.

According to Bazzanella (2001: 225), DMs can be defined as

> quegli elementi che, svuotandosi in parte del loro significato originario, assumono dei valori aggiuntivi che servono a sottolineare la strutturazione del discorso, a connettere elementi frasali, interfrasali, extrafrasali e a esplicitare la collocazione

dell'enunciato in una dimensione interpersonale, sottolineando la struttura interattiva della conversazione.

[those elements that, emptying themselves from part of their original meaning, assume additive values that serve to highlight discourse structure, to connect sentences, inter-sentence and extra-sentence segments, and to make explicit the interpersonal dimension of the utterance, which highlights the interactive structure of the conversation.]

A formal categorization of DMs is hardly possible due to the fact that the concept comprises elements of various length and complexity which mostly have 'counter parts' in different word classes and linguistic units such as adjectives (*bueno*), adverbs (*entonces*) or verbs (*mira*). DMs have evolved from these word classes in a process of pragmaticalization and now coexist alongside them. They are therefore usually considered a distinct functional class. Its elements fulfil functions on the metadiscursive (opening, closing stretches of discourse), cognitive (connection, coherence between stretches of discourse) and interactional (e.g. turn-taking) level of the organization of discourse (cf. Bazzanella above as well as López Serena and Borreguero Zuloaga 2011). DMs are often considered as multifunctional inasmuch as a particular marker can accomplish different functions depending on the context in which it is used, and it can also fulfil various functions at the same time (Weidenbusch 2014: 16). This implies that the meaning or function of DMs is highly indexical and it can only be described with reference to the specific conversational context in which it is used.

In the lexicographical entry for these elements, *sí*, *claro* and *vale* are first and foremost not described as DMs.[2] In the *Diccionario de la Real Academia Española* (DRAE), for example, *sí* is defined as an adverb that expresses affirmation or confirmation and that is frequently used in order to respond to polar questions (*¿Fuiste ayer al teatro? – Sí* [*Did you go to the theatre yesterday? – Yes, I did*]). Besides its functions as an adjective and as a noun, *claro* also figures in the DRAE as an adverb that expresses agreement

2 For Spanish, however, we are fortunate to have at our disposal various dictionaries specialised in the systematic description of discourse markers (Fuentes Rodríguez 2009; Santos Río 2003; Briz et al. 2000ff.).

and confirmation (*¿Vendrás? – ¡Claro!* [*Will you come? – Sure!*]). Finally, the form *vale* is classified in the DRAE as an interjection used to express agreement and conformance. As affirmation particles, *sí*, *claro* and *vale* are able to form sentence equivalent utterances that constitute a turn constructional unit (TCU) and that prototypically occur as a second pair part, for example in a question-answer-sequence or as the reactive intervention of other adjacency pairs. However, in verbal interaction the propositional meaning and affirmative value of *sí*, *claro* and *vale* sometimes seems to be reduced while other, rather discursive functions on the interactional, metadiscursive or cognitive level, come to the fore. In these cases, *sí*, *claro* and *vale* are considered as DMs and can also appear in other positions and not only at the beginning of a second pair part. It has to be emphasized that this distinction is a gradual and not a discrete one. In concrete conversational contexts, *sí*, *claro* and *vale* can perform different values (cf. also Pons Bordería 2003: 223), and the two functions as agreement particle and DM are more or less overlap. Nevertheless, in most of the cases, a dominant function can be identified.

As an affirmation adverb, *sí* represents the positive answer to a polar question, approves a statement or accepts a speech act. It can also be used as a focus adverb in contrastive or non-contrastive contexts (cf. Santos Río 2003). Apart from these values, *sí* can also function as a DM. Martín Zorraquino and Portolés Lázaro (1999) classify it as a metadiscursive marker in conversation (*marcador metadiscursivo conversacional*). As such, *sí* has no propositional meaning and realizes interactional functions (indicating the reception of the message or the beginning of the reactive turn, cf. also Santos Río 2003 and Fuentes Rodríguez 2009):

> [*Sí* y *ya*] se utilizan para marcar recepción del mensaje (en una intervención replicativa) y, por tanto, de forma indirecta para iniciar un cambio de turno en el uso de la palabra. (Martín Zorraquino and Portolés Lázaro 1999: 4191)
>
> [[*Sí* and *ya*] are used to mark reception of the message (in a replicative intervention) and, therefore, to initiate indirectly a turn-changing.]

Claro as an affirmative particle is more emphatic than *sí*. Regarding the difference between *sí* and *claro*, Briz et al. state that

> el acuerdo manifestado por claro es más enfático. Se forma así una escala entre claro, sí y bueno, que expresan, respectivamente, 'acuerdo enfático' (*claro que sí*), 'acuerdo' (*sí*) y 'acuerdo atenuado' (*bueno/sí*). (Briz et al. 2000ff)
>
> [the agreement expressed in *claro* is more emphatic. A scale is then built from *claro*, *sí* and *bueno*, which express 'emphatic agreement' (*claro que sí*), 'agreement' (*sí*) and 'attenuated agreement' (*bueno/sí*), respectively.]

In contrast to *sí*, the particle *claro* has thus an additional modal value expressing the speaker's attitude or epistemic stance. Pons Bordería (2003: 223) describes these functions as 'speaker-related values'. The speaker 'adopts a stance with regard to the other(s) [...] or with regard to what has been said'. *Claro* in this sense forms part of the class of evidential markers among which it is the most frequent one in colloquial conversation (cf. also Martín Zorraquino and Portolés Lázaro 1999: 4155f.; Fuentes Rodríguez 2009: 67f.). However, in some usages, these values seem to be strongly reduced and more or less replaced by rather interactional and metadiscursive values concerning the organization of speakers and topics or the planning of the utterance (cf. also Freites Barros 2006).

Vale finally, derived by grammaticalization from the verb *valer* [to be useful], is described by Martín Zorraquin and Portolés Lázaro (1999) as a deontic modal marker which reflects the speaker's attitude. Its value is the expression of acceptance, admission and approval. In the last few decades, *vale*, which was originally a feature of youth language varieties, has become a generalized and very frequent marker in everyday language in Spain, which is sometimes pejoratively classified as '*muletilla*' or '*bordoncillo*' [*tag*] (cf. Martín Zorraquin and Portolés 1999: 4169). Serrano Reyes (2003) shows that *vale* actually performs a couple of interactional and (meta-)textual values such as marking the reception of a message (without necessarily agreeing with it) or closing the conversation (cf. also Briz et al. 2000ff: *vale*). In any case, the different uses are often not clearly distinguishable as the value of agreement is implicitly preserved even if the textual function is dominant (Serrano Reyes 2003: 142f.).

In summary, *sí*, *claro* and *vale* are frequently used markers in Spanish conversation that perform a large variety of functions: as agreement particles that approves the proposition of a prior intervention, as modal markers that expresses the speaker's attitude towards what has been said, as connectors between stretches of discourse and thoughts, organization of interaction, etc. These features make *sí*, *claro* and *vale* potentially 'attractive' for learners. They are, due to their high frequency, easily accessible and perform a wide range of functions – including their ability to signal co-operation and positive politeness at the interpersonal level. In addition, *sí* and *claro* have semantic and/or formal equivalents in the L1 of the German students (*ja* and *klar*), *vale* is somewhat comparable to the use of *okay* in German conversation.

Methodology

The empirical basis for the current results consists of the spoken Spanish of adult students with German L1 who study Spanish at university. This means that they usually have a strong interest in improving their language proficiency during an often-obligatory study abroad stay of at least three months, but usually six months or longer.

The data were collected via speech recordings before and after the time abroad. A first step was a storytelling task based on visual input using non-verbal comic strips. The second part was mainly a kind of simulation where the L2 speakers had to call native speaker representatives of different institutions (universities, cultural institutes, etc.) in order to ask for information on subjects related to the intended stay in the target country. In this experimental design, the participants were faced with several conversational tasks (e.g. to structure the discourse, to indicate topical changes, to maintain the contact, to confirm the information of the interlocutor and to show comprehension and co-operation).

To date, ten students of Spanish have been recorded with altogether almost four hours of speech in total. For the purpose of comparison, we simulated a comparable situation involving telephone calls between German native speakers talking in German as well as between Spanish native speakers talking in Spanish. All recordings were transcribed in the system GAT 2 system for conversational analysis (cf. Selting et al. 2009) and tagged with regard to all kinds of DMs and affirmative particles and their respective functions.

The proficiency level differs among the students ranged approximately from A2 to C1. Beside information about their learning history provided by the students in a questionnaire and the subjective impressions about their proficiency derived from qualitative diagnostics, we used – as a criterion for language proficiency – the fluency category[3] of speech rate, that is, words per minute. This is measured in the opening turn in the telephone conversations: after the initial greeting, we find in all dialogues a longer, uninterrupted turn of the student explaining his or her request, in several cases it is even the longest turn during the whole conversation. Nonverbal hesitation has not been counted, which means that this form of hesitation causes at the end a lower speech rate overall. As far as objective measurement is concerned, the number of words is still problematic owing to different definitions of the word concept. We have to be aware that the given speech rates have a limited validity in showing proficiency as they hardly reflect language accuracy. Neither do these rates show difficulties in concrete formulations depending on the topic nor do they reflect personal talking speed. In some cases, it could even be possible that the competent use of DMs compenses for a lower speech rate, as Sajavaara/Lehtonen (1980: 71) remark: 'To be fluent in the right way, the speaker has to know how to hesitate, how to be silent, how to self-correct, how to interrupt, and how to complete his expressions.' Nevertheless, the speech rates shall give an approximation of the language competence. All the measured results are clearly below the speech rate of a Spanish L1 speaker in our corpus who pronounces 176.5 words per minute in a similar turn.

3 Freed, Segalowitz and Dewey (2004: 285f.) report nine parameters to measure fluency levels: speech rate, hesitation-free speech runs, filler-free speech runs, fluent runs, repetition-free speech runs, grammatical-repair-free speech runs, total words spoken, duration of speaking time, longest turn.

Table 5.1. Speech rates in Spanish FL

Student	Speech rate (words per minute)	See in
AG-1[4]	108.8	-
AG-2	136.6	Table 5.3
AN-1	77.1	-
AP-1	121.6	-
AP-2	128.4	-
AW-1	94.0	Table 5.2, Transcript 5.1
CM-1	101.4	Table 5.4
CM-2	121.4	Table 5.4, Transcript 5.4
JR-1	75.5	-
JR-2	133.3	Transcript 5.2
JU-1	92.7	-
KS-1	112.5	Table 5.6
KS-2	139.4	Table 5.6, Transcript 5.3
MW-1	108.5	Table 5.5, Transcript 5.5
MW-2	104.7	Table 5.5
SS-1	130.2	-

Results

Comparing DM repertoires of intermediate and advanced learners

Having a simple look at two DM repertoires – one of an intermediate and one of an advanced learner – we can observe some considerable differences:

4 The numbers indicate if the recording has been made before (1) or after (2) the stay abroad (see also Figure 5.1). Those who appear only with the number 1 have not been recorded a second time.

Table 5.2. Number of markers in free dialogue speech: Intermediate proficiency level

[AW-1]	DM
sí	15
hm/hm_hm	11
ah	3
y	3
vale	1
okay	1
Total number of words: 235	

Table 5.3. Number of markers in free dialogue speech: Advanced proficiency level

[AG-2]	DM
sí	26
bueno	14
y	14
hm/hm_hm	7
claro	5
perfecto	4
es que	4
o sea	4
vale	2
exacto	2
ah	2
de acuerdo	1
cierto	1
¿no?	1
Total number of words: 758	

Whereas the absolute numbers simply indicate that the advanced learner (AG) talked more, she also handles a wider variety of DMs, some of them with more distinctive meanings and higher phonological and morphological complexity. We can also see that the DMs used by the intermediate-level learner have similar counterpartners in German like *ja, okay, und* for instance. DMs of the advanced learner like *es que* or *o sea* do not exist in equivalent forms in German. Except for basic connectors like *y* and *pero*, all of the DMs used on the intermediate level have a potential affirmative value. This group is still dominant on the advanced level. However, DMs with other values like *es que, o sea, ¿no?* appear, too.

Comparing DMs before and after the stay abroad: Three case studies

We will now present the quantitative results of three students who took part in our study twice. The aim is to show and to explain the changes in their language habits. Sometimes, the presentation of absolute numbers risks misinterpretation as the conversations before and after the stay abroad are not completely equal in length, topics and interaction behaviour. In all following tables, we only indicate markers which are used at least four times during one conversation.

Student I

In Table 5.4, we can observe changes in the verbal behaviour of a female student after having stayed in the south of Spain for one semester:

Table 5.4. Number of markers before and after the stay abroad (intermediate level)

[CM]	DM before	DM after
sí	24	38
ah + x	12	17
hm/hm_hm	15	8
vale		14
(muy) bien	5	9
y	8	4
claro		4
pero		4
Total number of words:	212 (before)	328 (after)

Most significant is the use of *vale* as an affirmation particle that had not been used in the first recording. This leads us to the assumption that the use of *vale* has been acquired or intensified during the stay abroad. *Claro* as an affirmation marker of higher emphasis than *sí* and *pero* as a disjunctive connector also appear only after the stay abroad although the number is not significantly high to manifest an acquisition process. Another perspective could focus on decreases: the nonverbal marker *hm* or *hm_hm* tends to decline and might be substituted by *vale* and *claro*. Although *hm* or *hm_hm* is a marker which seems to work more or less in the same way in many languages, the substitution with a language specific marker can be seen as an improvement not only when considering the more distinctive form, but also the more differentiated meaning.

Student II

The next student had already had a high proficiency level before he went to Spain. Nevertheless, some developments become visible in the table of accumulated markers:

Table 5.5. Number of markers before and after the stay abroad (advanced level)

[MW]	DM before	DM after
vale	36	31
hm/hm_hm	22	28
sí	17	10
y	5	8
claro	5	7
ah + x	10	2
(muy) bien	10	1
perfecto	5	2
entonces		7
¿no?	1	4
pero		4
Total number of words:	366 (before)	445 (after)

This time the use of *entonces* seems to be newly acquired, or at least intensified, as it does not appear in the first recording. Regarding the interjection *ah*, it has to be mentioned that it appears almost always in combination with another marker like *ah sí* or *ah vale*, forms which native speakers would mainly use in order to express surprise, whereas learners often employ it in contexts where the expression of surprise seems inappropriate (cf. for French in Thörle 2015: 7). So, the decrease of this marker within affirmation processes can be seen as positive. The diminution of *bien* (often as *muy bien*) as an affirmation marker is perhaps less obvious in the proficiency development, but especially in the form of *muy bien*, which usually shows a kind of enthusiastic agreement, it seems to be misplaced as a reaction to often rather neutral utterances (cf. Delahaie 2009: 18).

Student III

The last student we analyse in this section also showed a higher proficiency before and several modifications after her stay in Argentina:

Table 5.6. Number of markers before and after the stay abroad (advanced level)

[KS]	DM before	DM after
y	29	31
sí	36	23
hm/hm_hm	25	2
claro	8	15
bueno	10	10
pero	5	11
o sea		11
ah + x	10	
(muy) bien	7	
okay	7	
es que	4	2
Total number of words:	889 (before)	1257 (after)

Three effects we have already described as positive changes towards a more specific manner of expression are the decrease of the markers *hm* or *hm_hm*, *bien* or *muy bien*, and of the interjection *ah* in combination with other markers which disappear completely in this case. Another form that disappears is the marker *okay*. Although this international word exists also in Spanish, the use is rather restrictive compared to other languages like French or German. It can also be a characteristic of the Argentinian variety that *okay* declines in the repertoire. The Argentinean variety may be responsible for the fact that, here, *vale* is not used. The marker *o sea* as a DM for turn-holding and reformulation appears only in the second recording and seems to be newly acquired or intensified in use.

Interlanguage usages of *sí*, *claro* and *vale* on different proficiency levels

In this section, we will present usages of *sí*, *claro* and *vale* in our recordings that attracted our attention and that we consider as typical of the student's interlanguage.

Sí

The following example illustrates the characteristic use of sí:[5]

Transcript 5.1. Interlanguage use of *sí* (AW-1)

04	L:	hola:: (.) e:hm (-) habla (.)
05		eh hablo con ((name))? (-)

5 The most important symbols are:

L	– learner	(-) (--) (---)	– pauses < 1”
N	– native speaker	(2.6)	– pauses ≥ 1”
sí: sí:: sí:::	– lengthened sounds	QUIEro	– focal accent
[...]	– overlapping voices	, ?	– raising intonations
°h	– breathing	.	– falling intonation
(.)	– micro-stop	((noise))	– comments.

06 N: eh sí (con ella,)
07 L: **sí** (.) ehm soy ((name)) ehm (.)
08 y ehm estudio español en ((place)),
[...]
18 N: cuál es la primera;
19 L: ehm (.) **sí** ehm: me: gustaría e:hm (-) saber (.)
20 cuáles son las condiciones para la participación ehm en
21 (-) en ehm (-) este programa (.)
22 ehm por ejemplo ehm (-)
23 QUÉ nivel de lengua ehm (-)
24 tengo (.) que (-) ehm s:/ (--) te/ (.) tener (-) **sí**
25 N: bueno (.) por lo menos e:h (.) un (-) be dos
26 L: hm_hm
27 N: eh (.) un nivel be dos de lengua
28 L: **sí**
29 N: e::h o el ser e::h estudiante: (.)
30 de una licenciatura: (-)
31 mínimo (-) del cuarto semestre.
32 L: [hm_hm okay]
33 N: [eh usted] estudia una licenciatura?
[04 L: hello (.) e:hm (-) speak (.)
05 eh do I speak with ((name))? ( )
06 N: eh yes (with her,)
07 L: **sí** (.) ehm I am ((name)) ehm (.)
08 and ehm I learn Spanish in ((place)),
[...]
18 N: what is the first;
19 L: ehm (.) **sí** ehm: I: would like e:hm (-) to know (.)
20 what are the requirements to take part ehm in
21 (-) in ehm (-) this programme (.)
22 ehm for instance ehm (-)
23 what language level ehm (-)
24 I need (.) to (-) ehm s:/ (--) ha/ (.) have (-) **sí**
25 N: well (.) at least e:h (.) un (-) be two
26 L: hm_hm
27 N: eh (.) a be two language level
28 L: **sí**
29 N: e::h or to be e::h studying: (.)
30 at university: (-)
31 at least (-) in the fourth semester.
32 L: [hm_hm okay]
33 N: [eh are you] studying at university?]

As we see in Transcript 5.1, the learner (L) uses *sí* quite frequently (ll. 7, 19, 24, 28). In all of these incidences, the main function of *sí* does not seem to be affirmation in a narrow sense of the term. In l. 7, *sí* is placed at a transitional point between two sequences. After the short question-answer-sequence *hablo con ((name))? (-)* [*Am I speaking with ((name))*] / *eh sí (con ella,)* [*eh yes (with her,)*], L introduces herself and explains the reason for her call (not in the excerpt). The particle *sí* does not affirm the propositional content of the prior turn. It rather indicates the reception of the prior turn as well as the willingness of L to take up the turn and to go on with the conversation. The function of *sí* is thus a rather interactional one. Something similar holds for *sí* in l. 19 where *sí* is used in the prototypical position of the affirmation adverb at the beginning of an answer to a question. However, *sí* does not represent the answer to this (non-polar) question, but indicates again that L has received the question and is willing to answer. Together with *ehm*, it is placed within a filled pause so that it could also be interpreted as a strategy to hold the turn and to get through a wording problem. In l. 24, *sí* belongs to the first pair part of the question-answer sequence. It is placed in turn final position after L has addressed a question to N. As in the lines before, *sí* is not the answer to this question but closes L's turn and cedes it to the interlocutor. Its value is therefore an interactional and metadiscursive one. In l. 28, *sí* functions as a reception signal. It does not confirm the proposition of the prior turn (this would require that L knows the 'right' answer to her own question) but signals her attention to and reception of N's answer.

All usages of *sí* that we have seen in the excerpt do not correspond to *sí* as an affirmation adverb. The semantic value of approval or confirmation is highly reduced. If there is some kind of approval or confirmation, it does not concern the propositional but the metadiscursive or interactional level: the taking up and closing of the turn, the reception of the message, the validity of the wording process, etc.

This use decreases from the intermediate to the advanced level. If we compare the percentage rate of *sí* used as an affirmation adverb or pure reception signal on the one hand, and as a DM with interactional or metadiscursive functions on the other hand, and consider in all recordings plus the examples in the speech of four native Spanish speakers and including also the use of German *ja* in a comparable situation in a German native dialogue, we come to the following result:

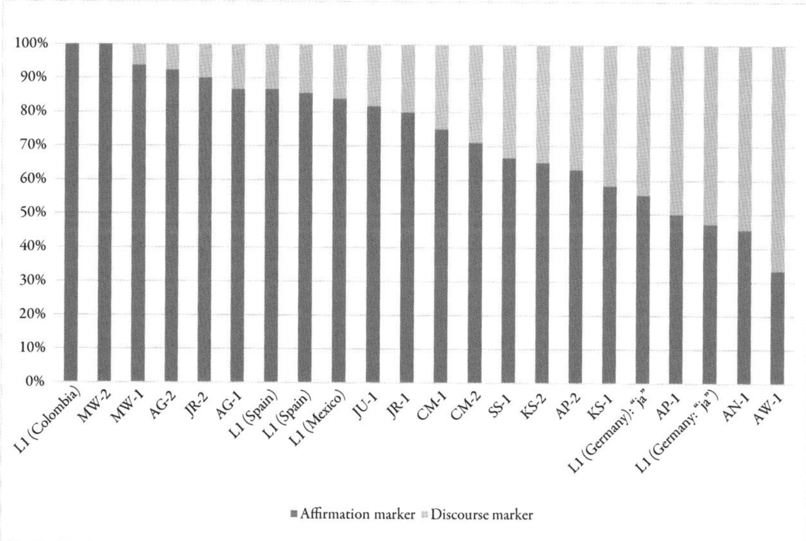

Figure 5.1. Percentage rate of *sí* as affirmation particle and as DM

We see that Spanish L1 speakers do employ *sí* as a DM, but the percentage is low (≤16%) compared to the German L1 *ja* (around 50%).[6] The ten Spanish students show a considerable variety, and it is remarkable that all the students (except CM) who were recorded a second time after the stay abroad – indicated by the number 2 – reduce the use of *sí* as DM but employ new DMs instead. Regarding the question why a polyfunctional use of the main affirmation marker *sí* appears mainly on lower proficiency levels of Spanish FL, an explanation could be found in the functional and formal equivalents in L1 German. Just as *ja* is a universal tool for a high number of discourse functions (cf. Fischer 2000: 68–97; Waltereit 2006: 56–62; Imo 2013: 158–200), learners could transfer this verbal behaviour to Spanish. However, *sí* as DM does not seem to be a phenomenon that shows exclusive characteristic for German learners.[7] So, a complementary hypothesis is that this marker forms part of the universal character of the

6 This calculation excludes completely the highly frequent German *ja* as a modal particle.

7 Cf. the use of English FL *yeah* in House 2013 or Italian *sì* in Guil et al. 2008, both times by speakers of Spanish L1.

interlanguage. *Sí* [*yes*] has the nature of a *passe-partout* marker which is easily accessible because of its frequency and simple pronunciation and which can be employed as an auxiliary particle in order to just utter something without risking any great modifications in meaning.

Claro

Interestingly, less fluent speakers such as AN, AW and JU do not use *claro* at all, although there is a quite similar form in German (*klar*). Other learners in our corpus like CM and JR, started using *claro* only after their stay abroad. In most of the cases, *claro* is employed as a backchannel signal (Transcript 5.2, l. 224) or a reaction to a tag question (l. 233). Then, *claro* can express a modal value by marking prior statements from the interlocutor as evident and thus signalling agreement with the latter.[8]

Transcript 5.2. Interlanguage use of *claro* (JR-2)

N:	y entonces también queremos que eso sea un beneficio,
	°hh para el estudiante extranjero.
L:	**claro claro**
N:	porque la capacidad de integración y de vivir
	realmente (--)
	como se <<laughing>vive [en realidad>]
L:	[((laughs))]
N:	es mucho mayor que en barcelona no? donde uno (-)
	donde uno (-) puede vivir perfectamente
	un año sin hablar (.)
	n:i español ni catalán ni nada no?
L:	**claro** ((laughs)) (-) H°
N:	entonces queremos evitar este tipo de:_ehm de relación
	solo con erasmus o solo con extranjeros.

8 For this reason, González (2014: 416f.) states that the function of *claro* in this context goes beyond the showing of agreement and backchannel. In evidential terms, *claro* is also used 'to cooperatively build up a common ground of trust and certainty that leads towards the final concluding argument'.

[222 N: and then we also want this to benefit,
223 °hh the foreigner student.
224 L: **claro claro**
225 N: because the ability of becoming integrated and to
226 actually live (--)
227 how people <<laughing>live [actually>]
228 L: [((laughs))]
229 N: is bigger than in barcelona right? where one (-)
230 where one (-) can perfectly live
231 one year without speaking (.)
232 neither spanish nor catalan nor any language right?
233 L: **claro** ((laughs)) (-) H°
234 N: so we want to avoid this kind of_ehm of interaction
235 only with erasmus or only with foreigners.]

In contrast to Transcript 5.2, where *claro* is 'reactive' and relates to the interlocutor's utterance, the use of *claro* in Transcript 5.3 refers to the speaker's own utterance:

Transcript 5.3. Interlanguage use of *claro* (KS-2)

155 N: y los conocimientos que ya tenía del español. (.)
156 le ayudaron?
157 L: **claro**. sí:
158 porque:: de hecho (.)
159 yo recuerdo la primera vez que fue a españa, (.)
160 **claro** ahí: (-) como al principio
161 no entendía to:do y me costa:ba °h (.)
162 pero ahora en: (.) en argentina:
163 no tenía ningún problema digamos (--)
164 y:: bueno. **claro**. al principio:: (.)
165 siempre me querían corregi:r,
166 porque **claro** los españoles hablan distin:to, (.)
167 N: hm_hm
168 L: pero: (-) bueno tampoco que: qu/ (--)
169 tampoco es que no lo respeten °h (.)
170 pero: (.) sí (.) me ayudaron los conocimientos

[155 N: and all the previous knowledge of spanish that you had.

156		was that helpful?
157	L:	**claro**. yes
158		because actually (.)
159		I remember the first time I went to spain, (.)
160		**claro** there (-) like at the beginning
161		I didn't understand everything and it was hard °h (.)
162		but now in (.) in argentina:
163		I had no problem so to speak (--)
164		and well. **claro**. at the beginning:: (.)
165		they always wanted to correct me,
166		because **claro** spaniards speak in a different way, (.)
167	N:	hm_hm
168	L:	but (-) it is not like qu/ (--)
169		like they don't respect it °h (.)
170		but (.) yes (.) the previous knowledge helped me]

While *claro* in l. 157 is used as an affirmation adverb, followed by *sí*, the monologic use[9] in ll. 160, 164 and 166 refers to the speaker's own utterance. It has modal value by marking what is said as obvious: the fact that the student did not understand everything when she went to Spain for the first time, and that Argentine people corrected her at the beginning because the type of Spanish in Argentina differs from the peninsular variety. By using *claro* and thus marking the content of the utterance as evident, the speaker initiates an inferential process inviting the interlocutor to activate the shared knowledge about the situation of language learners going abroad for the first time and about the different varieties of Spanish. The use of *claro* in this context is a way to establish intersubjectivity as well as solidarity and a certain sense of community between the interlocutors

9 González (2014: 411) distinguishes different functions of *claro* depending on the monologic or dialogic context: 'In a monologic segment, the speaker makes use of the evidentials to argue and share with the interlocutor his/her epistemological stance and perspective through an inferential reasoning process; the aim is persuasive and evaluative. In a dialogic segment, their role is that of truth-attesting and the negotiation of salient meaning.'

('You and I know how things are'). It can thus be interpreted as a strategy of positive politeness.

We find this use of *claro* only in more proficient learners from our corpus (i.e. in the telephone conversations of KS-1 and KS-2, AG-2, SS-1, JR-2 and MW-2). Among these learners, KS stands out, because she uses this monological variant of *claro* so often/excessively that we have to ask ourselves if *claro* does not also serve as an individual formulation strategy by which the speaker gains time for the wording process.

Vale

Similar to *claro*, *vale* is not considered very frequently by less proficient learners. In the data of the student CM, it appears only after her stay abroad (Table 5.4). Then *vale* is used mainly as a reception marker, sometimes combined with other forms like *ah vale* or *sí vale*, by which speaker accepts the proposal or statement of the interlocutor or simply confirms that the message has been received and understood as shown in Transcript 5.4:

Transcript 5.4. Interlanguage use of *vale* (CM-2)

75	N:	e:h tenemos un paquete de tres días,
76		y un paquete de cinco días. (.)
77	L:	°h **ah vale** ese (.)
78		e:hm mejor el con cinco díos? eh días creo que
79	N:	cinco días
80	L:	sí
[75	N:	e:h we have a three-day parcel,
76		and a five-day parcel. (.)
77	L:	°h **ah vale** that one (.)
78		e:hm better the with five days? eh days I think that
79	N:	five days
80	L:	yes]

The next example is taken from the recording of an advanced learner before his stay abroad. The interlanguage is characterized by its particularly frequent high and diversified use of the form *vale*:

Transcript 5.5. Interlanguage use of *vale* (MW-1)

N:	de acuerdo? °h muy bien.
	bueno eso no es problema,
	porque: nuestros programas pueden ser (-)
	de:: de una semana hasta un mes.
L:	**vale,**
N:	es decir dependiendo de sus intereses lo montamos (-)
	hm °h lo único es que como grupo, (-)
	°h tienen que hacer la:s inscripciones individualmente.
L:	**vale;**
N:	es decir no (.) no ad/ eh adoptamos grupos enteros
	como grupo que están juntos,
L:	**hm_hm,**
N:	sino (--) personas (.) individuales,
L:	**ah vale,**
N:	cada persona está en contacto con un estudiante de
	aquí.
	que es su tutor aquí.
L:	**ah vale, (-) muy bien**
N:	mh?
L:	**muy [bien, sí]**
N:	[pero igual] estas (.) las actividades y todo
	lo pueden hacer juntos después?
L:	**hm_hm,**
N:	pero digamos que todo el procedimiento es individual.
L:	**vale, (-) pues muy bien (.) maravilloso?**
N:	sí? (---) [muy] bien?
L:	[<<p>sí>]
N:	y:: no sé necesitan algún tipo de información de la::
	tenemos diferentes programas,
	no sé si (--)
	quiere saber qué programas tenemo:s (-)
L:	°h hm:: **VAle,** (-)
	n/ nosotros tenemos diferentes ideas, (.) °hh (.)

N: sí (.)
L: como:: (.) muchos días a barceLOna:: y (.) **vale** (.)
un dos días (-) no sé a figueres (.)
a (.) empordà [algo así,]
N: [hm_hm]

N: alright? °h very well.
well that is not a problem,
because: our programmes can last (-)
from:: one week to one month.
L: **vale,**
N: that is we can adjust it to your interests (-)
hm °h the only thing is that as a group, (-)
°h you need to do the inscriptions individually.
L: **vale;**
N: I mean we don't (.) we don't take/ eh take full groups
as groups that are together,
L: **hm_hm,**
N: but (--) people (.) individuals,
L: **ah vale,**
N: each person is in contact with one student
here.
who is their tutor here.
L: **ah vale, (-) muy bien**
N: mh?
L: **muy [bien, sí]**
N: [but it's the same] they can do
(some) the activities and everything together later?
L: **hm_hm,**
N: but let's say all the procedure is individual.
L: **vale, (-) pues muy bien (.) maravilloso?**
N: yes? (---) [very] well?
L: [<<p>yes>]
N: and don't you need any type of information about
we have different programmes,
I don't know whether (--)
you want to know what programmes we have (-)
L: °h hm:: **VAle,** (-)
w/ we have different ideas, (.) °hh (.)

68	N:	yes (.)
69	L:	like (.) a lot of days to barceLOna and (.) **vale**
70		one two days (-) I don't know to figueres (.)
71		to (.) empordà [something like that,]
72	N:	[hm_hm]

This excerpt demonstrates the omnipresence of *vale* in the interlanguage of a quite advanced student. Focusing on three distinct usages of *vale* (ll. 39, 66 and 69), we will show that *vale* is used by this student as a polyfunctional DM with different interactional and metadiscursive functions. In l. 39, *vale* does not mainly express agreement or conformance. The student is not familiar with the programmes and offers of the institution he is calling. *Vale* serves as a kind of reception signal. As we can see, the use of *vale* does not imply turn taking of L. The interlocutor N goes on with her explanation of the exchange programmes. This is different in l. 66. *Vale* is used here after N has ceded the turn to L. L starts with an audible inhaling which is followed by a hesitation phenomenon (*hm::*). *Vale* then confirms in a way that L is indeed taking his and indicates the beginning of L's contribution in which he presents his ideas. In l. 69, *vale* is used in the middle of the turn where it is preceded and followed by a pause. It serves here as a hesitation marker that helps to get through a wording problem.

In these three usages of *vale*, the semantic value of agreement is greatly reduced and replaced by discursive values such as interactional and metadiscursive marking. This interlanguage use of *vale* as a DM is highly polyfunctional, as we can observe at least three different functions within a very small stretch of discourse. What discourse function *vale* fulfils each time is indicated a) by the context and b) by prosodic features that are illustrated in the figures below. While *vale* as a reception signal (l. 39, Figure 5.2) is pronounced with a slightly rising intonation, typical for this kind of marker (cf. Pereira 2011: 94), *vale* as turn-opening marker (l. 66, Figure 5.3) is characterized by high intensity level and an accelerated and impulsive pronunciation. As a hesitation phenomenon, *vale* is pronounced with a low level of intensity and has a flat, suspended intonation curve (l. 69, Figure 5.4). By these prosodic means, the learner differentiates various usages of *vale* as a quasi-generalized DM and indicates each time the function that *vale* fulfils in the respective context.

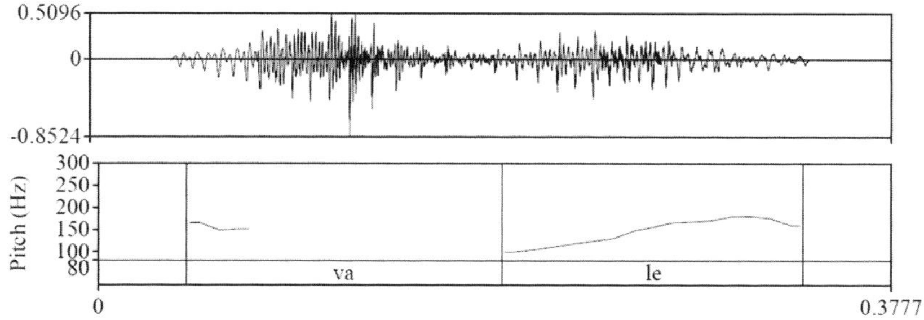

Figure 5.2. Intonation of *vale* in MW-1, line 39: reception signal

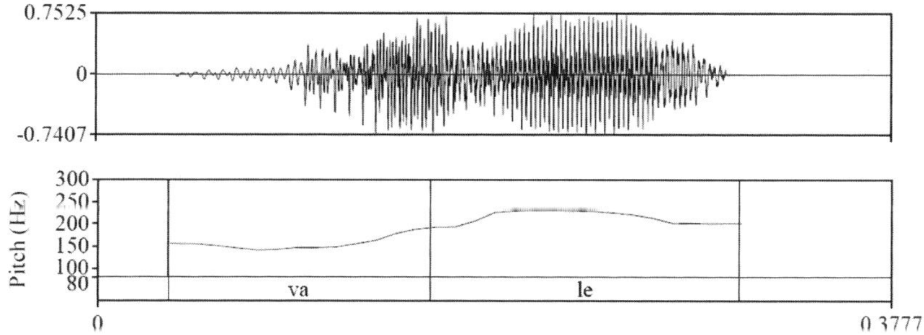

Figure 5.3. Intonation of *vale* in MW-1, line 66: turn-opening marker

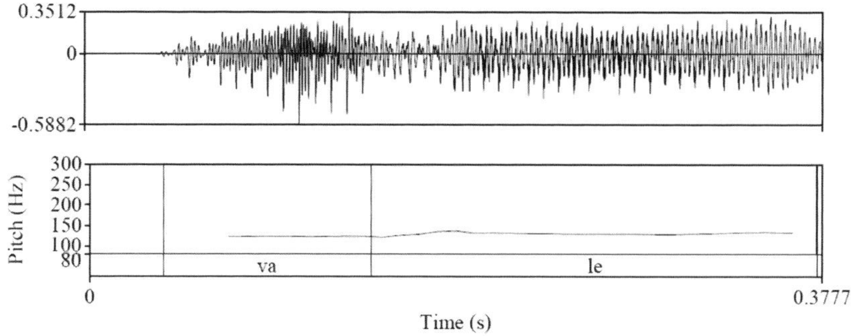

Figure 5.4. Intonation of *vale* in MW-1, line 69: hesitation marker

Discussion

The use of affirmation markers like *sí*, *claro* and *vale* is something to be expected in the context of exolingual telephone calls, where these particles can be interpreted as a politeness strategy with which participants confirm the reception and understanding of the messages, as well as signal their attention and their co-operation with the interlocutor. However, what we can observe is that, in learners' interlanguage, these particles are not only an important device of affirmation in learners' interlanguage but represent the most important type of DM – in the intermediate level the almost exclusive type of DM – that fulfils a broad range of discursive functions.

Looking at the repertoires of learners in different proficiency levels, we observe that the repertoire of the intermediate level consists – with the exception of simple connectives like *y* or *pero* – exclusively of affirmation markers among which *sí* plays an outstanding role due to its very high frequency and by the fact that its use as a DM appears very early in the acquisition process. In the advanced levels, affirmation markers are still dominant, but other DMs (e.g. *bueno*, *es que*, *o sea*, etc.) with other interactional, metadiscursive or cognitive values are used, too. The occurrence of *sí* within the repertoire decreases.[10] In higher levels of proficiency, we thus observe a diversification of forms and functional classes of DMs that is possibly accompanied by a functional specialization of the respective DM.

After the stay abroad, some students use a larger range of DMs than before. If particular DMs are used only after the stay abroad, these DMs (e.g. *entonces* or *o sea*) have possibly been acquired during the stay. Various students use even *claro* and *vale* only after their stay abroad. According to the diversification of forms, we observe a decrease of *sí* (with exception of CM). Other features such as nonverbal *hm_hm* or quite 'enthusiastic' expressions of reception and understanding (that in the given contexts might seem exaggerated) like *muy bien* and the change of state-token *ah*

10 While on the intermediate level, *sí* represents 44.1% of all DMs used by student AW, it constitutes only 29.9% of the DMs used by student AG (tab. 2 and 3).

decrease, too. From this, we conclude that learners have increased their mastery of discourse organizational devices so that they have to fall back to a lesser degree on compensation strategies in order to show their participation and co-operation in the conversation.

From a qualitative point of view, we have seen that *sí*, *claro* and *vale* are not used exclusively as affirmative means but are highly multifunctional. Besides the value of an affirmative answer and that of a reception signal, these forms have a range of other interactional (uptaking of the turn, turn holding), metadiscursive (wording, utterance closing) and even cognitive (modal) functions. However, the multifunctional use of the DMs – that, by the way, is not restricted to the interlanguage – does not imply that different discourse functions are not distinguished. As it has been demonstrated for *sí* and *vale*, the context-bound values of the DMs are indicated by prosodic devices and the position in the utterance. With regard to the acquisition process, we observed that the very multifunctional use of *sí* – which from a normative point of view can certainly be classified as an overuse – decreases. For *claro*, it has been shown that specific modal usages appear only at a quite advanced level of proficiency. Two of our learners stand out by the high frequency of *vale* and *claro* respectively which at we interpreted as personal routines that help the learners to take and to hold the turn and go on with the utterance construction. We hypothesize that this kind of overuse can also disappear or get reduced with the ongoing acquisition if this is not prevented by fossilization processes (Romero Trillo 2002). The acquisition of DMs could then be characterized as a process of recalibration of forms and functions (cf. also Pekarek Doehler 2013: 154).

Conclusions

This chapter focused on DM use in spoken Spanish FL by students with German L1. One question might be whether our observations are applicable to this language pair or are comparable to other language constellations, at least among the Standard Average European (SAE) group. One universal factor might be the nearness of DMs between L1 and FL in form and function, that is, learners use easier DMs in FL that are similar to their L1, even if these are not the most common ones. In fact, we saw that our intermediate learners use mainly forms that they perceive as equivalent in both languages. However, at this point, we could mention the lack of Spanish *ya*, a DM that none of our German students use despite the phonetic similarity to German *ja*. This may be explained, on the one hand, by the uncertainty about *ya* as a DM, since the students would mainly know the meaning of 'already'. On the other hand, it might be a more general strategy to avoid sounding 'too German'.[11] This example also shows that a potentially universal characteristic like nearness between the languages cannot be presumed without a closer examination of linguistic details. However, we think that many of the explanations given in this chapter can be adopted for other language constellations, as we have seen in and quoted from research findings in various other languages.

Such insights into DM acquisition through a stay abroad need to be incorporated into didactic approaches to language learning. Spending time in a target language country has an effect on the use of DMs. As they are hardly taught systematically in the classroom, immersion in a semester or a year abroad may compensate for this lack of exposure to them. The progress observed after the stay in the target language environment leads to the question whether such progresses can also or more efficiently be achieved in controlled language learning contexts. Our results may give access to focusing on the specific linguistic phenomena that should be treated in a way that goes beyond its purely grammatical content. Future work on this topic should lead to pedagogical suggestions about when and how DMs can be taught and learnt in the classroom. The improvement depends not only on the acquisition of knowledge of new forms, but mainly on the way of using them adequately in interaction. Thus, the crucial question is what methods are applicable to a systematic learning of spontaneous DM use in interaction as part of an adequate behaviour in FL.

11 A similar observation has been made by Delahaie (2009: 28) about Flemish students who avoid *okay* in French FL.

Bibliography

Bazzanella, Carla, 'I segnali discorsivi', in Lorenzo Renzi, Giampaolo Salvi, and Anna Cardinaletti, eds, *Grande grammatica italiana di consultazione* (Bologna: Il Mulino, 1995), 225–257.

Borreguero Zuloaga, Margarita, and Britta Thörle, eds, *Discourse Markers in Second Language Acquisition / Les marqueurs discursifs dans l'acquisition d'une langue étrangère. Studies on Italian and French as L2 / Études en italien et en français langues étrangères*. Special Issue of *Language, Interaction and Acquisition* 7/1 (2016).

Briz, Antonio, et al., eds *Diccionario de las partículas discursivas del español*. <http://www.dpde.es> (2000ff).

Delahaie, Juliette, '*Oui, voilà* ou *d'accord* ? Enseigner les marqueurs d'accord en classe de FLE'. *Synergies Pays Scandinaves* 4 (2009), 17–34.

Diao-Klaeger, Sabine, and Britta Thörle, 'Diskursmarker in L2', in Christoph Bürgel and Dirk Siepmann, eds, *Sprachwissenschaft – Fremdsprachendidaktik: Neue Impulse* (Baltmannsweiler: Schneider, 2013), 145–160.

Feldmann, Ute, *Pragmatische Aspekte im fremdsprachlichen Diskurs. Zur Verwendung von Gambits bei Spaniern und bei fortgeschrittenen Spanischlernern* (Heidelberg: Groos, 1984).

Fischer, Kerstin, *From Cognitive Semantics to Lexical Pragmatics. The Functional Polysemy of Discourse Particles* (Berlin/New York: Mouton de Gruyter, 2000).

Freed, Barbara, Norman Segalowitz, and Dan P. Dewey, 'Context of Learning and Second Language Fluency in French', *Studies in Second Language Acquisition* 26 (2004), 275–301.

Freites Barros, Francisco, 'El marcador de discurso Claro: funcionamiento pragmático, metadiscursivo y organizador de la estructura temática', *Verba* 33 (2006), 261–279.

Fuentes Rodríguez, Catalina, *Diccionario de conectores y operadores del español* (Madrid: Arco, 2009).

González, Montserrat, 'Evidentiality, Intersubjectivity and Salience in Spanish and Catalan Markers *claro/clar* and *la verdad/veritat*', *Intercultural Pragmatics* 11/3 (2014), 411–436.

Guil, Pura, et al., 'Marcadores discursivos y cortesía lingüística en la interacción de los aprendices de italiano L2', in Antonio Briz et al., eds, *Cortesía y conversación: de lo escrito a lo oral. Actas del III Congreso Internacional del Programa EDICE* (Universidad de Valencia y Programa Edice, 2008), 711–729.

House, Juliane, 'Developing Pragmatic Competence in English as a Lingua Franca: Using Discourse Markers to Express (Inter)Subjectivity and Connectivity', *Journal of Pragmatics* 59 (2013), 57–67.

Imo, Wolfgang, *Sprache in Interaktion* (Berlin: de Gruyter, 2013).

Iñigo Mora, Isabel, and Gloria Álvarez Benito, 'Marcadores kinésico-discursivos en español como L1 y en inglés como L2', *Oralia* 9 (2006), 145–166.

Koch, Christian, '*Sí, sí, estudio Lehramt, sí.* El uso de los marcadores de afirmación en el español de estudiantes germanohablantes', *Testi e linguaggi* 10 (2016), 159–172.

Koch, Christian, 'Lernen auf Spanisch zuzustimmen. Überlegungen zu einer Didaktik der Affirmationsmarker', in Daniel Reimann, Ferran Robles i Sabater, and Raúl Sánchez Prieto, eds, *Kontrastive Pragmatik und ihre Vermittlung. Deutsch, Spanisch und Portugiesisch im Vergleich* (Tübingen: Narr Francke Attempto, forthcoming).

López Serena, Araceli, and Margarita Borreguero Zuloaga, 'Los marcadores del discurso y la variación lengua hablada vs. lengua escrita', in Óscar Loureda Lamas, and Esperanza Acín Villa, eds, *Los estudios sobre marcadores del discurso en español, hoy* (Madrid: Arco, 2010), 415–496.

Martín Zorraquino, María Antonia, and José Portolés Lázaro, 'Los marcadores del discurso', in Ignacio Bosque and Violeta Demonte, eds, *Gramática descriptiva de la lengua española* (Madrid: Espasa Calpe, 1999), 4051–4213.

Pekarek-Doehler, Simona, 'Social-Interactional Approaches to SLA. A State of the Art and Some Further Perspectives', *Language, Interaction and Acquisition* 4/2 (2013), 134–160.

Pereira, Daniel Ignacio, 'Análisis acústico de los marcadores discursivos *a ver, bueno, claro, vale, ¿cómo?* y *ya*', *Onomázein* 24/2 (2011), 85–100.

Pons Bordería, Salvador, 'From Agreement to Stressing and Hedging: Spanish *bueno* and *claro*', in Gudrum Held, ed., *Partikeln und Höflichkeit* (Frankfurt am Main: Lang, 2003), 219–236.

Romero Trillo, Jesús, 'The Pragmatic Fossilization of Discourse Markers in Non-Native Speakers of English', *Journal of Pragmatics* 34 (2002), 769–784.

Sajavaara, Kari, and Jaakko Lehtonen, 'The Analysis of Cross-Language Communication: Prolegomena to the Theory and Methodology', in Hans W. Dechert and Manfred Raupach, eds, *Towards a Cross-Linguistic Assessment of Speech Production* (Frankfurt am Main: Lang, 1980), 55–76.

Santos Río, Luis, *Diccionario de partículas* (Salamanca: Luso-Española, 2003).

Selting, Maria, et al., 'Gesprächsanalytisches Transkriptionssystem 2 (GAT 2)', *Gesprächsforschung* 10 (2009), 353–402.

Serrano Reyes, Patricia, 'Análisis socio-pragmático del marcador conversacional *vale* como iniciador de intervención', *Estudios interlingüísticos* 1 (2013), 135–147.

Thörle, Britta, '*Oui* comme marqueur discursif polyfonctionnel en français langue étrangère', *Romanistik in Geschichte und Gegenwart* 21/1 (2015), 3–17.

Thörle, Britta, 'Turn Openings in L2 French. An Interactional Approach to the Discourse Marker Acquisition', *LIA – Language, Interaction and Acquisition* 7/1 (2016), 117–144.

Thörle, Britta, 'Sprachliche Mittel und Gesprächskompetenz. Die Rolle der Diskursmarker bei der Bewältigung von Sprecher- und Höreraufgaben in der Fremdsprache Spanisch', in Christoph Bürgel, and Daniel Reimann, eds, *Sprachliche Mittel im Unterricht der romanischen Sprachen. Aussprache, Wortschatz und Morphosyntax in Zeiten der Kompetenzorientierung* (Tübingen: Narr Francke Attempto, 2017), 311–332.

Waltereit, Richard, *Abtönung. Zur Pragmatik und historischen Semantik von Modalpartikeln und ihren funktionalen Äquivalenten in romanischen Sprachen* (Tübingen: Niemeyer, 2006).

Weidenbusch, Waltraud, 'Introduction', in Waltraud Weidenbusch, ed., *Diskursmarker, Konnektoren, Modalwörter. Marqueurs de discours, connecteurs, adverbes modaux et particules modales* (Tübingen: Narr, 2014), 11–25.

AN VANDE CASTEELE AND KIM COLLEWAERT

6 A pilot study on the use of discourse markers in the oral discourse of language learners of Spanish

On the concept of 'discourse markers'

It is generally acknowledged that the acquisition and the use of discourse markers tend to pose problems for foreign language learners. But, before discussing the peculiarities of discourse markers in language learners, it is necessary to mention that the concept of 'discourse marker' itself has been subject to many discussions (cf. Schiffrin 1987; Jucker and Ziv 1998; Martín Zorraquino and Montolío 1998; Martín Zorraquino and Pórtoles Lázaro 1999; Blakemore 2002; Fischer 2006; Pórtoles Lázaro 2007;[2] Martí Sánchez 2008; Loureda Lamas and Acín Villa 2010, etc.) and various terms (discourse/pragmatic marker/particle/connective/operator/...) have been adduced to refer to the same concept (see also the Introduction in this volume). In this chapter, the term 'discourse marker' will be further employed to refer to the multifunctional linguistic elements which, according to Fraser (1999: 950), constitute a 'pragmatic class' of 'lexical expressions drawn from the syntactic classes of conjunctions, adverbials, and prepositional phrases'. Schiffrin (1987: 328) underlines the extreme diversity in the set of expressions called discourse markers and suggests the idea of a 'core meaning'. As of their role in discourse, González (2004: 73) distinguishes two major functions. On the one hand, they adopt a structuring role in the discourse and serve to establish the discourse network and, on the other hand, they help listeners formulate a correct interpretation of the message by indicating the speaker's intentions and guiding the interlocutor in making possible inferences. Moreover, the 'core meaning' the markers are said to have is defined as 'procedural' and 'their more specific interpretation is 'negotiated' by the context, both linguistic and conceptual'.

As stated above, discourse markers are key devices in establishing discourse cohesion. They indicate how segments can be related and guide the interpretation of the message. In other words, by making connections between utterances, they process inferences and by doing this, they reduce the interpretative effort of the interlocutor and enhance an adequate comprehension of the message. Or, as Bazzanella (2006: 456) states:

> Discourse markers are items external to propositional content which are useful *in* locating the utterance in an interpersonal and interactive dimension, in connecting and structuring phrasal, inter-phrasal and extra-phrasal elements in discourse, and in marking some on-going cognitive processes and attitudes.

Another issue frequently discussed in the literature on discourse markers is their multifunctionality. There is not only a wide variety of discourse roles; discourse markers also belong to a heterogeneous group of syntactic items. The major difficulty lies in how to capture their meaning and pragmatic function. The fact that discourse markers are inherently multifunctional items relates to the fact that language on itself is multifunctional, as Schiffrin (2001: 62) argues:

> discourse markers function in cognitive, expressive, social, and textual domains, i.e. simultaneously on different planes of discourse. If language served primarily one or another function at different times [...] it would be relatively easy to decide on which plane to focus and to discover which aspect of discourse is indexed through a marker. But the language is multifunctional – as is certainly the case with discourse markers – it must be the data themselves that guide the selection of constraints to examine.

Although the aspect of multifunctionality has drawn a broad discussion, it is not seen as a real problematic issue in everyday language use. Aijmer (2002: 3) points out:

> Discourse particles are different from ordinary words in language because of the large number of pragmatic values that they can be associated with. Nevertheless, speakers are not troubled by this multifunctionality.

Discourse markers and second language acquisition

In brief, the meanings conveyed by discourse markers are complex and difficult to define. Their complexity does not seem to be problematic for native speakers but could explain why it does not appear evident for foreign language learners to accurately capture the different pragmatic roles the broad class of discourse markers can assume. Montolío Durán (1998), for instance, claims that their procedural role, which impedes defining them in conceptual terms, thwarts their acquisition and consequently, their solid usage. Nevertheless, as discourse markers are said to play a crucial role in guiding the communication process, their acquisition also relates to the acquisition of communicative competence, that is, the ability to act and interact with language. As such, Stubbs (1983) indicates that language learners can sound 'odd' by omitting discourse markers or by using them improperly, while Wierzbicka (2003: 341) states that 'if learners of a language failed to master the meaning of its particles, their communicative competence would be drastically impaired'. The starting point of the present study on the use of discourse markers by Dutch-speaking language learners of Spanish, however, was the statement of Martí Sánchez (2008) that second language learners seem to use discourse markers less frequently and in a less secure way than native speakers. After a previous study on the difference in the use of discourse markers in written discourse (Vande Casteele and Collewaert 2013), it appears that the difference mainly lies in the kind of discourse markers that are chosen. A corpus-based approach should enable us to verify if Martí Sánchez's hypothesis also holds for oral discourse.

Methodology

In order to investigate how learners of Spanish as a foreign language use discourse markers in oral discourse and which pragmatic roles in discourse are transferred, a corpus of oral narratives was composed. The participants are

Flemish learners of Spanish as a foreign language who approximately have an A2-B1 proficiency level according to the Common European Framework of Reference for Language. They are second-year students of the Spanish Linguistics and Literature Bachelor program at the *Vrije Universiteit Brussel* (VUB). We also recruited a control group of Spanish native speakers, who performed the same oral storytelling as the language learners. All participants were assigned an oral story-telling task, based on the Spanish telenovela *Yo soy Bea*. A compilation of seven fragments in which the telenovela's protagonists appear has been created for the task and reflects the rather complicated love story between Beatriz, an ugly secretary, and her boss Álvaro, the handsome manager of a fashion journal. As an illustration, an example of a sequence in a narrative of one of the learners and one of a native speaker (note that errors have not been corrected):

(1) 'Y eh aquí viene Beatriz y euh (reír) cuando él ve esta euh euh eh Beatriz no no le da un beso pienso euhm **y bueno** hay un ... ella está un poco soñando porque él, el hombre está muy guapo **y bueno** ella quiere quizas ser con él **pero** ella se realizo que no será posible.' (LL141504)

[and eh there comes Beatriz and ehh (laughs) when he sees this ehh ehh eh Beatriz he doesn't kiss her I think ehmm **and well** there is a ... she is a bit dreaming because he, the man is very handsome and well she maybe wants to be with him **but** she notice it will not be possible.]

(2) '**Entonces claro** él le está diciendo que se siente mal porque **en realidad** se siente como un actor que está utilizando una chica que es fea y que quiere acabar con esa mentira porque se siente muy mal y ella **claro entonces** se queda como sorprendida (silencio) y que no puede seguir viéndola como se acuesta con ella y vive con ella **pues** no puede seguir viéndola todas las mañanas ahí porque se siente muy mal' (N151604)

[**Then of course** he is telling her that he feels bad because he **actually** feels like an actor who is taking advantage of a girl who is ugly and that he wants to end with that lie because he feels very bad and **then of course** she feels a bit surprised (silence) and that he cannot go on seeing how he sleeps with her and lives with her **then** he can't go on seeing her every morning because he feels very bad]

The oral task was designed as follows: first, the participants watched the video with the sound on, while they had the opportunity to write down some key elements of the story that could help them achieve the second part of the task, namely the retelling of the story while watching the video for a second time, but this time without sound. This procedure allowed us to analyse recordings with a similar duration and avoid that participants kept to a mere summary of the history. Finally, the participants were not informed about the purpose of the study. The activity was presented to them as an ordinary oral task within a language acquisition course.

Afterwards, all narratives were transcribed and coded based on the following information: language learner (LL) or native (N), year of participation (ex. 1314 = academic year 2013–2014) and participant number (01, 02, etc.).

Results and discussion

In this chapter, we present some preliminary results of our pilot study on the use of discourse markers in the oral discourse of learners of Spanish. The aim is to examine which discourse markers the language learners preferably use and which functions in discourse the markers assume. First, some general results will be described, and then three specific conversational markers, namely *entonces*, *bueno* and *pues*, will be discussed in a more detailed way. The goal is to verify if language learners of Spanish show a lack of awareness in the use of discourse markers and if there is an overuse or underuse tendency for certain discourse markers. Not only typical discourse markers such as *o sea*, *bueno* or *en realidad* are taken into account, also connecting devices such as *pero* are considered in this study, because of the similar pragmatic roles they assume in the discourse (cf. Blakemore 2000, 2002).

General results

Distribution of the discourse markers in the language learners' corpus

The language learners' data set consists of 28 narratives, in which 112 discourse markers were used, providing an average of four discourse markers per text. If we also take into consideration the use of the prototypical contrastive device *pero*, which behaves in a similar way as the contrastive markers *sin embargo* and *no obstante*, our results drastically change: 368 markers were retrieved, which increases the average amount of markers to 13.1 per text. Appearing 256 times in our non-native corpus, which equals 70% of all markers found in the corpus, *pero* is by far the most used connective device in the learners' corpus. Besides, it is the only marker that appears in all the narratives produced by our group of language learners. This can easily be explained by the fact that *pero* is a relatively elementary conjunction, already acquired in the early stages of the acquisition of Spanish as a second language. It usually takes more time to acquire corresponding discourse markers such as *sin embargo* and *no obstante* and moreover, those are preferentially used in written discourse. This could thus explain their absence in our corpus, as we are examining oral narratives of rather early language learners of Spanish. Table 6.1 offers a summary of the discourse markers encountered in the oral narratives of the language learners of Spanish.

Table 6.1. Discourse markers by learners of Spanish

Language learners of Spanish		
Discourse marker	Number of occurrences	Number of narratives in which the marker appears
pero	256	28
bueno	28	5
pues	21	7
vale	19	3
después	17	9
entonces	14	8
por eso (que)	3	3
finalmente	1	1
luego	1	1
por fin	1	1
al final	1	1
al fin	1	1

últimamente	1	1
o sea	1	1
en realidad	1	1
por ejemplo	1	1
claro	1	1

On a closer analysis, we observe that the language learners frequently use the ordering device *después*, which appears 17 times in nine texts. Other preferred particles are *bueno*, *pues*, *vale* and *entonces*, which logically appear in the oral narratives, as they are conversational markers. However, the frequency of these markers is in sharp contrast with that of *pero*, which indicates that their use is mostly based on individual knowledge and preference, rather than on general knowledge of discourse markers and their use.

Distribution of the discourse markers in the native speakers' corpus

The native corpus, then, consists of seven narratives and thus is significantly smaller than the non-native corpus. As such, firm conclusions cannot be drawn, but nevertheless the results surely will present an indication on how discourse markers are used by native speakers of Spanish.

Table 6.2 lists the occurrences of the discourse markers in the native speakers' corpus.

Table 6.2. Discourse markers by native speakers

Native speakers		
Discourse marker	Number of occurrences	Number of narratives in which the marker appears
pero	86	7
bueno	66	5
entonces	49	7
pues	41	5
vale	17	3
luego	11	3

o sea	8	3
claro	7	2
en realidad	6	3
después	5	1
al final	2	1
primero	1	1
finalmente	1	1
vamos	1	1
por lo tanto	1	1
por eso	1	1
además	1	1

The dataset contains 304 discourse markers, providing an average of 43 markers per text, which is remarkably higher than in the language learners' corpus. As is the case in the learners' corpus, the connective device *pero* is used more frequently, although it is less prevailing, representing only a 28% of all markers (versus 70% in the learners' dataset). We also note that the native speakers choose typical conversational markers, such as *bueno, entonces, pues* y *vale*. In the case of *bueno, entonces* and *pues*, moreover, it seems that they belong to the standard repertoire of native speakers, as they appear in (almost) all the productions, while language learners seem to make more individual choices.

The use of conversational markers in the oral corpus

In the next section, a detailed analysis of some conversational markers will be provided. Three conversational markers that appear in both the learner and the native corpus, namely *pues, entonces* and *bueno*, will be analysed. We will first present the various meanings of these markers, before verifying to which extent the use of the three discourse markers by the learners of Spanish and by the natives correspond to the proposed meanings.

In line with Martín Zorraquino and Portolés Lázaro (1999), conversational markers are characterized as a group of discourse markers that realize discourse functions typical of oral discourse. As Martín Zorraquino and

Portolés Lázaro (1999: 4143) emphasize, oral discourse contains an important interactive role besides the informative function of written discourse:

> La conversación constituye una forma de comunicación peculiar que determina, o favorece, la presencia de ciertos marcadores del discurso. [...] Además de cumplir una función 'informativa' ('transaccional'), orientada hacia el mensaje – fundamental y predominante en el texto escrito – la conversación presenta una función 'interactiva' ('interaccional'), orientada hacia el interlocutor.
>
> [Conversation is a particular type of communication that determines, or favours, the presence of certain discourse markers. [...] Apart from having an 'informative' ('transactional') function, which is message-oriented – as well as key and mainstream in the written text – conversation also has an 'interactive' ('interactional') function, which is oriented at the interlocutor.]

Conversational markers, thus, contribute clearly to the interactive character of oral discourse and, according to Martín Zorraquino and Portolés Lázaro (1999), they can be divided into four categories: epistemic markers, deontic markers, metadiscursive conversational markers and alterity markers. In their analysis, Martín Zorraquino and Portolés Lázaro only mention *bueno*, which could be used as a deontic marker or as an alterity marker. However, a more recent study of Fuentes Rodríguez (2009) shows that the three markers in question – *bueno, pues* and *entonces* – all can act as conversational markers and, moreover, that they present a high degree of multi-functionality, covering a broad range of uses, which also complicates the acquisition process by learners of Spanish.

Therefore, in the following paragraphs, we explore to the extent to which all these meanings appear in our corpus and if language learners use them in a similar way as native speakers do. The use of these markers with their various meanings will be illustrated with examples from our corpus.

Some general results on the use of *pues, entonces* and *bueno*

Generally, there is a significant difference between the number of occurrences of the three conversational markers in the learners' corpus and in the native corpus. *Pues* appears 21 times in seven learners' narratives (i.e.

in 25% of all narratives), but 41 times in five native narratives (i.e. in 71% of all narratives). *Entonces* is found 14 times in eight texts (i.e. 29% of all productions) and appears 49 times throughout all natives' productions. Finally, the learners used *bueno* 28 times in five texts (or 18% of all narratives), while native speakers used it 66 times in five texts (or in 71% of all productions). As stated before, it appears that the use of these markers is much more consistent in native speakers, as they are used in the majority of the narratives. In contrast, the use of discourse markers by the language learners seems to be influenced by their individual interlanguage, that is, their level of knowledge of Spanish at the moment of the oral exercise.

Pues

Of the three conversational markers in question, *pues* is by far the most multifunctional device. In general, we can distinguish two major kinds of uses, namely its use as a connective device, on the one hand, and its function as a real, extrapredicative, discourse marker, on the other. As a connective device, *pues* shows three uses: first, it can appear as a causal conjunction, where it is used as synonym of *because* or *since*. Second, it can be used as a consecutive conjunction, equivalent to *therefore*. Finally, *pues* can also be a conclusive conjunction, such as *thus* or *in conclusion*. In its role as an extrapredicative discourse marker, *pues* shows an even more varied spectrum of uses, playing a role in discourse processing and conversation management. As such, it can be used to open a reaction or explanation, to repair or rephrase something, to maintain speech, to indicate contrast, to reinforce an opinion or to fill a pause, that is, as a tactic to gain time for reflection.

In our corpus, then, both the language learners and the native speakers prefer to use *pues* as a continuing element, that is, in order to maintain speech, as in (3) and (4). The native corpus also shows a tendency to use *pues* with its consecutive meaning, as exemplified in (5).

(3) 'los ven en los ojos y es un poco extraño/y **pues** vemos que Beatriz no puede entrar porque euhm el imagen es todo' (LL131411)

[they see them in the eyes and it is a little weird/and so we see that Beatriz cannot get in because ehmm image is everything]

(4) 'y cuando Bea se despierta **pues** quiere como escapar de aquí' (N151601)

[and when Bea wakes up **then** she wants like to escape from here]

(5) 'y entonces le dice que con la noche que tuvieron/**pues** que es normal que le bajaran las defensas o se encuentre mal' (N151604)

[and then she says that considering the night they had/**so** it is normal that her defences went low or that she felt bad]

Next, we would like to share some observations regarding the use of *pues* in both corpora. As stated before, the natives seem better at juggling the various uses of the several discourse markers, while the choices of the language learners rather reflect the status of their interlanguage. The cases where *pues* functions as a repairing or rephrasing marker perfectly illustrate this observation. Both corpora contain three examples of this specific meaning of *pues*, but while the three examples in the native corpus were uttered by three different participants, it was only one language learner who provided us with three examples of *pues* in its repairing role. As an illustration, (6) and (7):

(6) 'Hay el el Álvaro, el el tio guapo que entra en su despa– **pues** la compañía' (LL131401)

[There is this this Álvaro, the the handsome guy who goes into his off– **I mean** the company]

(7) 'y los hijos de un difunto hijo Julio **pues** los hijos de Julio que serían Cayetana y Diego' (N151602)

[and the children of a late son Julio, **I mean**, Julio's children who would be Cayetana and Diego]

Finally, it is noteworthy that the continuing function of *pues* seems to be the best acquired among language learners, as several of them use it with this meaning, while almost all the other uses (as consecutive conjunction, conclusion, opening of a reaction or as pause filler) can be ascribed to only two different participants. This confirms yet again that the status of their interlanguage plays an important role in the language learners' narratives.

Entonces

In the case of *entonces*, four different meanings can be distinguished, three of which coincide with those of *pues*. The classifications of Portolés Lázaro and Martín Zorraquino (1999) and Fuentes Rodríguez (2009) agree on the first one, namely its use as a consecutive device. Fuentes Rodríguez adds another three uses: *entonces* acts as a continuing element, used to maintain speech; *entonces* can assume a conclusive role (thus far, these meanings correspond to three of the meanings presented for *pues*); and, *entonces* can also function as a temporal device, in the sense of 'at that time, in those days'.

In our corpus, we note that both the language learners and the native speakers prefer to use *entonces* as a consecutive device or as a continuing element. The first use is illustrated in the examples (8) to (11), the latter in the examples (12) to (14).

(8) 'hay una discusión entre Diego y Álvaro/y pega a Diego pienso/pero de nuevo Beatriz es en lugar de Diego/entonces pega a Beatriz' (LL131402)

[there is a quarrel between Diego and Álvaro/and he hits Diego I think/but then Beatriz is in Diego's place/**so** he hits Beatriz]

(9) 'y los dos hombres de la conversación euhm entrar entran/y euhm quieren también saber qué se pasa/pero es la falta de los hombres que Beatriz euh es euhm in shock/**entonces** euhm Beatriz no dice nada' (LL141513)

[and the two men from the dialogue euhm they enter/and ehmm they want to know as well what it is going on/but it is the fault of the men that Beatriz eh is ehmm in shock/**so** ehmm Beatriz doesn't say anything]

(10) 'y Álvaro intenta convencerla de que habla con él/que recuerde quién es él/que puede confiar en él/pero ella ya sabe que no puede confiar en él/**entonces** no quiere hablar con él' (N141501)

[and Álvaro tries to convince her that she would talk to him/to remember who he is/**so** that she can trust him/but she knows already that she cannot trust him/so she doesn't want to talk to him]

(11) 'y parece ser que no tiene ningún tipo de sentimientos por ella/pero que está fingiendo un especie de amor por ella/**entonces** entendemos que viven juntos y duermen juntos' (N151601)

[and it seems that he doesn't feel anything for her/but rather that he is pretending some sort of love towards her/so we understand they live together and sleep together]

(12) 'ahora dice que está enfadada sobre la discusión entre los dos/**entonces** ahora hay Beatriz que está comiendo su cena' (LL131402)

[now she says she is upset about the quarrel between the two/**then** now there is Beatriz who is eating dinner]

(13) 'y ella cuando cae la cuenta se va corriendo/**entonces** antes de la entrevista la mujer se la queda mirando y la dice en este momento que el más importante en esta impresa [...] es que la imagen es lo que más cuenta' (N141501)

[and she when she realises she starts running/**then** before the interview the woman stares at her and tells her in that moment that the most important in that company [...] is that image is what matters most]

(14) 'y está como contando no sé/que tiene un blog y lo está contando a los seguidores que tenga vale/**entonces** nada cuando llega a la empresa sale Álvaro que es el director general' (N151604)

[and she is like telling something I don't know/that she has a blog and she is telling that to the followers that she may have/**then** when she arrives at the company appears Álvaro who is the general manager]

In a few cases in the learners' corpus, *entonces* is used to open an explanation, a function that is generally accomplished by the two other markers highlighted in the present study, *pues* and *bueno*. As an illustration:

(15) '**entonces** voy a mirar una serie de televisíon y comienzo comienza con una mujer que mira las mujeres perfectas' (LL131409)

[**so** I am going to see a TV series and I start it starts with a woman that watches the perfect women]

Bueno

As was the case with the previous discourse markers *pues* and *entonces*, the third and last marker that will be discussed here, *bueno*, is also highly multifunctional. Both Martín Zorraquino and Portolés Lázaro (1999) and Fuentes Rodríguez (2009) indicate the same meanings, using other descriptions though. All together, five uses of *bueno* can be distinguished. It can function as a deontic modal device, in order to accept or refuse what is being said. Nevertheless, this function is not likely to appear in our corpus, as it usually appears in dialogues. Second, *bueno* can be used as a corrective device. As an interactive marker, then, *bueno* marks the beginning of a turn, often indicating a change of theme or an anti-oriented reaction. Fourth, it can introduce the conclusion of a sequence and finally, it can be used to maintain speech, a function also found for *pues*.

Both the learners and the native speakers show a preference for the continuative meaning of *bueno*. As an illustration, (16) to (19):

(16) 'Después hay una pequeña fiesta del padre de Álvaro que se despide a la revista que es el fundador con otro señor creo **y bueno** hace un speech despide a todos' (LL131408)

[Later there is a small party organised by Álvaro's father who is leaving the magazine who is the founder with another man I think **and well** he gives a speech he says goodbye to all]

(17) 'Aquí ven ve-ven euhm el hombre en que se enamorado euhm/y se siente mal porque todos todas las mujeres son guapas pero ella no es euhm/**y bueno** todas las mujeres euhm euhm aman euhm el hombre euhm Álvaro euhm (risa) **y bueno** euhm hay (silencio) euhm' (LL141506)

[Here you see ehmm the man she has fallen in love with ehmm/and she feels bad because all the women are beautiful but she is not ehmm/**and well** all the women ehmm ehmm love euhm the man ehmm Álvaro ehmm (laughs) **and well** ehmm there is (silence) ehmm]

(18) 'la preguntan qué la ha pasado y qué la pasa de qué la ha pasado/hasta que la lleven al despacho/como ves ya no se puede tener en pie/**y bueno** está ... se encuentra mal' (N141501)

[they ask her what has happened to her and what happens to her and what happened to her/until they took her to the office/as you see she cannot stand any longer/**and well** she is ... she feels bad]

(19) 'la recogen/la sientan en un sofá rojo/**y bueno** la van calmando/la intentan calmar' (N151602)

[they take her/they sit her down in a red sofa/**and well** they calm her down/they try to calm her down]

In comparison to the previous markers *pues* and *entonces*, the occurrences of *bueno* appear to be more spread across its different meanings. As such, we also found several instances in both corpora of the corrective (examples 20 and 21), the interactive (examples 22 and 23) and the conclusive meaning of *bueno* (examples 24 and 25).

(20) 'Ahora tenemos una nueva cena donde los dos hombres euhm ... **bueno** hay mucho tensión' (LL141504)

[Now we have a new dinner where the two men ehmm ... **well** there is a lot tension]

(21) 'y cuando él le habla ella no contesta **bueno** no contesta nadie' (N131402)

[and when he talks to her she doesn't answer **well** nobody answers]

(22) '**Bueno**, todo empiezo euhm en un euhm en una impresa de euhm una para hacer una revista de modelas' (LL141504)

[**Well**, everything started ehmm in a ehmm in a company to ehmm a to do a magazine of models]

(23) '**Bueno** aquí comienzo el fragmento/y lo que vemos es un un ordenador con una cámara web' (N151601)

[**Well** here start the fragment/and what we see is a a computer with a web cam]

(24) 'Hay Álvaro y su mejor amigo en el baño y también hay Bea en un baño que está arreglando algo, pero no es su cara entonces no veo, parece parece un pie o algo euhm **bueno**' (LL131401)

[There is Álvaro and his best friend in the bathroom and also there is Bea in a bathroom who is fixing something, but it is not her face so I don't see, it seems it seems a foot or something ehmm **well**]

(25) 'y [dice] que le va a dar pasa a Álvaro que es el protagonist ahora de todo esto/ **bueno**/y aplauden todos' (N151604)

[and [she says] she is going to give pass to Álvaro who is the protagonist now of all this/**well**/ and all applaud]

Again, it should be observed that *bueno* only appears in 18% of the learners' narratives, but the data still present an indication of the multifunctionality of this marker throughout the productions of the language learners. As stated before, firm conclusions cannot yet be drawn, but it seems that the learners know the different meanings of *bueno* better than those of *pues* and *entonces*, where they showed strong preferences for some meanings or where the use of several meanings did depend more on individual knowledge.

Conclusions

The starting point of this study was the statement of Martí Sánchez (2008) that non-native speakers of Spanish use discourse markers less frequently than native speakers, and in a less secure way. In our corpus of oral narratives, it seems that the first hypothesis of Martí Sánchez holds, that is, the native speakers use more frequently 'pure' discourse markers in their narratives than the language learners (218 vs 112), even though the native dataset only consisted of a limited number of seven productions while 24 learner narratives were analysed. If we take into consideration the prototypical contrastive device *pero*, however, these numbers drastically change: the language learners then produced 368 markers, the natives 304. This already indicates that the production of the language learners depends on the status of their interlanguage, as *pero* is one of the first connective devices acquired by language learners of Spanish and as such, is frequently used. The fact that the interlanguage of the learners plays an important role in the choice of the discourse markers was also illustrated in the analysis of three specific discourse markers, namely *pues*, *entonces* and *bueno*. The choice of these markers can be considered a highly individual one, given the low frequencies of learners that used them. More precisely, language learners generally showed a preference for one specific meaning out of the variety of uses ascribed to these markers, and if another use was chosen, it again proved to be a rather individual decision depending on the learner's interlanguage.

Bibliography

Aijmer, Karin, *English Discourse Particles. Evidence from a Corpus* (Amsterdam: John Benjamins, 2002).

Bazzanella, Carla, 'Discourse Markers in Italian: Towards a "Compositional" Meaning', in Kerstin Fischer, ed., *Approaches to Discourse Markers* (Amsterdam: Elsevier, 2006), 449–464.

Blakemore, Diane, 'Procedures and Indicators: *Nevertheless* and *But*', *Journal of Linguistics 36* (2000), 463–86.

Blakemore, Diane, *Relevance and Linguistic Meaning: The Semantics and Pragmatics of Discourse Markers* (Cambridge: Cambridge University Press, 2002).

Fischer, Kerstin, 'Frames, Constructions and Invariant Meanings: The Functional Polysemy of Discourse Particles', in Kerstin Fischer, ed., *Approaches to Discourse Particles* (Amsterdam: Elsevier, 2006), 427–448.

Fraser, Bruce, 'What are Discourse Markers?', *Journal of Pragmatics 31* (1999), 931–952.

Fuentes Rodríguez, Catalina, *Diccionario de conectores y operadores del español* (Madrid: Arco Libros, 2009).

González, Montserrat, *Pragmatic Markers in Oral Narrative: The Case of English and Catalan* (Amsterdam: John Benjamins, 2004).

Jucker, Andreas H., and Yael Ziv, eds, *Discourse Markers. Description and Theory* (Amsterdam: John Benjamins, 1998).

Loureda Lamas, Óscar, and Esperanza Acín Villa, eds, *Los estudios sobre los marcadores del discurso en español, hoy* (Madrid: Arco Libros, 2010).

Martí Sánchez, Manuel, *Los marcadores en español L/E: conectores discursivos y operadores pragmáticos* (Madrid: Arco Libros, 2008).

Martín Zorraquino, María Antonia, and Estrella Montolío Durán, eds, *Los marcadores del discurso. Teoría y análisis* (Madrid: Arco Libros, 1998).

Martín Zorraquino, María Antonia, and José Portolés Lázaro, 'Los marcadores del discurso', in Ignacio Bosque and Violeta Demonte, eds, *Gramática descriptiva de la lengua española. Tercera parte. Entre la oración y el discurso. morfología* (Madrid: Espasa Calpe, 1999), 4051–4213.

Montolío Durán, Estrella, 'La Teoría de la Relevancia y el estudio de los marcadores discursivos', in María Antonia Martín Zorraquino and Estrella Montolío Durán, eds *Los marcadores del discurso. Teoría y análisis* (Madrid: Arco Libros, 1998), 93–119.

Portolés Lázaro, José, *Marcadores del discurso* (Barcelona: Ariel, 2007).

Schiffrin, Deborah, *Discourse Markers* (London: Cambridge University Press, 1987).

Schiffrin, Deborah, 'Discourse Markers: Language, Meaning, and Context', in Deborah Schiffrin, Deborah Tannen, and Heidi Hamilton, eds, *The Handbook of Discourse Analysis* (Malden, MA: Blackwell, 2001), 54–75.

Stubbs, Michael, *Discourse Analysis* (Chicago: The University of Chicago Press, 1983).

Vande Casteele, An, and Kim Collewaert, 'The Use of Discourse Markers in Spanish Language Learners' Written Compositions', *Procedia: Social and Behavioral Sciences 95* (2013), 550–556.

Wierzbicka, Anne, *Cross-Cultural Pragmatics: the Semantics of Human Interaction* (Berlin: Mouton de Gruyter, 2003).

MARILISA BIRELLO AND ROBERTA FERRONI

7 The appropriation of discourse markers by students of Italian as a Foreign Language in a sequence of action-oriented learning tasks

Introduction

Face-to-face conversation is the result of a collaboration and continuous process of negotiation, which implies the participants' active involvement in the interaction in order to co-construct the message. Bazzanella compares face-to-face conversation to a piece of fabric 'in which the contributions from the speaker and the interlocutor(s) are woven together to a point where they almost blend into one another to create one single product' (Bazzanella 1994: 62, own translation). This fabric, as conversation analysis has masterfully shown (see, among others, Schegloff 1972; Sacks, Schegloff and Jefferson 1974), is internally organized by mechanisms that make it an orderly activity governed by its own rules,[1] like traffic.[2] The conversation flow is characterized by anything but linear turn-taking, being instead broken by a series of linguistic elements, which, together with the 'words of the body' (parole del corpo, Poggi 2006:11, own translation),[3] work to establish an atmosphere of participation and interest among the participants and contribute to characterizing spoken language as a unique

1 For turn-taking and repair mechanisms we refer to Schegloff (1972) and Sacks, Schegloff, and Jefferson (1974), among others.

2 Goffman (1981) identified a principle of order which controls an activity which is, after all, as chaotic and unclear as traffic.

3 'the words expressed by hands, eyes, body, face, trunk and legs movement and posture, physical contact and the distance we put between us and the others (Poggi 2006: 11).

form of communication.[4] More specifically, these elements are phenomena which have been extensively dealt with in conversation analysis (see, among others, Schegloff 1981; Sacks, Schegloff and Jefferson 1974), such as: dialogic repetitions,[5] appositional beginnings, used by speakers in turn taking;[6] self-initiated and other-initiated interruptions;[7] 'simultaneous starts' (Bazzanella 1994:178);[8] overlapping; hesitations such as 'mmmmm …', 'ehhhh …' and 'ehmmmm'; sound elongation; lexicalized and non-lexicalized pauses; self-initiated and other-initiated repairs; and discourse markers,[9] used by both the speaker and the interlocutor.[10]

The final element does not seem to have been addressed enough in materials that are especially designed for foreign language teaching (on this subject, see Pernas et al. 2011). In the specific case of Italian as a Foreign Language (henceforth, IFL), a careful analysis carried out on a wide range of IFL course books used in the *Escuelas Oficiales de Idiomas* in Spain (Gillani and Pernas 2013, 2014) has revealed that much of the oral input contained

4 For more detailed studies on spoken Italian, we refer to Sornicola (1981), Berruto (1987), Voghera (1992), Bazzanella (1994).

5 Repetitions are here understood as 'identical or partial repetitions of one or more lexical items from the previous speaker's turn by the current speaker' (Bazzanella 1994: 210). For a categorisation of the functions of repetitions, see Bazzanella (1994).

6 For instance, *bene, ma, e, allora.*

7 For a definition of interruption, refer to Bazzanella (1994).

8 Simultaneous starts occur when two speakers start talking simultaneously, and, successively, one of them gives up the turn (Bazzanella 1994: 178).

9 In Italian, many terms have been used to identify discourse markers. Berretta (1984), for example, calls them textual connectors (*connettori testuali*), Bazzanella (1995) prefers discourse markers (*segnali discorsivi*), Stame (1999) uses the term pragmatic markers (*marcatori pragmatici*). In this work, we will adopt exclusively the term discourse markers, as it is the most widespread.

10 Bazzanella (1995, 2001) groups discourse markers (DM) into two macro-categories: interactional DMs, considered from the speaker's and interlocutor's points-of-view, are used by the participants in the interaction to highlight the co-construction of the message and the development of the interaction; the metatextual DMs are used by the speaker to signal the sequencing of different parts of the text (opening, development, closing and the relationship between the topics and the subjects addressed in the dialogue).

in the textbooks used for this study is characterized by a copious amount of discourse markers (henceforth DM), especially interactional DMs, to such an extent that interactions almost suffer from 'a certain forced ritualism' (Gillani and Pernas, 2013: 82). However, the activities that these same course books propose in order to develop students' dialogic and interactive competences in foreign language (henceforth, FL) are not as efficient from a teaching perspective (Pernas at al. 2011).

In this study, we follow the assumption that being exposed to authentic speech,[11] together with the 'meaningfulness' of interaction (Pernas et al. 2011: 132) and 'participative involvement' of the students (Pernas et al. 2011:75), represent the cornerstones of the development of 'awareness' (Pernas et al. 2011: 77) and, consequently, the ability to use DMs. The results obtained in this investigation, clearly suggest that the majority of textbooks in the market are still resistant to IFL teaching practices that favour the 'management of verbal interaction' (Pernas et al. 2011: 66), either because they use input that rarely reproduces the typical features of oral speech, or because they do not propose meaningful activities.

In order to fill this gap, some operational proposals have been put forward so that learners of IFL and Italian as a second language can develop a greater sensitivity towards a pedagogy inclined to 'co-constructing conversation, turn taking and interrupting' (Pernas et al. 2011: 66, own translation). In this respect, we refer to the didactic sequence described by Pugliese (2015), who, influenced by a task-based approach (Willis and Willis 2007; Ellis 2009), presents some activities to promote the development and ability to use the DM *figurati*. In previous research carried out by the authors of this work (Ferroni and Birello 2016)[12] which examines the way in which course books present the DMs *va bene, ok, allora, certo!, no dai, beh, dai, e va bene, eh no, eh sì, ma, dunque, va bene ok, sì*

11 By authentic language the authors refer to a language that contains phenomena which are typical of the oral language and not necessarily a language that has been recorded live (Gillani and Pernas 2013, 2014).

12 The material used in class corresponded to Unit 6 of the Italian as a Foreign Language textbook Bravissimo!3-B1.

certo dai,[13] it emerged that one IFL textbook that follows the principles of the TBLT approach:

> shows a balanced sequencing and alternation between discovery activities and practice activities, sufficient to guarantee effective progress in the acquisition of DMs [...]. Moreover, not only does the material proposed in Unit 6 of the textbook *Bravissimo!3-B1* present and analyse DMs, but it also expects learners to reuse them in a meaningful work context, through some 'interactive spaces' in which students become more aware and test the rules that manage the co-construction of conversation in a FL without worrying about losing face, as these 'interactive spaces' are shared with peers. (Ferroni and Birello 2016: 49, own translation)

Considering that the development of authentic and meaningful pedagogical activities is a necessary condition for learning DMs (Pernas et al. 2011), the aim of the following work is:

- To explore how IFL learners start to use and understand the meaning of DMs *dai, no dai* while performing *analytical* activities taken from unit 6 of the textbook *Bravissimo!3-B1*;
- Verify if and how the use of these DMs occurs in the *free practice* activities that are performed in groups and are part of the same unit.

We will base our study on the analysis of two *corpora*, both collected among IFL university students at level B1 of the Common European Framework of Reference for languages (henceforth, CEFR, 2002). The students' mother tongue (henceforth MT) is similar to the FL: Brazilian Portuguese in the first case (henceforth, BP) and Spanish and Catalan in the second case (henceforth, SC).

In the following pages, after describing the approach that inspires the textbook *Bravissimo!3-B1* and analysing the context in which the research was carried out, we will conduct a microanalysis of the dialogic speech of Italian learners who performed activities among peers and whose MT is

13 These are DMs used by the speaker and the interlocutor (Bazzanella 1995, 2001) to express agreement and disagreement, to add information, to take the turn, to interrupt the turn and signal disagreement, to support the current speaker.

similar to the FL. This microanalysis, based on conversational studies (Sacks, Schegloff and Jefferson 1974), will allow us to verify how the DMs *dai, no dai* are perceived and ritualized for the purposes of the co-construction of conversation in a context favourable to action teaching. Finally, in the last section we present the conclusions.

Action-oriented approach in the textbook *Bravissimo!*

As anticipated, the activities observed for this study were taken from Unit 6 of the IFL course book *Bravissimo! 3-B1*, entitled *A tavola non s'invecchia* (Birello and Vilagrasa 2014). It is an IFL textbook that, following an 'action-oriented approach' (Birello and Vilagrasa 2014: 2), aims to promote teaching practices that focus on the abilities necessary to perform tasks by resorting to a variety of resources that range from communicative-linguistic to cognitive and affective. Through this methodology, the concept of communicative competence is enriched by the concept of action competence (Long and Doughty 2009), which is understood as the ability to linguistically interact with other individuals in a participative and message-oriented way in order to complete a task and achieve specific goals.

The adoption of such an approach shall be analysed schematically in order to see the effect it has on teaching practice. This approach presents the following characteristics:

- It values co-operative learning, since interaction among peers promotes language practice and negotiation, which are fundamental activities for FL learning/acquisition. Namely, practice allows the learner to notice and test their hypotheses (Swain 1985) and negotiation makes input comprehensible (refer to Long 1996, among others);
- It focuses on the text as the central piece in the organization of pedagogical activities, since the text is the basic unit of communication and 'there can thus be no act of communication through language without a text' (CEFR 2002: 93);

- It favours teaching based on tasks, which 'involves learners in comprehending, manipulating, producing or interacting in the target language while their attention is focused on mobilising their grammatical knowledge in order to express meaning, and in which the intention is to convey meaning rather than to manipulate form' (Nunan 2004: 4);
- It promotes linguistic reflection through procedures that lead to the discovery of language regularity and favour reflective and metanalytical activities based on the texts (Long and Robinson 1998);
- It considers the intercultural dimension as integral to the communicative dimension, with implications on the affective, cognitive and communicative/behavioural level (Byram and Fleming 1998);
- It promotes students' autonomous learning abilities in the learning process (Nunan 1988).

To foster action-oriented learning, each unit of the course book *Bravissimo!3-B1* contains a series of activities that learners perform so as to complete a final task, presented in a section called *Il nostro progetto* [*Our Project*]. In this section, there are situations similar to those experienced outside the classroom, which strongly encourage linguistic action among partners and use of a type of communication that comes very close to everyday conversation.

Before moving on to describing the activities in detail, we believe it is important to clarify the nature of the input included in Unit 6 of *Bravissimo!3-B1*, since, as was stated in the introduction, presenting spontaneous language that contains mechanisms and discourse conventions typical of face-to-face speech is a necessary condition to appropriately learn the mechanisms and procedures typical of conversation (Gillani and Pernas 2013, 2014). Based on the categorization proposed by Pernas et al. (2011), the input presented in the unit on which we are focusing in this study is semi-authentic, that is, it presents dialogues that 'although created with pedagogical aims, starting from a simple outline or prompt, present intrinsic characteristics of oral language, such as false starts, overlapping and reformulations, which make them similar to spontaneous speech' (Pernas et al. 2011: 85, our translation).

To complete the final task, learners must work through a series of stages called 'sections'. Unit 6 of *Bravissimo!3-B1* consists of 45 activities distributed along the sections as illustrated below (Table 7.1):

Table 7.1. Activities in unit 6 of *Bravissimo! 3-B1*

Primo contatto [First contact	Testi e contesti [Texts and contexts]	Alla scoperta della lingua [Discovering language]	Qualcosa in più [A little something extra]	Risorse e un po' di allenamento [Resources and some practice]	In azione e ... il compito! [In action and ... the task!]
2	7	22	3	3	8

In the first section, called *Primo contatto [First contact]*, the students – first individually and later in a discussion with classmates – have to activate their previous knowledge in identifying some typical Italian restaurants and eateries (*trattoria, osteria, tavola calda, piadineria, bar*), and then practice expressing their thoughts on these places. In the second section, *Testi e contesti [Texts and contexts]*, after students have familiarized themselves with both oral and written texts about different eating styles (*street food, slow food, fast food*), they will present their favourite type of food to their classmates. At this stage, in the section *Alla scoperta della lingua* [*Discovering language*], students are encouraged to observe the use of the imperative form and to come up with a rule to determine the position of pronouns when they are preceded by the imperative, based on an Italian recipe. After noticing the connectors used to sequence the stages of a recipe in the past (*in primo luogo, intanto, adesso, infine*), and the DMs (*va bene, ok, allora, certo!, no dai, beh, dai, e va bene, eh no, eh sì, ma, dunque, va bene ok, sì certo dai)*, learners will apply the rules they observed to their own productions and will expand their culinary vocabulary. Based on the example, learners will write a personal recipe for a 'carbonara'. In the section *Qualcosa in più* [*A little something extra*], students are provided with content that will give them access to more lexical and sociocultural aspects connected to the topic of the unit.

Later, we move on to the section *Risorse e un po' di allenamento* [*Resources and some practice*], which aims to conceptualize the resources in the unit in order to check and revise the rules that were learned. More specifically, the contents dealt with are: the imperative conjugated in the second person plural, and the infinitive, both used to give instructions; agreement between the pronoun and the imperative in the affirmative and negative forms; connectors of time and sequence; reflexive verbs. The unit ends with the section called *In azione e ... il compito!* [*In action and ... the task!*], during which students autonomously and creatively use the tools presented and analysed previously. In order to complete the final task, which consists of setting up a classroom food blog used to share recipes, typical products, tips and tricks, advice, and news, the students will engage in a series of collaborative and organizational tasks which require both individual and group participation. At this point, students will have to draw on the knowledge and strategies acquired in the previous sections – including those about DMs – in a process that stimulates interaction and FL practice.

In relation to the activities on DMs, it is important to notice that they are distributed throughout the different sections of the unit and correspond to three typologies: *introductory activities, analytical activities* and *free practice activities*[14] (Table 7.2).

Table 7.2. Types of activities proposed in Unit 6 based on Ferroni and Birello's categorization (2016)

Unità 6 *Bravissimo!3-B1*	Total	Introductory Activities	Analytical Activities	Free Practice Activities
	11	1	8	2

According to the categorization proposed by Ferroni and Birello (2016), *introductory activities* are participative and aim to motivate and get students involved in the topic presented in the unit. At this stage, the learner observes the functions of the DMs.

Analytical activities encourage students to notice the DMs and their pragmatic functions through a type of controlled practice that, based on

14 For a more detailed description of the different typologies in the unit, see Ferroni and Birello (2016).

the idea of *scaffolding* (Bruner 1983; Ellis 2003), makes use of examples, images, useful words and grammar tables.

Finally, in *free practice activities*, the student will have to autonomously and creatively use the tools previously presented and analysed.

Methodology

The data that will be analysed was collected in two universities where Italian is learned as a FL and where the MT is similar to the FL: Brazilian Portuguese in the first case and Spanish and Catalan in the second.

The Brazilian group consisted of 18 students[15] who were enrolled in the course *Lingua Italiana IV* (Italian Language IV).[16] These students, aged between 20 and 28 (the mean age being 23),[17] were given fictitious names for the purpose of anonymity. The course is aimed at students graduating in Italian Language and Literature from the Faculty of Philosophy, Languages and Literature and Human Sciences of the University of São Paulo in Brazil and it corresponds approximately to level B1 of the CEFR (2002).

The lessons took place twice a week[18] and were taught by a teacher who is an Italian native speaker, who graduated from an Italian university, and who had lived in São Paulo for at least nine years when the study was carried out. Out of 18 participants, only one had been to Italy, having stayed there for five weeks to do an intensive course in Italian. The rest declared that the only contact they had had with the FL was in the classroom.

15 Of these 18 students, 16 are female and two are male. All participants signed a consent form.

16 *Lingua Italiana IV* is a compulsory course that lasts a semester, as stated in the study plan of the Italian Language and Literature undergraduate course at the University of São Paulo. In order to enroll, it is necessary to be registered in the fourth semester.

17 In order to assess the sociolinguistic profile of each student before starting the research, the students were asked to fill out a questionnaire.

18 The course consisted of 50 hours of taught classes. Each lesson lasted about one hour and 40 minutes.

The Spanish group consisted of seven students, and it was very heterogeneous in terms of age, academic background and previous experience in learning foreign languages.[19] Out of these seven participants one had spent one semester in Italy on an Erasmus scholarship and two participants had frequent contact with Italians but had never lived in Italy. The B1 level course is one of the courses offered by the Academic Language Centre at the University of Barcelona, and the students who attend these courses are mainly university students who gain university credits for attending the courses; however, the courses are open to everyone. The participants had a wide linguistic repertoire, in addition to Spanish and Catalan, all of them had already studied English and some of them had studied French. A student from Morocco, who had lived in Barcelona since her childhood, spoke Arabic, French and German as well as Catalan and Spanish.

The classes took place twice a week, totalling four hours per week.[20] The teacher was an Italian native speaker who had graduated from an Italian University and who had lived in Barcelona for over 20 years when the study took place.

In both contexts, the material used in class was taken from the course book *Bravissimo! 3-B1*.

Data collection

This research, which used the tools offered by an ethnographic approach (Hammersley 2006), was conducted by observing two classes. The BP *corpus* is a total of eight hours and 20 minutes long and consists of audio and video recordings, taken over the course of five lessons. The SC *corpus* consists of six hours of recordings, taken over the course of three lessons.

In both contexts, data was collected using a camera on a tripod and positioned in a fixed corner of the classroom by the teacher-researcher. Audio data was also collected: in the Brazilian context, two portable

19 All students were given fictitious names. As with the Brazilian context, each participant was given a consent form.

20 The total amount of taught classes in the course amounted to 50 hours.

recorders were handed out to two groups at the beginning of the lesson and it was recommended that the students turn them on while performing the activities in pairs. Depending on the type of activity and on personal preferences, some students turned the recorder on from the beginning, whereas others decided to turn it on only after the activity had begun. To guarantee more uniform data, we opted to always record the same students. In the Spanish-Catalan context, three portable recorders were distributed and turned on from the beginning of the activities. Although students were free to turn them off and turn them on again, the three groups decided to record everything. As it was a small class, the teacher deemed it necessary to change the pairs. Each change was recorded in the teacher-researcher's field notes.

In both contexts, students were informed about the aims of the study. During peer interactions, the teachers tried to keep their interventions to a minimum, preferring to postpone them to the stage of whole group interaction.

The BP *corpus* groups were identified by numbers 1 and 2. The members of group 1 were Karla and Luciana and of group 2 were Laura and Marta.[21]

There were three SC *corpus* groups and students tended to organize themselves into two groups of two and a group of three students and, as anticipated, the members of each group changed throughout the lessons based on class dynamics.

Unit 6 of *Bravissimo! 3-B1* consists of 45 activities in total. Due to time constraints, we had to make some methodological decisions, therefore, in both contexts, 25 activities were performed, allocated as follows (Table 7.3).[22] Of these activities, 11 are focused on DMs. Due to the similarities of the two contexts – in both students are at the same level, their MT is similar to the FL and the material, the approach and the procedures followed to collect the data are practically identical – we opted to treat the collected data as one *corpus*.

21 As we only had simple portable recorders the groups were chosen based on which students had the clearest tone of voice to facilitate the transcription.

22 Activities lasted a maximum of 10 minutes.

Table 7.3. Total number of activities and activities that were actually performed out of Unit 6 of *Bravissimo! 3-B1*

Primo contatto [First contact]	Testi e contesti [Texts and contexts]	Alla scoperta della lingua [Discovering language]	Qualcosa in più [A little something else]	Risorse e un po' di allenamento [Resources and some practice]	In azione e ... il compito! [In action and ... the task!]	Total activities
2	5	12	1	0	5	Activities that were actually performed
2	7	22	3	3	8	Number of activities in unit 6 of the course book

In the following pages, we aim to illustrate how IFL learners gradually start understanding and using the DMs *dai, no dai*. We will describe how the learners noticed and ritualized these DMs in dialogic speech, so as to co-construct the conversation while performing *analytical* and *free practice activities* taken from Unit 6 of the course book *Bravissimo!3-B1* in small groups.

Results and discussion

In Examples 1, 2 and 3, starting from some initial oral input which was also presented in written form, students are engaged in performing comprehension and analytical activities to acquire a range of competences and better understand the uses and functions of the DMs *certo!, no dai, va bene, eh no, ma, va bene ok, sì certo dai*. Referring to Bazzanella's (1995, 2001) taxonomy, the DMs *certo! va bene, si certo dai, dai, va bene ok* are used by interlocutors to express agreement; DMs *no dai! eh no* and *ma* help speakers signal turn-taking, interrupt the previous turn and show disagreement about the current speaker's propositional content.

In Example 1 Laura and Marta, BP *corpus* students, are focused on an *analytical activity* that consists in inferring the function of the DMs that appear in the initial input.

Esempio 1	Example 1
T1. Laura: ((mentre svolge l'attività)) che è *no dai*? T2. Marta: ah è anche un un'espressione che serve::: serve per tante cose per esprimere accordo disaccordo è::: sospettamento disospettamento anche per ((muovendo le mani)) dare coraggio *dai* facciamo la torta *dai*! T3. Laura: per esprimere accordo io ho scelto ((leggendo)) certo va bene va bene ok sì certo T4. Marta: sì T5. Laura: e per esprimere disaccordo ((leggendo)) eh no ma ma dai T6. Marta: sì d'accordo T7. Laura: sei d'accordo? T8. Marta: certo ((sorridono)) T9. Laura: vou chegar na Italia e vou falar *dai dai dai dai* T10. Marta: *dai* T11. Laura: eh no! *dai!* ((mentre ridono))	T1. Laura: ((while doing the activity)) what's *no dai*? T2. Marta: oh it's also an expression which is used::: is used for many things to express agreement disagreement uh::: suspicion insuspicion even to ((moving hands)) encourage *dai* let's make the cake *dai*! T3. Laura: to express agreement I chose((reading)) certo va bene va bene ok sì certo T4. Marta: yes T5. Laura: and to express disagreement ((reading)) eh no ma ma dai T6. Marta: yes, I agree T7. Laura: do you agree? T8. Marta: certo ((they smile)) T9. Laura: I'll go to Italy and say[23] *dai dai dai dai* T10. Marta: *dai* T11. Laura: eh no! *dai!* ((while laughing))

In this conversation, Laura, who is focused on identifying the DMs' functions, consults Marta and, using a direct question, asks for her help in understanding the function of DM *no dai* (Turn 1). Marta, given her better

23 Here the learner switches to Portuguese, her MT.

linguistic competence,[24] takes the role of more expert learner and, talking to Laura in the FL, explains the meaning of the DM *no dai* through a series of strategies that clearly reveal that not only has Marta fully grasped the use of this DM, but she is also capable of explaining it and coming up with an example to help her classmate understand its meaning and use (Turn 2). She first points out that it is used to express many functions: agreement, disagreement, but also surprise and, finally, encouragement. After that, to be more specific, she uses an illustrative gesture as she explains (Poggi 2006) and, shaking her hands, she comes up with a sentence in which the last meaning of the DM is contextualized: *dai facciamo la torta dai!*. In other words, by analysing the context, Marta proves she has understood the paradigmatic polyfunctions specific to the DM *no dai* (Bazzanella 2015: 37). From Turn 3 to Turn 5, the students compare their responses. It is important to notice that, while Laura reads the functions she identified for each DM, Marta uses the DM *sì, d'accordo* to show she agrees (Turn 6). Laura, realizing her classmate has used the DW perfectly, answers ironically, using an 'interactional repetition' (Bazzanella 1994: 209) of the DM *d'accordo*, which signals involvement and participation in the interaction (Turn 7). Marta plays along and answers in a playful tone using the DM *certo* to confirm her agreement (Turn 8). This way, the students' linguistic activities alternate with metalinguistic activities (Camps 2015), allowing for moments focused on code and moments focused on communication (Bange 1992). Turn 9 is when the speakers switch from Italian to Portuguese when Laura makes her classmate laugh by saying that, when she goes to Italy, she will only use the DM *dai*. A ludic interactive space is opened where the two students show off their interactional competence in Italian while playing with the DMs under analysis in a creative and natural way through a procedure that consists of 'dialogic repetition' (Bazzanella 1994: 210) of the DM *dai* (Turns 10 and 11).

Basically, we can notice that this activity opened up a space in which the students were given the opportunity to: 1) reflect and focus their attention on how to use the DMs to encourage someone to do something (*dai*), to

24 Marta, unlike the other students, had already lived in Italy for a while.

express agreement (*sì d'accordo, certo!*) and disagreement (*no dai!*); 2) reuse DMs to express agreement (*sì d'accordo, certo!*) in a context that encouraged their natural and spontaneous use by promoting reciprocal involvement and a collaborative attitude. This is particularly true for the second category of DMs, as it shows in the example, as they help to make the adjacent Turns that constitute the conversational exchange more cohesive and articulate, proving that the type of task achieved its goal, namely to develop the ability to linguistically interact with other individuals in a participative and message-oriented way.

Let us move on to see how learners Eva, Inma and Lola, from the SC *corpus*, understand the meaning of the DMs *dai* and *no dai* and use them while doing the same *analytical activity*.

Esempio 2	Example 2
T1. Eva: è come per dire a qualcuno di cominciare a fare qualcosa T2. Inma: sì T3. Eva: no? T4. Inma: come il nostro venga T5. Lola: sì, no? T6. Inma: no leggi dopo *dai*! T7. Lola: sì ma per esempio si usa in senso positivo ma ha un senso negativo anche T8. Eva: mh mh T9. Lola: porque ti va bene *dai no dai* ((risate)) sì non so io credo che per::: T10. Eva: no ma ce n'è altri per esempio qiu e::: qui e::: sì T11. Lola: ah sì T12. Eva: lo leggi dopo *dai*! qui c'è la T13. Inma: è come per enfatizzare no? T14. Lola: sì sì T15. Inma: ma si usa per tutto	T1. Eva: it's like saying to someone to start doing something T2. Inma: yes T3. Eva: right? T4. Inma: like our venga T5. Lola: yes, right? T6. Inma: no leggi dopo *dai*! T7. Lola: yes but for example it's used with a positive meaning but it also has a negative meaning T8. Eva: mh mh T9. Lola: porque it's ok for you *dai no dai* ((laughter)) yes I don't know I think that to::: T10. Eva: no but there are others for example here and::: here and:: yes T11. Lola: oh yeah T12. Eva: lo leggi dopo *dai*! Here there's the T13. Inma: it's like to emphasize, right? T14. Lola: yes yes T15. Inma: but it's used for everything

T16. Eva: sì sì **i** tanto! ((pausa 25 secondi)) T17. Eva: ya están uno dos tres o cuatro? T18. Inma: sì sì (...) T19. Lola: sì allora la prima lo leggi dopo dai la seconda forse *va bene dai* T20. Inma: *dai dai dai*! ((ridono))	T16. Eva: yes yes **i** a lot! ((25 second pause)) T17. Eva: ya están uno dos tres o cuatro? T18. Inma: yes yes (...) T19. Lola: yes, then the first lo leggi dopo dai the second maybe *va bene dai* T20. Inma: *dai dai dai*! ((they laugh))

In Turn 1, Example 2, Eva immediately points out the function of the DM *dai*, which is used to encourage someone to do something. In Turns 2–4, the students show they still have doubts and look to each other for confirmation. In Turn 4 Inma solves the problem by code-switching and comparing the DM *dai* with the Spanish DM *venga*, which has the same function.[25] Lola, in Turn 5, shows she does not feel confident yet and asks for confirmation, so Inma, in turn 6, as a reply, reads the example with *dai* from the input. Lola takes the turn again and expresses her doubts about the uses of *dai* and *no dai* (Turn 7 and 9) to the others. Eva, after thinking about it (Turn 8), points out to her classmate that there are other examples with the DM *dai* in the input (Turn 10) and reads an example again (Turn 12). In Turn 13, Inma proposes to her classmates that *dai* is used to emphasize something. The classmates agree and Inma concludes that the DM *dai* can be used in many cases (Turn 15), proving that she is aware of the paradigmatic polyfunctions of this DM (Bazzanella 2015:37). After a pause during which each learner checks their answers individually, in the three following turns (Turns 17–19) the students check the activity together and make sure they did what the teacher had asked. Inma closes this interactive exchange using the DM *dai* in a playful way, which makes the group laugh. In the CS *corpus*, as well as in the BP one, we observe that, once students have become aware of the uses and functions of the DM under analysis, they use the DM *dai* sometimes to talk about DMs and sometimes to clarify their functions and spontaneous use in the co-construction of the interaction. It is clear that students alternate linguistic activity with metalinguistic activity. Furthermore, at the end of the task, they feel confident

25 Diccionario de Partículas Discursivas del Español, <http://dpde.es>.

they understood the meaning and comfortable enough to use the DM *dai* in an appropriate and playful way.

After completing the activity described above, the groups act out the dialogue in pairs and then proceed to a more detailed analysis of the DMs *dai* (used to encourage someone to do something), *va bene* (used to express agreement), and *va bene* (to show the speaker was convinced and accepted what the interlocutor proposed).[26] Finally, to consolidate the learning of DMs *ma, no dai, e va bene, eh no, no dai sì certo*, students ritualize the different forms improvising situations similar to those in real life (*role-play*). Group 1 of the BP *corpus* decided to create a dialogue in which to use the DMs *dai* and *no dai* to convince some friends to eat out (Example 3).

Esempio 3	Example 3
T1. Karla: allora scegliamo questo perché ci sono più persone ((indicando il biglietto)) T2. Luciana: va bene ok = T3. Karla: =((mentre scrive)) andiamo al ristorante alla pasta stasera? È una trattoria nuova andiamo alla nuova trattoria quella quella ... in via ((muove la testa)) in via ... = T4. Luciana: =in via garibaldi ((ride))	T1. Karla: so we choose this because there are more people ((pointing to the paper)) T2. Luciana: all right ok = T3. Karla: =((while writing)) let's go to the restaurant *alla pasta* this evening? It's a new *trattoria* let's go to the new *trattoria* that that ... on road ((moves the head)) on road ... = T4. Luciana: =on garibaldi road ((laughs))
T5. Karla: ok garibaldi in via garibaldi ((mentre scrive)) in via garibaldi come si chiama *dai*? ((scrivendo)) mangio tutto certo? T6. Luciana: ((mentre ride)) *no dai* io ho un'altra cosa T7. Karla: ((mentre scrive)) *no ma dai* T8. Luciana: io ti ho fatto T9. Karla: io ti ho preparato ((mentre scrive e consulta il libro))	T5. Karla: ok garibaldi on garibaldi road ((while writing)) on garbaldi road what's the name *dai*? ((writing)) mangio tutto certo? T6. Luciana: ((while laughing)) *no dai* I have something else T7. Karla: ((while writing)) *no ma dai* T8. Luciana: I've made you T9. Karla: I've prepared you ((while writing and checking the book))

26 Refer to Bazzanella (1995, 2001).

T10. Luciana: *ma no dai* io c'ho preparato una lasagna alla puttanesca ((ridono)) ed è proprio buona T11. Karla: ah no perché non l'hai detto prima T12. Luciana: e va be volevo farti una sorpresa T13. Karla: certo certo tanto la trattoria resta sempre lì *va bene dai* mangiamoci questo capolavoro	T10. Luciana: *ma no dai* I've prepared a *lasagna alla puttanesca* ((they laugh)) and it's really good T11. Karla: oh no, why didn't you say so before? T12. Luciana: *e va be* I wanted to surprise you T13. Karla: *certo certo* the *trattoria* is always there anyway *va bene dai* let's eat this masterpiece

In Turn 1, Karla self-selects and takes her turn through the DM *allora*, here used as appositional beginning (Sacks, Schegloff and Jefferson 1974). By doing this, she performs an act of power towards Luciana as she decides, without consulting her classmate, the topic they will have to talk about. Turn 2 consists in the completion of the adjacent pair (Schegloff 1972), where Luciana accepts Karla's proposal through the DM *va bene ok*.

Luciana and Karla overlap when Karla starts to write and dictate out loud the beginning of the dialogue (Turn 3). However, as she cannot find a proper Italian name for the street, she starts using repetitions, vowel elongation and body gestures in her speech, which makes it possible to infer that she is willing to give the turn to her classmate. Luciana sees Karla struggling and, close to the transition relevance place (Sacks, Schegloff, and Jefferson 1974), comes to her rescue suggesting the name of a street '*in via garibaldi*' (Turn 4). Karla accepts the suggestion using the DM *ok* and then continues to write the text and to dictate it out loud proposing the utterance '*come si chiama dai? mangio tutto certo*' (Turn 5). The irony contained in the name of the restaurant makes Luciana laugh but, following the instructions in the task, she refuses Karla's invitation and uses the DM *no dai* at the beginning of her turn (Turn 6). Karla accepts the proposal (Turn 7), while Luciana is still uttering her sentence (Turn 8), which is repaired in the following turn by Karla (Turn 9). Luciana accepts the repair substituting the verb *fare* with *preparare* and continues to produce her counterproposal, which provokes laughter again '*ma no dai io c'ho preparato una lasagna alla puttanesca ed è proprio buona*' (Turn 10). Karla accepts the invitation using the DM *ah no* at the beginning of the turn to emphasize her surprise (Turn 11), while Luciana replies with the DM *e va bene* to accept. The dialogue ends when Karla accepts Luciana's invitation using the DMs *certo* and *va bene dai* (Turn 13), contextualized in the sentence '*certo certo tanto la trattoria resta sempre lì va bene dai mangiamoci questo capolavoro*'.

From this episode, some interesting observations about the use of DMs can be pointed out. Firstly, it is evident that the type of task provoked, on the one hand, a 'forced' use of the DMs, which were the study topic of the unit. Consequently, at an interactional level, there is an 'abundance' of the DMs *dai, va bene dai, no dai,* to the point that the fabricated dialogue is only at times plausible (the frequent laughter that interposes it could confirm this hypothesis). Furthermore, it is important to notice that the DMs used in the example do not correspond exactly to the target language. For instance, the DM *certo*, as it happens in BP, appears in the final position of the turn and is uttered by Karla with a rising intonation (Turn 5) as she wants 'support for the conversational progression or to request discursive approval' (Urbano 1997:96, own translation).[27]

On the other hand, apart from the repetitive style of the fabricated dialogue, there is another interactional thread, which is essential in order to weave the activity together. In fact, the learners' speech mirrors face-to-face conversation considerably more than the fabricated dialogue does. What makes the learners' speech more akin to face-to-face real conversation is the use of DMs, encouraged by the task procedures, which, as it has been mentioned before, were designed to promote collaboration. For instance, the DMs *va bene ok* (turn 2) and *ok* (turn 5) are inserted into the second turn of adjacent pairs to help the interlocutor support the current speaker.

At this point, after a guided practice that gradually turned into freer practice (Ferroni and Birello 2016), students came to the point where they had to perform the final task, which involved all the language content that was presented and worked on throughout the unit. The final task represents the ultimate free practice activity as it requires students to comprehend, manipulate, produce, interact (Nunan 2004) and use the unit contents and other linguistic resources they had already acquired autonomously. In the specific case

27 In Italian *certo!* is used by the interlocutor to express their agreement (Bazzanella 1994: 158).

of Unit 6, the task consisted of creating a food blog. In order to complete it, the students had to decide on the format and contents to use in the blog and did so through peer discussion. We will now look at Example 4, taken from the SC *corpus*, where Sara, Marta, Beatriz and Lucia discuss their ideas. In the negotiation that we will present here, the four students have just decided that their blog will be dedicated to fusion cuisine and move on to structure the contents of the blog in detail. Sara, who is the most fluent in the group and who frequently deals with food and wine because of her job, takes the role of the leader and suggests creating links for each ingredient. However, she does not know, or does not remember, the word 'link' and resorts to an explanation in which she refers to the colour blue, which distinguishes it, making her classmates laugh (Turn 1).

Esempio 4	Example 4
T1. Sara: e a volte anche quando mette l'ingrediente puoi metterla in azzurro in color azzurro e::: e quindi c'è l'azzurro? ((ride)) non trovo le parole ((inc)) ((risate)) trovi trovi trovi una una parola e che mette dentro ti spiega l'origine il significato	T1. Sara: and sometimes even when you put the ingredient you can make it blue the colour blue and::: and then there's blue? ((laughter)) I can't find the word ((inc)) ((laughter)) you find find find a a word and that puts inside and it explains the origin the meaning
T2. Marta: ah sí! un link –	T2. Marta: oh yes! a link –
T3. Sara: tipo un link – esatto::: entri ti spiega la proprietà come hai detto tu per esempio l'origine::: e l'azzurro ((inc)) ((risate)) Io devo studiare italiano per la mattina perché di pomeriggio ... ((risate))	T3. Sara: like a link – exactly::: you click on it and it explains the properties as you said for example the origin::: and the blue ((inc)) ((laughter)) I have to study Italian in the morning because in the afternoon ... ((laughter))
T4. Marta: ((inc)) siamo stanche. ok	T4. Marta: ((inc)) we're tired. ok
T5. Sara: metti la freccia in azzurro ((riferendosi a una compagna che sta scrivendo)) ((risate))	T5. Sara: colour the arrow blue ((referring to a classmate who is writing)) ((laughter))
T6. Beatriz: ok?	T6. Beatriz: ok?
T7. Marta: *dai*	T7. Marta: *dai*
T8. Sara: allora	T8. Sara: so
T9. Lucia: *dai* ((cercando di riprodurre, esagerandola, l'intonazione italiana)) ((risate))	T9. Lucia: *dai* ((trying to reproduce Italian intonation, but overdoing it)) ((laughter))

T10. Beatriz: dunque dunque:::	T10. Beatriz: so so:::
T11. Marta: dunque facciamo questo no? si mette diverse::: pagine	T11. Marta: so let's do that, right? We'll have lots of::: pages
T12. Sara: facciamo due	T12. Sara: let's make two
T13. Marta: du-due?	T13. Marta: tw-two??
T14. Sara:una tradizionale e una fusione	T14. Sara: a traditional one and a fusion one
T15. Marta:ok	T15. Marta: ok

In Turn 2, Marta suggests the word and Sara, in Turn 3, accepts the suggestion, explaining the reason why she is having difficulties finding the word, then she leaves the utterance incomplete and Marta completes it in the following turn (Turn 4). The turn ends with the DM *ok* to signal that the negotiation on the blog structure has ended. Everything happens in a relaxed atmosphere, as proved by the classmates. At this point, Sara self-selects (Turn 5) and makes a joke about the use of the colour blue, making a link to what was said in Turns 1 and 3.

From Turn 6 to Turn 10, the utterances consist of a series of DMs used by the students in the following order: to express agreement (*ok*), encourage to continue the activity (*dai*) and organize speech (*allora, dunque*). In Turn 9, Lucia uses *dai*, trying to imitate Italian intonation, which provokes the classmates' laughter. Sara and Beatriz use *allora* (Turn 8) and *dunque* (Turn 10), respectively, intending to close this interactive exchange and move on. The last part (Turns 11–15) is a dialogue between Marta and Sara. In turn 11, Marta uses the DM *dunque* again to introduce the proposal that puts an end to this part of the negotiation. Sara, in Turn 12, expresses the final decision, which surprises Marta (Turn 13). In Turn 14 Sara gives further information and in turn 15 Marta uses the DM *ok* to accept. This example extracted from the interaction that took place when the students were performing the final task shows that the learners have understood the meaning of and used the DMs that were analysed and practiced in the sequence of activities. After a lateral sequence in the beginning when a communication problem is solved, the students use a series of DMs whose functions are, in the following order: to close the lateral sequence and show agreement (*ok?* In Turn 6 and *dai* in Turn 7), and to organize speech (*allora* in Turn 8 and *dunque* in Turn 10). Furthermore, it can be noted that the use of DM *dai* provokes new laughter, showing that the attempt to reproduce the DM with Italian intonation is not a source of frustration, but rather a source of amusement. We need to stress that the attempt to reproduce the intonation of the DM *dai* (Turn 9) is consciously exaggerated, conveying irony. We can conclude that the interactive spaces that are opened in the sequence of activities of an action-oriented approach not only promote activities to reflect on and to use DMs, but also create opportunities for students to show the acquired fluency through irony.

Conclusions

The aim of this study was to explore how IFL learners understand the meaning of and use the DMs *dai, no dai* while performing *analytical activities* and to verify whether and how these learners use these DMs in the *free practice* activities taken from Unit 6 of the Italian textbook *Bravissimo!3-B1*. The analysis was carried out with university students at level B1 of the CEFR (2002) whose MT is similar to the FL. The results show that, during the analytical activities, group interaction consisted of exchanges that encourage metalinguistic activity, that is, activity that is focused on how the language works (Camps 2014). In these exchanges, the DMs *dai* and *no dai* became the object of reflections in which learners become aware of the DMs' paradigmatic polyfunctions (Bazzanella 2015) and of their use, thanks to a series of strategies such as code-switching from the FL to the MT (Example 1) and comparing the presence of similar phenomena in one's own language (Example 2). Although the roleplay activity encouraged a 'forced' use of the DMs *dai, no dai*, in this case we noticed a playful attitude in the learners, triggered by their awareness of the use of the DMs which were the focus of the activity (Examples 1, 2 and 3). As the guided practice gradually turns into free practice, metalinguistic activity leaves room for metacommunicative activity, that is, activity that is focused on communication (Ciliberti 2016). In these interactive spaces, we noticed that the use of DMs *dai* and *no dai* became gradually more natural and spontaneous, while laughter, which is limited to the attempt to imitate Italian intonation in an exaggerated way (Example 4), gradually disappears.

Moreover, we can state that collaborative work, which is present both in the *analytical* and *free practice* activities, favoured the spontaneous use of the DMs *sì, va bene, ok, d'accordo, certo* deployed by the speaker and the interlocutor with interactional function (Bazzanella 1995, 2001). These were used as well as a series of DMs which had previously been analysed by students, such as *allora* and *dunque*.

Bibliography

Bange, Pierre, 'A propos de la communication et de l'apprentissage de L2 notamment dans ses formes institutionnelles', *Acquisition et interaction en langue étrangère* 1/1 (1992), 53–85.

Bazzanella, Carla, 'I segnali discorsivi', in Carla Bazzanella, eds, *Le facce del parlare* (Firenze: La Nuova Italia, 1994), 145–174.

Bazzanella, Carla, 'I segnali discorsivi', in Lorenzo Renzi, Giampaolo Salvi, and Anna Cardinaletti, *eds, Grande grammatica italiana di consultazione*, vol. III (Bologna: Il Mulino, 1995/2001), 226–257.

Bazzanella, Carla, 'Segnali discorsivi a confronto. Dati e teoria, un percorso integrato', in Margarita Borreguero Zuloaga, and Sonia Gómez-Jordana Ferary, eds, *Marqueurs du discours dans le langues romanes: une approche contrastive* (Limoges: Lambert-Lucas, 2015), 35–46.

Berretta, Monica, 'Connettivi testuali in italiano e pianificazioni del discorso', in Lorenzo Coveri, ed., *Linguistica testuale* (Roma: Bulzoni, 1984), 237–254.

Berruto, Gaetano, *Sociolinguistica dell'italiano contemporaneo* (Firenze: La Nuova Italia, 1987).

Birello, Marilisa, and Albert Vilagrasa, *Bravissimo! 3 Corso d'italiano* (Barcellona: Edizioni Casa delle Lingue, 2014).

Bruner, Jerome, *Child's Talk: Learning to Use a Language* (New York: Norton, 1983).

Byram, Michael, and Michael Fleming, *Language Learning in Intercultural Perspective* (Cambridge: Cambridge University Press, 1998).

Camps, Anna, 'Metalinguistic Activity in Language Learning', in Teresa Ribas, Xavier Fontich and Oriol Guasch, eds, *Grammar at School. Research on Metalinguistic Activity in Language Education* (Brussels: Peter Lang, 2014), 25–41.

Ciliberti, Anna, 'Pratiche discorsive e processi sociali in classi multilingue', *Rassegna Italiana di Linguistica Applicata* 2/3 (2016), 133–139.

Consiglio d'Europa, *Quadro comune europeo di riferimento per le lingue: apprendimento insegnamento valutazione* (Firenze: La Nuova Italia-Oxford, 2002).

Briz, Antonio, Salvador Pons, and José Portolés, co-ords, *Diccionario de partículas discursivas del español.* <http://www.dpde.es> (2008).

Ellis, Rod, *Task-Based Language Learning and Teaching* (Cambridge: Cambridge University Press, 2003).

Ellis, Rod, 'Task-Based Language Teaching: Sorting Out the Misunderstandings', *International Journal of Applied Linguistics* 19/3 (2009), 221–246.

Ferroni, Roberta, and Marilisa Birello, 'Meta-analisi e applicazione di una proposta didattica orientata all'azione per l'apprendimento dei segnali discorsivi in italiano LS', *Italiano LinguaDue* 1/8 (2016), 30–53.

Gillani, Eugenio, and Paloma Pernas, 'Input orale e competenza dialógica: Le scelte dei manuali di italiano Ls', *Studi Italiani di Linguistica Teorica e Applicata* 42/1 (2013), 61–99.

Gillani, Eugenio, and Paloma Pernas, 'La trasmissione del parlato nei libri di testo di italiano LS: dall'oralità madrelingua all'input orale', in *Atti del XII Congresso SILFI Società Internazionale di Linguistica e Filologia Italiana* (Helsinki, 18–20 June 2012), 'Dal manoscritto al web: canali e modalità di trasmissione dell'italiano. Tecniche, materiali e usi nella storia della lingua' (2014).

Goffman, Erving, *Forms of Talk* (Philadelphia: University of Pennsylvania Press, 1981).

Hammersley, Martyn, 'Ethnograph: Problems and Prospects', *Ethnography and Education* 1 /1 (2006), 3–14.

Long, Michael, 'The Role of the Linguistic Environment in Second Language Acquisition', in William Ritchie, and Tej Bhatia, eds, *Handbook of Second Language Acquisition* (San Diego: Academic Press, 1996), 413–468.

Long, Michael, and Catherine Doughty, *Handbook of Language Teaching* (Oxford: Blackwell, 2009).

Long, Michael, and Peter Robinson, 'Focus on Form: Theory, Research and Practice', in Catherine Doughty and Jessica Williams, eds, *Focus on Form in Classroom Second Language Acquisition. Focus on Form in Classroom Second Language Acquisition* (Cambridge: Cambridge University Press, 1998), 15–41.

Nunan, David, *The Learner-Centered Curriculum: a Study in Second Language Teaching* (Cambridge: Cambridge University Press, 1988).

Nunan, David, *Task-Based Language Teaching* (Cambridge: Cambridge University Press, 2004).

Pernas, Paloma, Eugenio Gillani, and Annamaria Cacchione, 'Costruire testi, strutture conversazionali: la didattica dei segnali discorsivi come elementi pivot dell'interazione verbale', *Italiano LinguaDue* 3/1 (2011), 65–138.

Poggi, Isabella, *Le parole del corpo. Introduzione alla comunicazione multimodale* (Roma: Carocci, 2006).

Pugliese, Rosa, 'Figurati, tra i segnali discorsivi. Una prospettiva pedagogica', in Elena Pistolesi, and Rosa Pugliese, and Barbara Gili Fivella, *eds, Parole, gesti, interpretazioni. Studi linguistici per Carla Bazzanella* (Roma: Aracne 2014), 163–207.

Sacks, Harvey, Emanuel Schegloff, and Jefferson Gail, 'A Simplest Systematic for the Organization of Turn-Taking in Conversation', *Language* 50/4 (1974), 696–735.

Schegloff, Emanuel, 'Sequencing in Conversational Openings, in Joseph Gumperz, and Dell Hymes, eds, *Directions in Sociolinguistics: The Ethnography of Communication* (New York: Holt, 1972), 346–379.

Schegloff, Emanuel, 'Discourse as an Interactional Achievement: Some Uses of "uh huh" and Other Things That Come Between Sentences', in Deborah Tannen, ed., *Analyzing Discourse: Text and Talk* (Washington, DC: Georgetown University Press, 1981), 71–93.

Sornicola, Rosanna, *Sul parlato* (Bologna: Il Mulino, 1981).

Stame, Stefania, 'I marcatori della conversazione', in Renata Galatolo, and Gabriele Pallotti, *eds, La conversazione: un'introduzione allo studio dell'interazione verbale* (Milano: Raffaello Cortina Editore, 1999), 169–186.

Swain, Merrill, 'Communicative Competence: Some Roles of Comprehensible Input and Comprehensible Output in its Development', in Susan Gass, and Madden Carolyn, eds, *Input in Second Language Acquisition* (Mahwah, NJ: Lawrence Erlbaum), 235–253.

Urbano, Hudinilson, 'Marcadores conversacionais', in Dino Preti, ed. *Análise de textos orais* (São Paulo: Editora Humanitas, 1997), 81–101.

Van Lier, Leo, *The Classroom and the Language Learner* (London: Longman, 1988).

Voghera, Miriam, *Sintassi e intonazione nell'italiano parlato* (Bologna: Il Mulino, 1992)

Willis, Dave, and Jane Willis, *Doing Task-based Teaching, A Practical Guide* (Oxford: Oxford University Press, 2007).

MARGARITA BORREGUERO ZULOAGA

8 Expressing agreement in L2 Italian: Strategies and discourse markers in Spanish learners

Introduction

This paper aims at analysing the linguistic strategies employed by Spanish learners of L2 Italian when expressing agreement in interaction. Expressing agreement is one of the most frequent conversational moves, both in formal and informal interactions, and it has proved to be one of the best indicators of linguistic competence in a foreign language as it requires comprehending what has been said by the conversational partner and overtly expressing both comprehension and solidarity with the content of the previous utterances.

One of the main problems when analysing lexical markers of agreement[1] is the difficulty to disentangle agreement from signalling understanding because in all cases the same lexical units may be used to fulfil different discourse functions related to a positive stance (cf. Kerbrat-Orecchioni 2016: 34). The situation is even more complicated in L2 interactions because in this case speakers do not master the use of lexical markers and tend to overuse or underuse them or to assign them some functions that are not conveyed by those lexical units in native speakers (NSs).

However, providing positive evidence is particularly frequent in L2 interactions, especially in non-native speakers (NNSs) with a low linguistic competence because it is a way of encouraging each other to go on with the interaction and a way of reassuring mutual understanding. According to Condon and Čech (2007), there are at least three types of positive evidence

1 In this paper, we will not take into consideration non-lexical markers such as prosody or other paralinguistic elements or non-linguistic means (mimics and kinesics).

in interaction (i.e. means of showing understanding): presupposition of understanding, assertion of understanding and display of understanding. We will now explain briefly the difference between them. Any response to a partner's contribution presupposes understanding, so in this case understanding is the 'default assumption'. On the other hand, assertions of understanding require the use of acknowledging signals, normally discourse markers which define the 'backchannel verification'. Finally, answers to explicit questions or repetition and paraphrases of what has been said are means of displaying and exemplifying understanding.

In this paper, we are mainly interested in the way learners use discourse markers (henceforth DMs) linked to assertion of understanding to express agreement with their interlocutors. Expressing agreement presupposes understanding of the interlocutor's utterance but, as we will see, the same lexical units that are employed to express agreement are also used as part of backchannel verification, that is, they are used to assert understanding and not necessarily agreement. We will explore how learners with different competence in L2 Italian employed DMs that perform both functions.

DMs contribute to the turn-taking structure of conversation and to the dynamic interaction among speakers; they function as cohesive devices and allow speakers to express their emotions, viewpoints and intentions. Therefore, they constitute an essential element of linguistic competence and their absence may cause misunderstandings and oddness when interacting with native speakers. The theoretical studies in this field have only recently had direct applications to language acquisition and teaching, and it has been found that NNSs have strong difficulties to use these elements when developing their oral competence and that little attention has been paid to them in language teaching (cf. Pernas et al. 2011 for a revision of the treatment of DMs in L2 Italian language coursebooks).

Previous research has shown that DMs are not easy to acquire due to their polyfunctionality and mobility in the utterance, that L2 learners use a very reduced number of them compared to native speakers (NSs), and that NNSs tend to attribute many functions to this reduced inventory, overwhelming them with functions that are not found in the L1 and reaching a stage known as fossilization (Romero Trillo 2002).[2] In this study, we have first analysed which lexical items are acquired to express agreement along with the development of communicative competence and, second, which functions they may assume that are not found in L1 native speakers.

The investigation is based on the data collected from a learner corpus of L2 Italian speakers whose mother tongue is Spanish (the A.Ma.Dis. Corpus). The data were elicited through role-play interactions between informants with symmetric and asymmetric linguistic competence. Participants in the role-play interactions were supposed to negotiate on different issues (such as buying a present for a friend) where agreement played a prominent role as a conversational strategy.

This research is part of a wider project on the acquisition of pragmatic competence in Italian by Spanish speakers, with especial attention to the use of linguistic devices, such as discourse markers and information structure to manage turn-taking alternation and thus to move forward in conversation, which is not always an easy task for NNSs, especially beginners. Our focus lies on the path of acquisition of these devices in closely related languages (Spanish and Italian); thus, with this purpose, we have analysed the speech of learners belonging to three different levels of competence (beginners (A2), intermediate (B1.3), advanced (C1)).

The results of previous studies show that DMs are present since the initial stages of the acquisition process, but in these first stages beginners use a few of these elements; for example, back-channel signals (such as interjections *hm, uhm, ah*), DMs phonetically closed to their L1 (*sì*) or to other previously acquired L2 (*ok, d'accordo*). All DMs in beginners' interlanguage have the peculiarity of being phonetically light (one or two syllables) and similar to DMs in the L1 or another L2 (Guil 2015: 373). In intermediate and advanced learners, the inventory is enriched with new elements, but the acquisition process is far from linear: Some lexical elements are never

2 Specific studies devoted to the acquisition of DM are relatively frequent in acquisitional linguistics. For L2 English the most complete study is Müller (2006) who studies the acquisition of some conversational DMs in German speakers. In this paper we will refer specially to studies on L2 Italian, which has been one of the languages where DM have been more widely studies since Andorno's (2000) pioneer research.

acquired, some are used with different functions than in NSs, and some are overused (cf. Guil 2015, Borreguero 2017, Borreguero et al. 2017 for comprehensive panoramic of the acquisition process based on the data of the A.Ma.Dis. Corpus). There is no significant difference between symmetric and asymmetric interactions as far as the use of DMs is concerned. This means that there is not a 'mirror-effect' in asymmetric interactions, that is, NNSs do not repeat the DMs employed by NSs during the conversation.

The expression of agreement in closely related languages

We are interested in the function of expressing agreement in interaction, which is considered to be one of the most basic and frequent discursive functions, both in formal and informal interaction. Expressing agreement is closely tied to politeness strategies in discourse; in fact, when the interlocutor gives positive feedback, the speaker's positive face is reinforced.[3] Moreover, by expressing agreement speakers contribute to interactively establishing the situational context. This is done both by signalling understanding and by signalling agreement, which presupposes understanding as we have seen above. 'Participants display their understanding of each other's utterances and the relationship that holds between these utterances to each other. These interpretations may be ratified or challenged by the coparticipants in the following turn' (Fischer 2007). This process is known as the 'grounding' process.[4]

3 This does not imply that they cannot admit ironic uses and become a strategy of impoliteness (Gras 2003). This author also explores other uses of these DMs as concessive and focus makers.

4 According to Fischer (2007), the main difference between DMs (or discourse particles) and modal particles is that while the first ones are very actively in the grounding process, modal particles refer to the common ground of an interaction, that is, what is shared by the communication partners, which is usually unproblematic and thus implicit.

Languages have a wide range of lexical units and phrases to express agreement with different degrees of intensity. In Spanish, the most frequent ones are *sí, vale, bien* (quite neutral), *bueno* (which can be used for partial agreement), *por supuesto, claro* (emphatic), *desde luego, no faltaba más, sin (lugar a) duda(s)* and the adverbs *ciertamente, naturalmente, obviamente* (very emphatic). In Italian, *sì*[5], *ok, d'accordo, bene, va bene* are the most common markers for agreement (Bazzanella 1995, 2006) while *certo, certamente, senz'altro, infatti, in effetti, ci mancherebbe* include increasing levels of emphasis and therefore subjectivity. We will deal with some important differences in use between these DMs below.

For some of them, expressing agreement is their core meaning and function (Sp. *vale*, It. *ok, d'accordo, bene*), while others have been traditionally considered evidential adverbs that indicate not only the source of information (mainly inferential in these cases) but also a high level of certainty about the information reported in the interlocutor's utterance; indicating this certainty becomes a way of expressing agreement, as it can be seen in (1).

(1) A: ¿Vienes a la fiesta?
B: *Sí*
A: ¿Llevamos un regalo, no?
B: ¡*Claro*!

[A: Are you coming to the party?
B: Yes
A: We will bring a present, won't we?
B: Of course!]

In (1), the fact that one has to bring a present when invited to a party is part of the common cultural knowledge of both speakers, and there is no

5 Andorno (2016), contrary to Bazzanella and following previous studies by Bernini (1996) and Andorno and Rosi (cf. References in Andorno 2016) does not consider *sì* a confirmative marker, but only an affirmative one which indicates the polarity of the utterance. We have no doubt that this is the case with NSs, but the situation with NNSs is far more complex, although we will not deal with it the present study, as this author shows in Andorno (2007: 102). Cf. also Koch's (2016) study on the use of Sp. *sí* by Geman spakers of L2 Spanish.

need for negotiation. In this sense, B responds *¡Claro!* to indicate that the relation between going to a party and bringing a present is expected, and therefore, that s/he agrees with A's proposal. But B responds *Sí* to the first question because there is no presupposition about what B is going to do in A question (or in B's response to that question), and it is thus presented as open to negotiation.

The number of evidential adverbs (or adverbial phrases) employed to express agreement is higher in Spanish than in Italian, and there is also an increasing number of studies devoted to their analysis, often from a comparative perspective, to try to delimit their meaning and contexts of appearance: *(muy) bien*, *bueno* (Fuentes 1993c and Blas Arroyo 2011), *claro* (Fuentes 1993a, Gras 2003, Pons 2008, Solís 2013), *cómo no*, *de acuerdo* (Ruiz Gurillo 1999), *desde luego* (Fuentes 1993b, Pérez Canales 2003, Alvarado and Ruiz Gurillo 2011, Solís 2012a), *efectivamente / en efecto* (Pérez Canales 2003, Solís 2012a. Llopis 2015), *por supuesto* (Fuentes 1993b, Ruiz Gurillo 1999, Gras 2003, Pérez Canales 2003, Solís 2013) and some model adverbs ending in *–mente* such as *naturalmente*, *ciertamente*, *obviamente*, etc. (cf. Fuentes 1993b). There are also more comprehensive views of all (or almost all) these elements such as Fuentes (1991, 1995), Martín Zorraquino and Portolés (1999) and Solís (2012b). Researchers are, however, far from reaching an agreement on how to classify these markers in a general taxonomy. Solís (2012b: 17–43) – and to a lesser degree Pérez Canales (2003) – review the different conceptualizations in the most recent grammars, the main dictionaries of DMs (Santos Ríos 2003, Briz et al. 2008 and Fuentes 2009) and most of the monographic studies mentioned above.[6]

In the case of Italian, *sì* (Bernini 1995, Andorno 2016) and *bene* and its variations (*va bene*, *be'*, *va be'*) have attracted most of the attention (Frank-Job 2006, Lindbadh 2015a/b), while to our knowledge other DMs of this group have been almost ignored until today in L1 Italian (but see Mandelli (2006) about *in effetti* and Andorno (2016) about *esatto*, *infatti* and *okay*). The situation is not different in a L2, where the pair *sì/no* in positive and

6 Fuentes (1991) offers a no longer up-to-date revision of the descriptions of the so called modal or modality adverbs in the main monographic studies on the classification of adverbs in English, French and Spanish.

negative questions of L2 Italian speakers has been analysed by Andorno (2007, 2008) and Andorno and Rossi (2016). From a contrastive perspective, we would like to highlight Calvo (2001) and for overview approaches, cf. Bazzanella (1995, 2006).

These DMs appear more frequently in conversation than in written texts, or to be more precise, in immediate communication than in distant communication, so they are usually considered conversational markers or markers with a main interactional function, which means that their main discursive function is to regulate the turn-taking alternation; overtly agreeing with the interlocutor is often a way of encouraging the discourse flow.

All of them share some characteristics: they may appear both as part of an utterance or constituting an utterance by themselves; for example, acting as answers to questions or as responses to invitations (see (1) above). Regarding their procedural meaning, most authors consider that they present the content of the utterance or the relation between one utterance and the previous one (or implicit information) as obvious, evident and unquestionable; that is why they are considered evidential adverbs (or adverbial phrases).[7] However, as Solís (2012a, 2012b: 55–68 and *passim* and 2013) has shown, most descriptions do not allow to clearly establish in what contexts they can or cannot be used. Here, we follow her proposal, which is based on the speaker's attitude towards the interaction and not towards the content of the utterance itself. In fact, our focus of attention lays on what the speaker is doing when using one or the other DM to express agreement.

However, we cannot forget that some of these lexical units function as acknowledgement tokens in both languages, together with a variety of interjections (*aha*, *uhm*, etc.): Sp. *sì*, *vale*; It. *sì*, *ok*. This polyfunctionality is also shown in L2 learners.

The above-mentioned interest in the speaker's intention has led us to stress the study of pragmatic functions. Therefore, we have adopted an

7 The differences are linked to the degree of pre-existing necessity between the connected parts of discourse (for example, the necessity pre-exists for *por supuesto*, but it does not for *claro*, cf. Gras 2003) or to the expectations of the interlocutor: for example, *en efecto* and *efectivamente* confirm what the speaker thinks it was expected by the hearer (Pérez Canales 2003: 1538).

onomasiological approach that is focused on the pragmatic function – not on the semantic value – and analyses which lexical (or paralinguistic) elements fulfil this function in the learners' variety.[8] As in previous studies, we follow the functional taxonomy in López Serena and Borreguero (2010), which distinguishes three discursive macrofunctions: interactional, metadiscursive and ideational.[9] Following Bazzanella (1995), the interactional macrofunction is subdivided in control function, contact function and reactive function. The interesting point for us in this research is that the same lexical elements, when functioning as DMs, may fulfil different interactional functions; for example, *ok* can manifest agreement, but it functions also as a back-channel signal, that is, as a sign of phatic function, which is part of the contact function, that is, it encourages the speaker to keep the floor. The situation is much more complicated for DMs such as Sp. *bueno* or It. *bene* (cf. Calvo 2001). The high degree of polysemy of these DMs is one of the reasons why we deem the onomasiological approach (from function to lexical element) to be a most appropriate perspective in the task of tracing their acquisitional path in NNSs.

In adopting an acquisitional perspective, one of the difficulties for the analysis in the case of Spanish and Italian is that the minimal expression of agreement is phonetically identical in both languages (It. *sì*, Sp. *sí*), so it is difficult to identify a real process of acquisition.[10] For this reason, we will analyse all the DMs found in our corpus to express agreement with

8 The onomasiological approach is increasingly being used in studies on pragmatic acquisition. For the acquisition of discourse markers in L2 Spanish and Italian, cf. Jafrancesco 2015, Pascual Escagedo 2015, Borreguero 2009, 2017, Borreguero et al. 2017.

9 For a full presentation of the taxonomy, cf. López Serena and Borreguero (2010) and Borreguero (2015). For a shorter presentation in English, cf. Borreguero (2017).

10 This difficulty is present also in other DM: disagreement marker such as *no* or the most difficult adversative Sp. *pero* and It. *però*, with a different accent position in each language which is often neglected by learners and makes almost impossible to decide whether the Spanish learner of L1 Italian is using a Spanish connective or has just acquired the lexical component but not the prosodical one of the Italian connective (cf. Borreguero 2009a/b for the use of adversative connectives in written and oral L2 Italian).

the exception of *sì/sí*, which represents a challenge that deserves an independent study.[11]

There are, of course, other DMs fulfilling this discursive function which present phonetic similarities, such as It. *certo* / Sp. *cierto*, It. *d'accordo* / Sp. *de acuerdo*, It. *bene* / Sp. *bien*, but they are not so close as to prevent the analyst from deciding whether the learner is using a L1 or a L2 unit. However, as we will see, there are phonetically similar lexical elements that do not share the same function, as the pairs It. *buono*[12] / Sp. *bueno* or It. *chiaro* / Sp. *claro*, where only the Spanish member functions as a DM. The use of the most phonetically similar element for expressing agreement to supply a lack of linguistic competence in interaction is one of our more interesting findings and will be discussed below.

Methodology

The corpus

Our research is based on data collected from a learner corpus of L2 Italian speakers whose mother tongue is Spanish. The corpus contains 36 video-recorded interactions with informants of three different levels of proficiency (12 are symmetric conversations between learners and 24 are asymmetric

11 The few studies on *sì* L2 Italian (D'Alfonso 2016) and L2 Spanish (Koch 2016) does not concern close-related languages. For example, the Pavia project and studies based on Siena's ADIL corpus focus on the acquisition of Italian by NNSs whose mother tongue is typological very distant from Italian (Giacalone Ramat 2003, D'Alfonso 2016, respectively). This is one of the reasons why our results are difficult to compare with Andorno's (2007, 2008) based on Chinese and Tigrine speakers and with Nigoević and Sučić's (2011) on Croatian learners. Other studies on French or Spanish NSs do not focus specifically on DMs expressing agreement (Manili 2001, Jafrancesco 2015).

12 In some varieties *buono* can function as a DM, mainly under the form *va buo'* or *va buono* in Tuscan Italian.

ones with a native speaker). We also recorded a small corpus of Italian native speakers (see Table 8.1). The corpus was collected in 2006 and the informants were students from the Public School of Languages in two Spanish cities (Segovia and Valencia).[13] It has a total duration of around 400 minutes, and it contains 38,000 tokens.

Table 8.1. A.Ma.Dis. learner corpus: Number and type of interactions

	Initial level	Intermediate level	Advanced level	Native
Symmetric interactions[14]	4	4	4	4
Asymmetric interactions	8	8	8	24

Participants were provided with very simple instructions to take part in role-play situations which were designed to produce semi-spontaneous interactions. Three of these situations were task-oriented: choosing a present for a friend, deciding what to do when facing a rise in the rent of the apartment and a job interview for a babysitter position. The fourth one was a not task-oriented, free talk with an Italian visitor at a friend's house. The first two situations were chosen for the symmetric interactions (between NNSs with similar linguistic competence) and the other two for asymmetric interactions with a NS and needed a more formal register.

13 The corpus is entirely available online at <http://www.marcadores-discursivos.es>. This website contains also information about the Project and the main publications of the members of the A.Ma.Dis. research group. More information about the corpus in Guil et al. (2008), Guil (2015) and Borreguero (2017) (among others). All the NNSs were university graduate women between 25 and 45 years old.

14 The number of tokens increases through the three levels because, as expected, learners with higher linguistic competence become more fluent, thus they are able to produce a higher number of tokens in similar time slots (around 10 minutes). As far as symmetric interactions is concerned, the corpus contains 4,974 tokens at the beginner level, 7,538 at the intermediate level and 8,344 at the advance level, a number that matches the 8,141 tokens of the NS symmetric interactions.

The theoretical framework

In the analysis of these DMs, we will follow Solís' (2012a/b, 2013) analyses, which identify the invariant meaning of DMs and distinguish it from their contextual meaning effects in order to find a convincing explanation of their mutual differences. According to this author, expressing agreement is not the basic meaning of these DMs but only a contextual effect derived from their use in certain contexts. But when a speaker uses *claro* or *desde luego* as a response to invitations or questions, he is not agreeing upon anything but just providing an affirmative answer different from a simple *sí* (cf. Pons 2008 who proposes two different markers in the case of *claro* to explain these two different functions). The strong argument in Solís' proposal is that the invariant meaning of these markers does not lie on the speaker's attitude towards the propositional content but towards the interaction and his/her interlocutor (this is what she calls the metalinguistic dimension, cf. Solís 2012b: 47–49), in other words, the grounding process. In her analysis, she offers a very detailed and convincing analysis of the most used Spanish markers to express agreement, an analysis that allows her to get rid of tags such as 'emphatical', 'argument reinforcer', and 'evidential', which are often vague and ambiguous in this case, because they appear in the descriptions of almost all of them.

We will claim that by using these DMs the speaker expresses his/her point of view about the relationship with the interlocutor and about the act of producing an utterance, adopting a certain particular position (Solís 2012b: 66). The five parameters to describe these DMs are: a) the degree of commitment of the speaker;[15] b) the presence or absence of expectations about this commitment; c) the dependency of this commitment on external circumstances or on the speaker's decision; d) the fact that this commitment is up for negotiation or not; and e) the relationship of the commitment with the extralinguistic world (Solís 2012b: 82–92). Using these five parameters, we will describe the DMs found in our corpus.

15 An explicit commitment allows to distinguish DMs such as *de acuerdo*, *en efecto* or *por supuesto* from others such as *al parecer* o *por lo visto*, which lack the commitment of the speaker (Gaviño 2011).

Results and discussion

We have extracted automatically the number of occurrences of the most frequent DMs employed in our corpus to express agreement (see Table 8.2).[16] Although DMs are highly polyfunctional in discourse, we have considered only their main function in each occurrence.

As Table 8.2 shows, the four most frequent DMs in the learners' variety (*d'accordo, ok, va bene, bene*) have a basic meaning of agreement, but there are important differences between them, as we will see below. By having a quick look at Table 8.2, it can be easily verified that: a) these DMs are very frequent in our corpus, they represent almost the 0.8% of all the tokens; b) these DMs are present since the very first stages of language acquisition (95 occurrences just in the initial level); c) there is no clear progression through the three levels, and above all there is no quantitative progression: some DMs are more frequent at the initial level (*d'accordo, va bene*), others at the intermediate level (*ok*) and others at the advanced level (*bene*); and d) contrary to previous expectations, these DMs are more frequent in the NNSs' speech without exception.

Table 8.2. Most frequent DM expressing agreement in the A.Ma.Dis. Corpus

DM	Initial	Intermediate	Advanced	Total (NNS)	NS	Total
d'accordo	58	1	25	84	46	130
ok	13	37	5	55	50	105
va bene	22	10	2	34	9	43
bene	2	4	11	17	6	23
Total	95	52	43	190	111	301

16 We have found no adverbs or adverbial phrases which are considered to have evidential meaning in our corpus and this may be due to two reasons: a) these DMs are not part of the lexical inventory of learners with a low competence of L2 Italian and neither do they seem to be acquired later on neither; b) they belong to more formal registers in language so they are not very frequent in oral spontaneous conversations, not even in the ones which are more formal, such as the job interview. This confirms what has been found for Spanish NNSs (Solís 2012: 9 and the quoted references, Pascual Escagedo 2015).

These DMs share some common discursive properties regarding their semantic and their position in the utterance. They have the possibility of constituting a turn on their own or of being part of a more complex turn, divided in discursive units (acts and subacts),[17] in which they are accompanied by other discursive units that offer an explanation of the agreement (Gras 2003). When they constitute a turn on their own, they establish an anaphoric link with the previous utterance that allows the recovery of the part of the utterance that is not repeated.

(2) A: Vieni questa sera a cena?
B: *Sì* (vengo stasera) / *Certo* (che vengo stasera), etc.

[A: Are you coming tonight for dinner?
B: Yes (I'm coming tonight) / Sure (I am coming tonight), etc.]

Contrary to what has been noticed about DM *sì/sí* [*yes*],[18] the main discursive function of these DMs is to express conformity with what has been said by the interlocutor and thus help the conversation to go on. This discursive function derives from an invariant meaning related to the assertion of a predicative relation to which these elements anaphorically refer.

According to Solís (2012b), DMs such as *sí, de acuerdo* and *vale* (equivalents to It. *sì* and *ok*) are different from all the other agreement DMs because they are oriented to the extra linguistic word.[19] This means that

17 The minimal structural units in conversation have been called acts and subacts by the researchers of the Val.Es.Co. group (2003, 2014). Act units have been classified in substantive or adjacent acts according to their semantic and pragmatic contribution to the conversation. A DM expressing agreement constitutes a substantive act, because it is autonomous and can substitute the whole turn.

18 In the case of *sì/sí*, there is still a debate going on about the nature of these elements. They have been traditionally considered as affirmation adverbs or presentences (Bernini 1995) due to their anaphoric nature and their capacity of substituting a whole sentence. However, they have a variety of functions: as DMs they not only express agreement but also function as backchannel signals, that is, as markers of reception and comprehension of the interlocutor's message.

19 Martín Zorraquino and Portolés (1999) considered *vale* and *de acuerdo* as 'deontic modality markers' while *sí* is a 'conversational metadiscursive marker'. All the other DMs expressing agreement are considered evidential (epistemic) markers. We will not discuss different taxonomies in this paper, but we would like to highlight that

the speaker expresses a commitment which considers not only the predicative relation of the previous utterance but also some possible future action in the extra linguistic world. In (3), M proposes to carry on with an action already agreed upon by the speakers and N not only confirms the predicative relation 'we first do that' but expresses her commitment to actually take the action.

(3) M: no / dai prima facciamo quello che [hai=]
N: [**ok**]
M: = detto te (3VA2, 164–166)

[M: no / come on we first do what you said
N: ok']

D'Accordo

Likewise, *sí* and *de acuerdo* are different from all the others DMs because they do not convey any expectation about the commitment of the speaker, that is, the speaker simply confirms a predicative relation but without presupposing that his/her commitment is taken for granted. As in the case of *ok* (see (3) above), the speaker confirms not only a predicative relation but also commits him/herself to take some action in the extra linguistic world when agreeing with the prepositional phrase *d'accordo* – the expression arises from the phrase *essere d'accordo*, literally 'to be in agreement', 'to agree'. The main difference with *ok* is that this commitment is not taken for granted by the speaker, that is, s/he does not consider that his/her commitment should be obvious for the interlocutor (Solís 2012b: 129–131).

According to the data in Table 8.2, the most frequent DM employed by our learners is *d'accordo* (84 occurrences), which almost doubles the number of occurrences found in NSs data (46). However, it is necessary to look at these numbers carefully because most of these occurrences belong to

there is some agreement on the fact that DMs such as *sí*, *vale*, *ok* have a special status in the family of the so-called affirmation operators or affirmation markers.

the same informant, which happens to be a French teacher with a very low level of linguistic competence in Italian and whose interlanguage is scattered with several elements from her L1 (French). We could claim, without being too adventurous, that the presence of *d'accordo* in this informant is a positive transfer of Fr. *d'accord*, but interference with Sp. *de acuerdo* cannot be discarded either.

Although expressing agreement is not the only function fulfilled by *d'accordo*, it is the most important one. This does not mean that, in certain contexts, this DM does not have other secondary functions, but in most of the occurrences this is its only function. Among its secondary functions, we highlight taking the floor (43 times), closing the interaction (10), phatic function (7), closing a topic (7), topic shifting (3), online planning (2) and introducing a digression (1).

In fact, Table 8.2 gathers only the occurrences of *d'accordo* when expressing agreement is its main function, but looking at the global numbers of our corpus (Table 8.3), we can see that *d'accordo* accomplishes two other functions: a phatic/backchannel function and asking for confirmation.

Table 8.3. Total number of occurrences of *d'accordo* divided by main functions

Discoursive functions of *d'accordo*	Beginner	Intermediate	Advanced	Total (NNS)	NS	Total
Total	81	1	37	119	59	178
Expressing agreement	58	1	25	84	46	130
Phatic function	20	0	11	31	0	31
Asking for confirmation	3	0	1	4	13	17

The phatic function is hardly found in NSs and can be considered an overuse of this DM instead of *sì*, which is far more frequent in this function in NSs. As shown in Table 8.4, there is no single occurrence of *d'accordo* with this function in NSs, but we have 20 in NNSs. One good example of this overuse is (4), where Ch uses *d'accordo* [*I agree*] as a phatic cue in an inadequate context (Ch is the learner with 66 occurrences of this DM in our corpus):

(4) Ch: uhm / ti piacee ↑ / ti piace iil→ // ehm / la cena?
L: ma / è molto buona / guarda / perché sono cose nuove / completamente nuove per me ↑ / mi piace→ tantissimo sì / questa insalata che hai fatto è ottima / direi / [sì sì]
Ch: [**d'accordo**]
/ la car– la carne tu– → / ti piace? (1SG6, 4–6)

[Ch: uhm / do you enjoy / do you enjoy the // ehm the dinner?
L: it is really good / listen / because they are new things / completely new for me / I like it so much really / this salad you made is excellent / I would say / yes yes
Ch: I agree / the meat the meaty you / do you like it?]

We must say, however, that when the phatic function is the primary function, expressing agreement is present as secondary function in four occurrences, although in the other cases taking the floor is the secondary function.

On the other hand, the use of *d'accordo* with interrogative intonation to ask for confirmation about a previous agreement is present in NSs speech and very scarcely used by NNSs (only four occurrences). Normally in these cases, *d'accordo* has no other secondary functions:

(5) L: [ok] / perfetto / allora facciamo così ↓ / io // la– le faccio sapere appenaaa / appena possibile insomma ↓ / e comunque anche lei sì / ecco / ci pensi ↑ / ee / e ne riparliamoo→ / tra qualche giorno ↑
Ch: **d'accordo** [signora=]
L: [***d'accordo*?**]
Ch: = una– una dema– [una domanda] (1SG5, 235–238)

[L: ok / perfect / then we do this way / I // will inform you as soon / as soon as possible then / and anyway you too / right / you think about it / eeh / and we talk again about it / in a couple of days
Ch: I agree madam
L: do you agree?
Ch: one one question]

To sum up, the presence of *d'accordo* in our corpus is mainly biased by the fact that one learner overuses this DM both in the expression agreement function and in the phatic function (a fact already noticed by Guil 2015). In fact, the numbers at the three levels are completely unbalanced (81 occurrences at the initial level, only one at the intermediate level and 25 at the advance level; see fn. 13 about number of tokens in each level). It is important to notice that the 81 occurrences at the initial level are produced by three informants: C (1), T (13) – also a teacher of French – and Ch (67). This is a good example of how idiosyncratic uses can alter results of research if they are not detected in time, as in this case. Moreover, if we consider NSs productions, we see that one native speaker from Tuscany produces 30 occurrences (half of them), while the numbers are lower for a NS from Piemonte (15) and even lower for a NS from Padova (3). Therefore, there seem to be preferences in use by NSs linked to their diatopic (and probably diastratic) variety.

Ok

A number of studies about how English NSs employ *ok* in conversation (cf. Fischer 2006, Condon and Čech 2007 and the references quoted in these studies) agree that *ok* has intertwined discourse functions: one of its functions is related to the structure of the interaction and marks transitions in discourse, in fact it often appears at structural boundaries;[20] another one is related to asserting the understanding of current discourse; and the other displays understanding of the common ground which is being built during conversation.

According to Andorno (2016: 108–109, 112–114), the difference between *ok* and all the other Italian DM usually employed to confirm the interlocutor's utterance is that *ok* expresses agreement with a state-of-the-art that is not directly accessible to the speaker, but it is just being presented

20 This function has been analysed in decision-making interactions (face-to-face and human-to-computer) by Condon and Čech (2007), who found that *ok* more frequently seems to signal that the previous decision routine has been completed and a next decision routine is initiated. This is not necessarily linked to verbal interaction but to extra linguistic actions. 'When *ok* marks the transition from one decision sequence to the next, it does not necessarily do so in response of an utterance from the conversational partner'.

by the interlocutor and thus it modifies the speaker's previous knowledge in a certain situation. This specific function explains why *ok* can appear as a response to directive utterances contrary to other DM such as *esatto* or *infatti* as in (6).

(6) A: Avvicinati!
B: okay / ?esatto / ?infatti (adapted from Andorno 2016: 113)

Bearing in mind these insightful descriptions, we will describe the use of It. *ok* in our corpus adapting the description of Sp. *vale* in Solís (2012b: 97–99). To our knowledge, there is no study about how and whether It. *ok* has preserved all and every function of Eng. *ok* but we will hypothesize that this is the case in Spanish learners' speech: there is probably a convergence of their linguistic competence on L2 English and the uses of the equivalent Spanish DM *vale*. We consider that *ok* expresses the speaker's commitment (that the speaker takes for granted) to undertake some action in the extralinguistic world. Its meaning is therefore very close to that of *d'accordo*, but expectation plays here a key role. This explains why it appears frequently at the end of an interaction or at the end of a sequence inside the interaction, once an agreement about what to do next has been reached.

The numbers are not more trustable in the case of *ok*, and there is no clear progression along the three levels (cf. Table 8.4). The scarce presence at the initial level may be explained by the concurrence with *d'accordo*, but it is important to bear in mind that the 13 occurrences are produced by just one learner (C). The number rises suddenly at the intermediate level (37 occurrences) and decreases again at the advanced level (5 occurrences).[21] It is not easy to explain why the apparent progression from the initial to the intermediate level is abruptly interrupted at the advanced level. But looking at the other DMs, we can observe that their frequency is always lower in this level (except in the case of *d'accordo*, which is practically absent at the

21 In fact, not all learners employ this DM with the same frequency: we can find *ok* in only one learner at the initial level (with 28 occurrences, cf. Table 8.4), two learners at the intermediate level produce 45 and 31 occurrences respectively (76 out of 80) and at the advanced level one participant eight occurrences out of 18 are to be attributed to the same learner.

intermediate level). The reason for that may be that when L2 speakers are more confident, they do not need to constantly display politeness strategies to encourage the interlocutor, which is a very common strategy at the initial level. Therefore, the number of DMs with this primary function is drastically reduced. However, once again the use of *ok* at the intermediate level is better explained as an idiosyncratic phenomenon: some learners privilege some DMs to display certain discursive functions.

As it was also the case with *d'accordo*, '*okay* functions basically in two ways: it signals discourse boundaries and thus indicates agreement about topic boundaries (the discourse marker use), and acknowledges what is being said (the feedback signal use)' (Fischer 2007). This is clearly shown in Table 8.4, where it is easy to see that expressing agreement and phatic functions are the most frequent functions in our corpus. While the expressing agreement function is balanced in the number of occurrences between NNSs and NSs, the phatic function – as it was also the case with *d'accordo* – is much more frequent in NNSs. These numbers evince the learners' necessity to constantly assert their understanding of what is uttered by their communication partner to reinforce their positive face, as it can be observed in (7), where learner C shows understanding of what is being explained by the native speaker E:

(7) E: § stanno facendo lezioni private / in Italia di spagnolo per avere una minima idea / però / &eh / ecco / avrei bisogno di una persona che parli spagnolo e italiano per stare con loro durante l'estate
C: ***ok***
E: in modo tale che / quando inizia il nuovo corso ↑ (1VA3, 61–63)

[E: they are having some Spanish home tutoring / in Italy to have a minimal basis/ but/ &eh / right/ I would need a person who speaks Spanish and Italian to be with them during the summer
C: ok
E: so that/ when the new school year begins]

In this function, *ok* marks internal boundaries within discourse, and its occurrences help the speaker to organize his/her discourse in information chunks. Thus the phatic function is both an interactive and a metadiscursive function, as it helps to assemble discourse internally.

In our corpus, *ok* covers at least nine different functions (taking into account only the primary functions), therefore it can be considered a highly polyfunctional DM if compared to *d'accordo* or to *bene/va bene*, as we will see below. But the number of occurrences for other functions (mainly related to turn-alternation) is noticeably lower and only in the case of taking the floor *ok* is more frequent in NSs than in NNSs. Besides, agreement expression is frequently the secondary function of these occurrences.[22]

Table 8.4. Total number of occurrences of *ok* divided by main function

	Initial	Intermediate	Advanced	NNS (Total)	NS	Total
Total	28	80	18	126	98	224
Expressing agreement	13	37	5	55	50	105
Phatic	11	24	6	41	19	60
Taking the floor	2	8	2	12	20	32
Closing conversation	1	1	3	5	1	6
Asking for confirmation	0	1	1	2	3	5
Leaving the floor	1	1	1	3	1	4
Online planning	0	4	0	4	1	5
Keeping the floor	0	4	0	4	1	5
Topic shift or topic closing	0	0	0	0	2	2

22 Of course, occurrences whose main function is agreement may also have secondary functions. For example, we have found the following: taking the floor (38 occurrences), marking internal boundaries by signally topic shift or recovery or by closing conversation (10), leaving the floor (7), keeping the floor (1) and paraphrastic reformulation (1).

Finally, we would like to point out the fact that *ok* and *d'accordo* are frequently combined in our corpus, both in NSs (8) and in NSSs (9) as well as with other agreement markers, such as *perfetto* [*perfect*] (found only in NSs). These combinations appear mainly when speakers want to close the interaction (cf. 8) and evince the necessity of closing negotiation by assessing an explicit, reinforced and emphatic agreement.

(8) L: *ok* / *perfetto* / posso chiamarla in qualsiasi mo[mento?]
Ch: [sì / in] qualche momento perché si noon sonoo da uno èè un al– un [altro ↓]
L: [***ok*** ↓] / *perfetto* ↓
/ ***d'accordo*** ↓ / io la ringrazio infinitamente ↑ / e le le faccio sapere allora ↓
Ch: **d'acco[rdo** / grazie]
L: [prego ↓ / l'accompagno] / venga /// arrivederci] (1SG5,96–100)

[L: ok / perfect / may I call you at any time?
Ch: yes / at any time because if you don't reach me in a place you can reach me in the other
L: ok / perfect / all right / many many thanks / and I will keep you informed then
Ch: ok / thank you
L: you are welcome / I accompany you / come /// bye]

(9) E: è tutto spesato / non ti preoccupare
MJ: **ok** / ***d'accordo***
E: poi quello che vuoi fare tu nel tuo tempo libero logicamente no (3VA5, 191–193)

[E: everything is covered / don't worry
MJ: ok / all right
E: but what you want to do in your free time it is logically not]

Bene and va bene

Italian modal adverb *bene* [*well*] has gone through a desemantization process to express not that an action is performed in an adequate way, as in *Scrive bene [He writes well]*, but that the speaker agrees with what has been said or gives his/her consent to a situation. This desemantization process has been accompanied by a change in utterance position from the internal predicative relation – where it precedes or follows the verb – to an independent position as a separate utterance (holophrastic use). Both desemantization and greater mobility are part of a grammaticalization process (Hopper and Traugott 2003). This is a well-described process for English *well* or Spanish *bien* (Fuentes 1993; Blas Arroyo 2011), among others, and the result is a highly polyfunctional DM which tends to conform complex DMs by adding new elements (the case of It. *va bene* or Sp. *muy bien, pues bien, ahora bien*) or by reducing its phonetic substance (the case of It. *be'* or *va be'*).

All these markers have kept the acceptance of information or situation as their invariant meaning, and from this meaning they have developed a variety of pragmatic functions: expressing agreement is one of them, but metadiscursive functions such as topic shift and pre-closing markers are also frequent (Borreguero 2017). However, It. *bene* and Sp. *bien* are not symmetrical in their uses, although they may share some of these functions. *Bene* is much more frequent in interaction, and its functions are equivalent to those of Sp. *bueno*, which is a source of confusion and transfer phenomena in learners, as we will see in the next section. It. *bene* and Sp. *bueno* have as many interactional metadiscursive functions, including not only discourse organization but even reformulation in the case of *bueno* (cf. Martín Zorraquino and Portolés 1999 and the references quoted in this work).

Bene is the less frequent of the four DMs analysed here, and it has been found to fulfil only two closely related functions in our corpus, as we have seen in the analysis of *ok*: expressing agreement and the phatic function. Numbers are slightly superior for NNSs, and it is easy to observe a good progression from the initial to the intermediate level. After this level, however, the situation seems to become stagnant, as there is no significant change in the advanced level, except a slight reduction of the number of occurrences.

Table 8.5. Total number of occurrences of *bene* divided by main function

	Initial	Intermediate	Advanced	NNS (Total)	NS	Total
Total	4	17	12	33	12	45
Expressing agreement	2	14	11	27	6	33
Phatic	2	3	1	6	6	12

But what is remarkable in these data is that NSs hardly ever use *bene* as a DM (only 12 occurrences out of 45 belong to NSs' speech), especially in the function of marking an explicit agreement. This proves that *bene* is progressively abandoning its interactional functions in NSs' speech (Lindbladh 2015b).

On the other hand, the grammaticalized predicate *va bene* [*ok, all right*] is more present in both the NNSs and the NSs' speech and displays a wider range of functions, as it is shown in Table 8.6. *Va bene* overtly expresses acceptance of the situation or the information conveyed by previous utterances, and it is one of the most co-operative DMs in conversation. This explicit acceptance reduces its capability of becoming just an acknowledging signal (the phatic function), a function we have only found at the initial stages of acquisition.

Table 8.6. Total number of occurrences of *va bene* divided by main functions

	Initial	Intermediate	Advanced	NNS (Total)	NS	Total
Total	26	11	2	39	18	65
Expressing agreement	22	10	2	34	9	43
Topic shift	0	0	0	0	4	4
Taking the floor	0	1	0	1	2	3
Phatic	3	0	0	3	0	3
Closing interaction	1	0	0	1	3	4

Notwithstanding the low number of occurrences in NSs' speech in our corpus, we would like to highlight that *va bene* occurs frequently as preclosing DM in NS interactions: in fact NSs employ *va bene* as a pre-closing signal (directly preceding the greetings) in three out of four symmetric conversations among NS (Lindbladh 2015a), as in (10):

(10) L: = chiaramente / cioè a quelle condizioni o noi / ci cerchiamo qualcos'altro / poi vedrà lui / insomma §
O: § °(perfetto)° §
L: § quello che vuole fare

O: ***va bene*** / ti saluto che devo andare→ / [(( ))]
L: [ok]
O: ciao
L: niente / ci vediamoo ↑ / stasera / ciao
O: ciao (NAT1, 49–56)

[L: obviously / I mean with those conditions or we / look for something else / then he will see / so
O: perfect
L: what he wants to do
O: ok / I say bye I have to go
L: ok
O: bye
L: so / we see each other / this evening / bye
O: bye]

This function, which is shared also by *d'accordo* and *ok*, is hardly found in NNSs, hence we have again a functional dysimmetry.

Spanish DMs in the learner corpus: The role of code-switching

The use of lexical elements from the L1 when interacting in L2 is a very frequent phenomenon. Previous studies (Borreguero 2017) have shown that code-switching is particularly recurrent in the case of DMs as if the need to use these elements were so strong that it would make the learner turn to his/her L1 when the lexical unit is not available in his/her L2. The agreement function is no exception but, in our corpus, Spanish markers expressing agreement are less frequent than DMs with metalinguistic functions like reformulation or online planning.[23]

23 For example, we have found three occurrences of Sp. *bueno* with the function of introducing a new discursive topic or subtopic in conversation and oneoccurrence with the function of summing up; eight occurrences implying online planning, that is, to take time to plan the ongoing discourse (and one more occurrence under the

Most of these markers appear at the initial level. We have found the following: *ya* (2), *bueno*, *claro*. We will not deal extensively with these DMs as they do not constitute the focus of this paper, but we will just give some examples to show how code-switching works in expressing agreement. In the case of Sp. *ya* (ex. 10 and 11), the function as DM derives from its adverbial use to express present tense (*ya* can also express past and future tense) but mostly from its ability to signal that something that was not happening before is happening now. As a result of the change in the situation, the expectation that nothing was going to change is rejected, as in *Ya llega el tren [The train is already arriving]* (cf. Bazzanella et al. 2005: 67–74). *Ya* is mainly used as a DM to acknowledge understanding. This function is a result of a grammaticalization process: the speaker informs the interlocutor that his/her words in the previous turn have produced a change in his/her knowledge, but the idea of a change taking place (not in fact but in mental representations) is still there. This is what can be observed in (11) and (12), where, besides the phatic function, it is easy to observe an agreement with the previous turn (the area is expensive and the old city is too big to be visited properly in just one day):

(11) C: [ti piace que]sta zona // vuoo– / vuoi continuare→
MJ: ma è molto caro
C: ***ya*** ma / [forse se la casa è più piccola] (1VA2, 32–34)

[C: [do you like] this area // do you want to continue
MJ: but it is too expensive
C: right but / [maybe if the house is smaller]

(12) C: e la città vecchia ti ha pi– ti ha piaciuto?
E: la città vecchia ↑ / ooddio!/ l'abbiamo vista così un po' alla svelta
C: ***ya*** / soltanto sei un giorno qui! (1VA6, 100–102)

[C: and did you like the old part of the city?
E: the old part of the city/ Oh my God!/ we saw it a little bit quick C: right / you are only one day here!]

---

form of *buono*, which is a literal translation of *bueno*, because It. *buono* [good] does not function as a DM) and eight occurrences with reformulation functions (cf. Borreguero 2017, Borreguero et al. 2017).

As it has been pointed out by some authors (cf. Martín Zorraquino and Portolés 1999: 4192, Guil in Bazzanella et al. 2005: 71), *ya* expresses a lesser degree of involvement than Sp. *sí* with which it shares both functions (phatic and expressing agreement). In fact, in its holofrastic occurrences it could express either the idea 'I have already understood' or the idea 'I already knew'. In this last case, the agreement is reached based on a common piece of knowledge and the speaker conveys the idea that the information is not new to him/her. This means that his/her interlocutor's previous turn was not informative at all. Therefore, it is less co-operative than other DMs, and it is frequently used to take the floor to introduce some information that constitutes an alternative to what has been just said, which indicates clear mitigation functions. For example, in (12), the agreement about the expensiveness of the area is followed by the proposal of living in a smaller house in this same area and not by a proposal of moving to other area, as it would be expected if *ya* indicated a true agreement.

Another Spanish DM with this function in our corpus is *claro*, one of the most frequent agreement DMs in spoken Spanish. Contrary to what happened with *ya*, *claro* appears in the advanced level, but it does not exactly express agreement with a previous turn. According to Solís (2012b: 94–97; 2013: 354), *claro* confirms the predicative relation between a subject and a predicate (as we have seen in (1)) indicating that the agreement is somewhat expectable. It can be considered a common-ground particle (Fischer 2007) because it relates the utterance to an aspect of the common ground. The context surrounding (13) is the discussion about the possibility of sharing the flat with someone else, but E raises the problem that the flat has other rooms, but only two beds. And she does so by asking something that it is clear to her, that is, that is part of the common ground of both interlocutors: the owner will not buy another bed. *Claro* underlies the fact that she has no doubt about the owner's will, and this reinforces the previous statement: the problem is the beds. The best Italian equivalent in this case would probably be *certo*.

(13) E: § ma ci sono più stanze! / il problemaa / i letti
P: eh ↓ §
E: § perché **claro** / lei vorrà comprare un altro? (5VA2)

[E: but there are more rooms! / the problem / the beds
P: eh
E: because obviously / you would like to buy another one?]

Conclusions

Expressing agreement DMs play an important function during interaction because they serve the purpose of building the grounding process: they signal the way speakers understand each other's contributions and their position towards the facts expressed in those contributions. DMs are by no means the only technique employed by speakers to build the grounding process and to display understanding: continued attention, acknowledgement resources (such as nodding or using a variety of interjections: *uh-huh*, *hmm*, and *aha*) and actively taking part in the conversation by using verbal and non-verbal means all serve the same purpose. Besides, DMs do not only contribute to the grounding process, but they also refer to the common ground, that is, the result of the grounding process, the set of relevant assumptions to that particular situation shared by communication partners. Speakers must display their understanding of the common ground to make the utterances interpretable (Fischer 2007). Their fundamental role in both building the grounding process and referring to the common ground explains why these DMs are so frequent in spoken interactions, even in NNSs interactions since the first stages of language acquisition.

Following previous studies, we consider that expressing agreement is not the invariant meaning of any DM, but it is rather a common pragmatic or discursive use of many DMs. In this study, we have focused our attention on Italian DMs and especially in the most frequent DMs in an interlanguage corpus: *d'accordo*, *ok* and *bene* (and its derivate *va bene*). The invariant meaning of these DMs is related to the position the speaker adopts towards his/her utterance: if s/he feels responsible for what s/he has said and if s/he considers that the predicative relation conveyed by the utterance was expectable according to the common ground shared by the participants. That is the invariant meaning of these DMs, which have usually been described by two of their pragmatic uses: to express agreement and to sign reception (phatic cues).

In NS informal interactions, there is no predictable expectation about the tendencies to ratify or to challenge information previously presented by the interlocutor, but in learners' interaction – especially among initial learners – one can expect an overwhelming presence of ratifying utterances and a deliberate avoidance of conflict with the interlocutor. This tendency is based on the scarce linguistic competence and the surely stressing situations in which the corpus was collected, but it is mainly sustained by the fact that learners find it easier to make the conversation go forward by agreeing with their partner and by being co-operative. This would explain why DMs expressing agreement are more frequent in NNSs than in NSs in our corpus.

From our data, we can conclude that Spanish learners of L2 Italian use a variety of DMs to express agreement with their interlocutor since the very first stages in acquisition. However, the number of DMs with this discourse function does not increase significantly along with the development of the linguistic and communicative competence. Moreover, there does not seem to be a clear acquisitional path in Spanish learners as the number of DMs does not constantly increase throughout the three levels, an observation already made for metadiscursive markers in a previous work (Borreguero 2017). Besides, the analysed DMs share one important semantic feature: the commitment of the speaker to some kind of action in the extra linguistic world. In fact, other DMs can also be used to express agreement but do not involve this commitment (for example, It. *infatti*, *in effetti* 'indeed', *certo* 'sure, for sure' are absent from our learners' corpus). Nothing is taken for granted, nothing is considered an expectable predicative relationship, everything is open to negotiation and must be positively asserted as such.

Finally, we would like to highlight some interesting differences between NSs and NNSs: phatic uses of these DMs are much more frequent in learners than in NSs, and this constitutes a piece of evidence of a greater necessity to make explicit the grounding process and the references to the common ground in learners' interaction, probably linked to the reinforcement of the positive face, which makes the partner confident in his/her speech, especially in symmetric interactions.

The analysis has given us the opportunity to reflect upon different issues. Some of these are of a methodological nature and refer to the way in which results can be biased by idiosyncratic production (as in the case of *d'accordo* in the initial stage); or are related to the difficulty of drawing apart grounding functions (such as expressing agreement) from common ground functions (such as phatic functions) when both are fulfilled by the same DM. Others are related to language teaching suggestions drawn from this acquisitional study. As we have seen, DMs are often overused, and they assume discursive functions that are not present in NSs speech. Their inventory is very reduced and hardly enriched in upper levels, but the necessity of marking understanding and agreement is stronger than the capacity to use lexical means in L2, and this explains why learners resort to some L1 DMs. Language teaching should focus on providing learners with a wider range of DMs and in delimiting their functions in interaction; two actions which require explicit attention to these units in the language learning process (cf. Pernas et al. 2011).

Bibliography

Alvarado Ortega, M. Belén, and Leonor Ruiz Gurillo, 'Un acercamiento fraseológico a *desde luego*', *RILCE* 27/2 (2011), 305–320.

Andorno, Cecilia, 'Apprendere il lessico: elaborazione di segnali discorsivi (*sì, no, così*)', in Marina Chini et al., eds, *Imparare una lingua: recenti sviluppi teorici e proposte applicative* (Perugia: Guerra, 2007), 95–121.

Andorno, Cecilia, 'Entre énoncé et interaction: le rôle des particules d'affirmation et négation dans les lectes d'apprenants', in Christine Dimroth, and Monique Lambert, eds, *La structure informationnelle chez les apprenants L2*. Special issue of *Acquisition et Interaction en Langue Étrangère* 26 (2008), 173–190.

Andorno, Cecilia, 'Quando affermare non è confermare. Per uno studio di *sì* a confronto con *esatto, infatti, già* (e *okay*)', in Inmaculada Solís, Juliette Delahaie, and Nicoletta Gagliardi, eds, *Sistemi e strategie di affermazione nella interazione*. Special issue of *Testi e linguaggi* 10 (2016), 89–127.

Andorno, Cecilia, and Fabiana Rosi, 'Confirming or Asserting? Conflicting Values and Cross-Linguistic Influence in the Use of *Yes/No* Particles in L2 Italian', in Margarita Borreguero, and Britta Thoerle, eds, *Discourse Markers in Second Language Acquisition – Studies on French and Italian as L2*. Special issue of *Language, Acquisition and Interaction* 7/1 (2016), 17–43.

Bazzanella, Carla, Cristina Bosco, Emilia Calaresu, Alessandro Garcea, Pura Guil, and Anda Radulescu, 'Dal latino *iam* agli esiti nelle lingue romanze: verso una configurazione pragmatica complessiva', *Cuadernos de Filología Italiana* 12 (2005), 49–82.

Bernini Giuliano, 'Le profrasi', in Lorenzo Renzi, Giampaolo Salvi, and Anna Cardinaletti, eds, *Grande grammatica italiana di consultazione*, vol. III (Bologna: Il Mulino, 1995), 175–224.

Bini, Milena, and Almudena Pernas, 'Marcadores discursivos en los primeros estadios de adquisición del italiano L2', in Rafael Monroy Casas, and Aquilino Sánchez Pérez, eds, *25 años de lingüística aplicada en España: hitos y retos* (Murcia: Universidad de Murcia, 2007), 25–36.

Blas Arroyo, José Luis, 'From Politeness to Discourse Marking: The Process of Pragmaticalization of *muy bien* in Vernacular Spanish', *Journal of Pragmatics* 43 (2011), 855–874.

Borreguero Zuloaga, Margarita, 'Topic-Shift Discourse Markers in L2 Italian: Paths of Acquisition by Spanish speakers', *Language, Acquisition, Interaction* 8/2 (2017), 173–203.

Borreguero Zuloaga, Margarita, Paloma Pernas Izquierdo, and Eugenio Gillani, 'Metadiscursive Functions and Discourse Markers in L2 Italian', in Ana Paula Loureiro, Conceição Carapinha, and Cornelia Plag, eds, *Marcadores Discursivos e(m) Tradução* (Coimbra: Universidade da Coimbra, 2017), 15–58.

Calvo Rigual, Cesáreo, 'Italiano *bene/va bene, be'/va be'* e spagnolo *bien, bueno*: analisi contrastiva nel parlato', in Hang Ferrer and Salvador Pons, eds, *La pragmática de los conectores y las partículas modales*. Special Issue of *Quaderns de Filologia. Estudis Linguistics* VI (2001), 53–79.

Condon, Sherri L., and Claude G. Čech, '*Ok, next one*: Discourse Markers of Common Ground', in Anita Fetzer and Kerstin Fischer, eds, *Lexical Markers of Common Grounds* (Amsterdam: Elsevier (Studies in Pragmatics 3), 2007), 17–45.

D'Alfonso, Alberto,'Risorse linguistiche per la riposte affermativa in italiano L2: avverbi ed espressioni a inizio frase nelle produzioni orali (primi sondaggi)', in Inmaculada Solís, Juliette Delahaie, and Nicoletta Gagliardi, eds, *Sistemi e strategie di affermazione nella interazione*. Special Issue of *Testi e linguaggi* 10 (2016), 173–193.

Fischer, Kerstin, 'Grounding and Common Ground: Modal Particles and Their Translation Equivalents', in Anita Fetzer and Kerstin Fischer, eds, *Lexical Markers of Common Grounds* (Amsterdam: Elsevier (Studies in Pragmatics 3), 2007), 47–66.

Fuentes Rodríguez, Catalina, 'Adverbios de modalidad', *Verba* 18 (1991), 275–321.

Fuentes Rodríguez, Catalina, '*Claro*: Modalización y conexión', *Sociolingüística andaluza* 9 (1993a), 99–126.

Fuentes Rodríguez, Catalina. '*Desde luego, por supuesto, naturalmente*', *Sociolingüística andaluza* 9 (1993b), 127–160.

Fuentes Rodríguez, Catalina, 'Comportamiento discurso de *bueno, bien, pues bien*', *Estudios de Lingüística Universidad de Alicante* 9 (1993c), 205–221.

Fuentes Rodríguez, Catalina, 'Polifonía y argumentación: los adverbios de verdad, certeza, seguridad y evidencia en español', *Lexis* 19 (1995), 59–83.

Gras Manzano, Pedro, 'Diferencias lingüístico-discursivas en el usos de los marcadores *claro* y *por supuesto*: un enfoque cognitivo', *Interlingüística* 13/2 (2003), 309–319.

Guil, Pura, 'Segnali discorsivi come meccanismi di intensità in italiano L2', in Barbara Gili Fivela and Carla Bazzanella, eds, Fenomeni d'intensità nell'italiano parlato (Firenze: Cesati, 2009), 223–241.

Guil, Pura, 'Marcadores discursivos en la interlengua de aprendices de italiano L2', in Margarita Borreguero, and Sonia Gómez-Jordana, *Les marqueurs du discours dans les langues romanes: une approche contrastive* (Limoges: Lambert-Lucas, 2015), 374–385.

Kerbrat-Orecchioni, Catherine, 'Oui et ses variantes en français: l'expression de l'accord dans les débats présidentiels', in Inmaculada Solís, Juliette Delahaie, and Nicoletta Gagliardi, eds, *Sistemi e strategie di affermazione nella interazione*. Special Issue of *Testi e linguaggi* 10 (2016), 15–38.

Koch, Christian, 'Sí, sí, estudio Lehramt, sí. El uso de marcadores de afirmación en el español de estudiantes germanohablantes', in Inmaculada Solís, Juliette Delahaie, and Nicoletta Gagliardi, eds, *Sistemi e strategie di affermazione nella interazione*. Special Issue of *Testi e linguaggi* 10 (2016), 159–172.

Lindbladh, Sara, '*Va bene* e *va be*' nella sequenza conclusiva. Tra segnale di risposta e segnale di prechiusura', *Milli mála* 7 (2015a), 267–308.

Lindbladh, Sara, 'La semantica e pragmatica dei segnali discorsivi italiani – un confronto tra *bene, va bene, be*' e *va be*', Göteborg University, <http://svenska.gu.se/infoglueCalendar/digitalAssets/3097043168_BifogadFil_Sara%20Lindbladh,%20text,%20seminarium%2027%20okt.pdf> (2015b).

Llopis Cardona, Ana, 'Entre la modalidad y la conexión: la confirmación. El caso de *en efecto*', *RILCE* 31/2 (2015), 205–434.

López Serena, Araceli and Margarita Borreguero Zuloaga, 'Los marcadores discursivos y la variación lengua hablada vs. lengua escrita', in Óscar Loureda, and Esperanza Acín, eds, *Los estudios sobre marcadores del discurso en español, hoy* (Madrid: Arco/Libros, 2010), 415–495.

Nigoević, Magdalena and Patricia Sučić,'Competenza pragmática in italiano L2: l'uso dei segnali discorsivi da parte degli apprendenti croati', *Italiano LinguaDue* 2 (2011), 94–114.

Pascual Escagedo, Consuelo, 'Análisis de las funciones de los marcadores discursivos en las conversaciones de estudiantes italianos de E/LE', *Lingue e linguaggi* 13 (2015), 119–161.

Pérez Canales, José, 'Marcadores de modalidad epistémica: *en efecto, efectivamente, desde luego, por supuesto* …', in Manuel Casado Velarde, Ramón González Ruiz, and M. Victoria Romero Gualda, eds, *Análisis del discurso: lengua, cultura, valores. Actas del I Congreso Internacional*, vol. II (Madrid: Arco/Libros, 2003), 1525–1540.

Pernas, Paloma, Eugenio Gillani, and Annamaria Cacchione, 'Costruire testi, strutturare conversazioni: la didattica dei segnali discorsivi come elementi pivot dell'interazione verbale', *Italiano Lingua Seconda* 3/1 (2011), 65–138.

Pons, Salvador, 'Claro', *Diccionario de partículas del español* <http://www.dpde.es> (2008).

Ruiz Gurillo, Leonor, '*Por supuesto, estamos de acuerdo*: un análisis argumentativo de los operadores de refuerzo', *Oralia: Análisis del discurso oral* 2 (1999), 241–264.

Solís García, Inmaculada, 'Instrucciones procedimentales de los marcadores evidenciales *en efecto* y *efectivamente*', *Pragmalingüística* 20 (2012a), 239–254.

Solís García, Inmaculada, *Por supuesto et alii. Tomas de posición del enunciador* (Napoli: Pisanti, 2012b).

Solís García, Inmaculada, 'La toma de posición del enunciador por medio de los operadores *claro, desde luego* y *por supuesto*', *Archivium* LXIII (2013), 333–356.

PATRIZIA GIULIANO, ROSA RUSSO AND SIMONA ANASTASIO

9 Discourse markers, interlanguage level and social integration: The immigrant learners in the Naples area[1]

Introduction

In the present work, we analyse the types and functions of discourse markers in the dialogic and narrative speech of immigrant learners in the area of Naples (Southern Italy). The informants have different interlanguage levels and source languages and mostly learned Italian in a natural environment. In agreement with their different levels and types of acquisition (natural and/or tutored), we aim at identifying the different levels that our learners reached in the use of discourse markers.

The interviews that we conducted were semi-structured in the sense that the Italian interviewers prepared a battery of questions and narrative topics, but the interviewees were not previously informed about them. We also interviewed a group of native Italian speakers (reference group) using this same modality.

In our theoretical framework, discourse markers are seen as crucial for the construction of coherence and the processing of textual information in spontaneous communication. So, a socially well-integrated

1 Patrizia Giuliano wrote the chapter. All three authors, nevertheless, contributed to the analysis of the data used for the study, in particular, Giuliano analysed the data produced by the Italian informants, Anastasio studied the data of Polish learners and Russo focused her attention on the productions of Ukrainian, Senegalese and Sinhalese learners.

individual will have learned to manage and use discourse markers in his daily communication.

With respect to the classification that we adopted for discourse markers, which divides them into interaction markers and meta-textual markers, we shall demonstrate that the latter ones are particularly frequent in the interviews of advanced learners with plans to stay in Italy long term but less used by advanced informants not having this type of plan and by those with a lower interlanguage level. Moreover, in these last two groups, the meta-textual markers can be used in a non-native way. For all groups, the interaction markers are more frequent than the meta-textual ones.

From a sociolinguistic point of view, lower frequency and non-native use of discourse markers are strictly connected to the desire of going back to their own country and to a greater or lesser integration in the Italian community, even when the interviewees have been living in Italy for many years. A further result lies in the higher percentage of discourse markers with inferential functions in the interviews of less advanced informants. As a final observation, it is possible to hypothesize an implicational scale in the emergence of the functions that we can attribute to each discourse marker.

Previous studies and research goals

During the acquisition of a foreign language (L2), in order to create a successful linguistic interaction with the native community of speakers, a learner has to master not only the *sentence grammar* but the *discourse grammar* as well. In the functionalist framework, the latter has been depicted in more or less restricted terms: for some authors it is concerned with the way native speakers package and shape information while producing a text in a specific context (the 'rhetorical' styles of a language according to Slobin 1987, 1996, 2003, 2004; for this view, cf. also, among other works, von Stutterheim and Klein, 2002; von Stutterheim *et al.*, 2002, 2003; Carroll and von Stutterheim, 2003; von Stutterheim and Nüse, 2003;

Carroll *et al.*, 2004; Carroll and Lambert 2005, 2006; Von Stutterheim and Carroll, 2006; Carroll *et al.*, 2008); for others, it is necessary to more extensively consider the intentions of the speaker and the different manners of interacting in a specific context while producing a given type of text in a determined community of speakers (cf. Giuliano and Di Maio 2008; Giuliano 2012; Giuliano and Musto in preparation). Discourse grammars can vary according to the textual genre to produce (dialogue, narration, description, etc.): even though textual and interactive mechanisms are on the whole universal (conversational strategies, anaphoric devices, deixis, etc.; cf. Grice, 1975, 1989), the way of realizing them is *language specific*. So, it is possible to state that an L2 learner needs to master the discourse grammar (or better grammar*s*) in order for its communication to be successful.

Inside this type of grammars, the employment of discourse markers (henceforth DMs) is crucial and frequent but also variable across languages (cf. Engl. *so, well, why*, etc.; It. *quindi* [so], *allora* [so, then], *praticamente* [practically, actually], etc.). So, in our opinion, a learner who employs DMs is certainly an individual having intense contacts with the native community of speakers of a given language. The semantics and syntax of DMs is, however, neither obvious nor simple to learn for a foreign speaker, since they are strictly connected to the context of employment, as shown by the Italian use of *allora* (and its different translation in English) in the following examples:

(1) A: ma è vero che non vuoi venire alla festa di Cinzia?
B: *allora* io non ho mai detto che non voglio venire ma solo che forse non potrò!
[A: But is it true that you don't want to come to Cinzia's party?
B: *Well* I've never said that I don't want to come but only that maybe I won't be able!]

(2) Lavoravo dieci ore al giorno per neanche mille euro al mese *e allora* ho deciso di licenziarmi
[I worked ten hours a day for not even one thousand euros a month *so* I decided to quit.]

In example (1), the function of *allora* is that of a change of turn in a conversation (cf. Engl. *well*); in example (2), the same item marks instead an inferential function[2] (cf. Engl. *so*). The different translation of *allora* into English clearly shows the crosslinguistic variation of this type of means.

As Nigoević and Sučić observe,

> La funzione principale dei segnali discorsivi è collocare un certo enunciato nel contesto linguistico e extralinguistico. La loro funzione è emotiva, espressiva ... all'interlocutore offrono l'informazione sul co(n)testo in cui viene pronunciato un enunciato e gli permettono di classificarlo pragmaticamente. (Nigoević and Sučić, 2011: 95)[3]

So, the mastery of DMs is not an easy task since it demands a deep knowledge of the communicative processes in L2. As Borreguero Zuloaga puts it,

> Su contribución semántica no reside fundamentalmente en su contenido conceptual o en su función gramatical, sino en su capacidad de guiar las inferencias del intérprete en el procesamiento de la información textual y de gestionar la interacción que se basa en su sucederse de actos linguísticos. (Borreguero Zuloaga 2015: 153)[4]

Despite the crucial role that DMs play in languages, for Italian most of the available studies focus on the native variety (cf. the crucial work by Bazzanella 1995).[5] So DMs have not received much attention in the studies about Italian as L2 (cf. nevertheless, Nigoević and Sučić 2011; Andorno 2007, 2008). Furthermore, in the institutional teaching of an

2 For an overview of the functions of Italian DM, cf. Bazzanella (1995).

3 The main function of DMs is to locate a given utterance in a given linguistic and extra-linguistic context. Their function is emotional, expressive ... they offer the listener information about the co(n)text where an utterance is pronounced and let him pragmatically classify it (our translation).

4 Its semantic contribution [of a DM] does not fundamentally lie in its conceptual content or grammatical function, but in its capacity of guiding the inferences of an interpreter in the processing of textual information and of managing the interaction, which is based on a sequence of speech acts (our translation).

5 We support Bazanella's framework and by virtue of that we shall consider DMs as elements typical of oral interaction whose function is to regulate the turn taking and the relationship between interlocutors (for a discussion of the various definitions of DM across studies, cf. for instance Borreguero Zuloaga, 2015).

L2, the practice of these items is neglected if not completely omitted (also see the discussion on other markers in Chapters 2, 3 and 4), despite the fact that in spontaneous communication DMs are crucial for the construction of the textual and dialogical coherence.

For the reasons just mentioned and with respect to the present study, we hypothesize that an individual well integrated into a foreign community will have surely learned – at least partially – to master and use DMs in his daily speech. On the basis of this hypothesis, we propose an analysis of the DMs employed by different groups of L2 learners of Italian (interactions and narrations with Italian native listeners), who have all immigrated to the area of Naples, the biggest city in Southern Italy. The analysis will consider the relationship between several variables: the L2 level reached by the learners, the type of DM that they employ, the functions that they apply to them and their socio-biographical profiles. By doing so, we shall show that the lexically varied use of DMs and their functionally correct employment is directly related not only to the linguistic competence in L2 but also to the different personal aspirations of the informants concerning the target country.

Following the research objectives described above, we hope to contribute to the study of DMs in a new and more exhaustive manner with respect to the already available works on the acquisition of the Italian language as L2 in natural environment.

Methodology

Our study is based on an investigation that took place in Naples, a city that has had a high immigration rate in the last 20 years. We interviewed four groups of learners with different native languages (Ukrainian, Sinhalese, Pular, Wolof and Polish) and a group of Italian native speakers. All the informants live or come from the area of Naples.[6]

6 The Polish subjects (11) have been staying in Naples from a minimum of eight years to a maximum of 19; their education ranges from a high school diploma to a university

Among the learners, the Senegalese, Polish, and Ukrainian subjects have a high or very high proficiency in Italian (C1/C2 competence according to the Common European Framework of Reference for Languages), whereas most of the Sinhalese informants have a level just slightly higher than basic, with which they can satisfy only some essential communicative needs (cf. Klein and Perdue 1992, 1997).[7]

The interviews were based on a long conversation during which the interviewers asked questions about a large variety of topics (personal life, job, friends, hobbies, etc.). The questions were the same for all the learners but partly different with respect to the ones posed to the Italian speakers. All the interviews also involved the production of biographical narrations, the topics of which varied according to the informant.

All the data were transcribed by CHAT (MacWhinney 2000) and analysed using the two perspectives commented on above:

---

degree (for the latter three out of the 11 subjects); all of them had already studied at least another foreign language before coming to Italy (normally Russian); most of the subjects (8) have learned Italian in a spontaneous way; eight out of 11 have (or had) an Italian partner. For Ukrainians (10 informants), they have spent in Italy from 7 to 15 years; four out of ten have a university diploma; almost all of them studied Russian, one also studied French; just two people followed an Italian language course; three informants have an Italian partner. The Senegalese informants (3) have Italian partners; they have been staying in Italy from 11 to 15 years and have a university degree; they learned Italian language both in tutored and untutored way; their other L2s: French and Wolof. Concerning the Sinhalese group (3 subjects), they have been staying in Italy from ten to 15 years; all of them attended an Italian language course and just one also knows English; none of them has an Italian partner. As for the Italian group, all of them have a level of education from medium (high school diploma) to high (university degree) and come from the Naples area.

7 As Klein and Perdue (1992, 1997) have demonstrated, the acquisition of an L2 in a natural environment can involve the creation of a 'basic variety', that is to say an acquisitional stage essentially deprived of L2 inflectional morphology and syntax. In this variety, semantic and syntactic principles such as *focus last* and *controller first* compensate – as far as possible – the absence of grammatical principles. Now, some of our Sri Lankan learners have just a bit more than a basic competence. With respect to the European Framework for Languages the basic variety is not easy to be placed, since it satisfies some communicative needs (A2 / B1 levels) though *in absentia* of the very specific L2 grammar.

- A socio-biographical perspective: are the possible different use and types of DMs linked to the socio-biographical variables of the learner groups investigated?
- An interlanguage perspective: is there any relationship between the function and form of the DMs employed by the learners and their levels in L2?

Data analysis and results

Linguistic competence and socio-biographical variables

As Figure 9.1 shows, the stay in Italy of the L2 learners is always long term; but their proficiency in Italian is not necessarily high, as is the case for most of the Sinhalese speakers. The following histogram shows the correlation between the linguistic competence of our learner groups and the four biographical variables that mostly influence it.

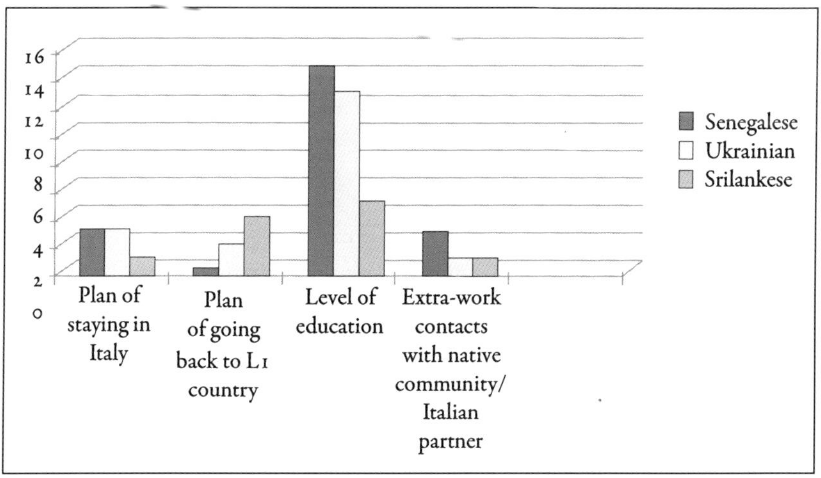

Figure 9.1. Linguistic competence and biographical variables

As Figure 9.1 illustrates, the variables which mostly correlate with an advanced language level are: education level, extra-work contacts with the native community and/or the fact of having an Italian partner, and long term plans for staying in Italy. Two of the most influential variables detected, namely contacts with the Italian community and the fact of having an Italian partner, necessarily involve a good integration in the native community.

Discourse markers: Percentage and functional evaluations

Our most proficient groups of informants, namely the Polish, Ukrainian and Senegalese ones, employ a relevant quantity of DMs, which are different from each other for the variety of functions that each of them can take on. Here is an extract from the interview of one of our Senegalese subjects:

(3) Pierre, Senegalese

@EXP: senti mi vuoi raccontare del tuo viaggio per arrivare in Italia?
@SUJ: ***guarda*** # è stato molto semplice # mh già sapevo quando venire perché tutto era preparato
ho avuto il visto facilmente perché venivo come studente e c'è un po' di agevolazione per quanto
riguarda ***diciamo*** le pratiche ...
@EXP: e magari non so non avevi il timore comunque di trovarti male in un Paese totalmente diverso poi dal tuo?
@SUJ: mh no no no più nel lato mh le apprensioni sono più legato ***magari*** non riuscissi a fare gli esami per la lingua perché ***cioè*** non capivo benissimo l'italiano ***no?*** ...
@SUJ: ***allora*** quando sono arrivato in Italia da Roma sono sceso ... e ho incontrato un agente ... e
lui ha detto di solito i senegalesi non vengono qua a studiare # ***allora*** già a primo impatto ...
@EXP: vuoi parlarmi un po' della tua famiglia in Senegal?
@SUJ: si una famiglia molto modesta ... poi man mano più o meno ha raggiunto una certa # un
certo benessere ***cioè no giustamente*** non è non è grazie a me non è grazie a me è grazie anche

i miei fratelli e le mie sorelle che hanno lavorato e continuano a lavorare in Senegal ... e ***comunque***
stanno mandando avanti la casa ... accogliamo sempre anche gente che non è della famiglia stretta
come si dice # cugini amici

[@EXP: Listen can you tell me about your journey to Italy?
@SUJ: *look* #it was very simple # mh I already knew when to come because everything was ready I easily got my visa because I was coming as a student and it's easier to get this type of visa of *let's say* the procedure
@EXP: And probably I don't know weren't you afraid however of living badly in a country completely different from yours?
@SUJ: mh no no no more with respect to +// mh the apprehensions were more concerned with *maybe* I wouldn't be able to take exams because of the language *I mean* I didn't understand Italian very well *no?*
@SUJ: *well* when I arrived in Italy I got off in Rome ... and I met a policeman ... and he said generally the Senegalese don't come here to study # *so* already during the first impact ...
@EXP: can you tell me a bit about your family in Senegal?
@SUJ: yes a very modest family ... then it has slowly more or less reached a certain # a certain wealth *well no I mean* it's not it's not thanks to me it's thanks also to my brothers and my sisters who worked and continue to work in Senegal ... and *however* they're keeping the family going ... we also always host people who are not from the immediate family *how you say* # cousins friends]

The passage contains several types of DMs: modulation mechanisms (*diciamo:* [let's say], *comunque:* [however], *magari:* [may be] in the context in question), turn-taking strategies (*guarda*: [look], *allora*: [well] in *allora quando sono arrivato in Italia ...*), request for confirmation (*no?*), self-reformulations (*cioè :* [I mean], *come si dice:* [how you say]), inferential function (*allora:* [so] in *allora già a primo impatto*). As *allora* shows, the same item can have different functions (in our example those of *well* and *so*). Conversely, a combination of several items can have just one meaning, as what happens with *cioè no giustamente* ([I mean no well]) having altogether a self-reformulation function.

Table 9.1 illustrates the type and frequency of DM in the Senegalese group (for demarcative and focus means, cf. examples *infra* from other groups).

Table 9.1. The Senegalese group: Dialogues[8]

Interactive functions: Dialogues	
Acceptation markings / Request for Confirmation (*No?, eh?, ti pare?, non è così?, esatto, ecco, giusto, certo*)	30 (14%)
Request of Attention and Verification of Correct Reception (*capisci?, sai/lo sapete, capito? eh?*)	19 (9%)
Modulations Mechanisms (*in qualche modo, praticamente, diciamo, veramente, proprio / davvero, magari, insomma, penso io*)	43 (19%)
Pause fillers (*Eh, mh, cioè, non so, come (posso) dire, come si dice, diciamo*)	91 (41%)
Turn takings markings (*Allora / ecco / vabbé, guarda*)	38 (17%)
Total	220 (57%)
Metatextual functions: Dialogues	
Demarcative means (*Insomma, senti, a proposito, comunque*)	57 (38%)
Focalizers (*Ma, sì, dico / voglio dire, proprio / appunto, ecco*)	19 (13%)
Reformulators (*Cioè, diciamo, anzi, insomma, non so, mettiamo/prendiamo*)	73 (50%)
Total	149 (49%)
Inferential functions: Dialogues (*quindi / allora*)	14 (4%)

The interactive and meta-textual functions of DMs are very frequent in the interviews of the Senegalese subjects, who employ all the items in question in a native-like way and whose Italian sounds native-like except for the

8 *No?* [no?], *eh?* [isn't it?], etc., *ti pare?* [don't you think so?], *non è così?* [isn't it], etc., *esatto* [exactly], *ecco* [well], *giusto* [right], *certo* [definitively], *capisci?* [you understand?], *sai/lo sapete* [you know], *capito?* [understood?], *eh?* [isn't it], etc., *in qualche modo* [in a way], *praticamente* [practically], *diciamo* [let's say], *veramente* really], *proprio / davvero* [actually], *magari* [maybe], *insomma* [in short], *penso io* [I think], *Eh, mh, cioè* [I mean], *non so* [I don't know], *come (posso) dire* [how can I say, *come si dice* how do you say], *diciamo* [let's say], *Allora / ecco / vabbé*: [well], *guarda* [look], *insomma* [in short], *senti* [listen], *a proposito* [actually], *comunque* [however], *ma* [but], *sì* [emphatic use of *do*], *dico / voglio dire* [I mean], *proprio / appunto* [actually], *ecco* [well], *Cioè* [I mean], *diciamo* [let's say], *anzi* [rather], *insomma* [in short], *non so* [I don't know], *mettiamo/prendiamo* [let's suppose], *quindi / allora* [*so*].

prosodic aspects. So this group seems not to have problems with both the mastery of the communication processes (interactive functions) and the organization of the text that they are producing (meta-textual functions).

In the interviews of the Ukrainian subjects, the DMs are conspicuous as well and also varied with respect to the functions that they take on.

(4) Lesia, Ukrainian

@EXP: Mi racconti un po' com'è nata l'idea di partire dal tuo paese?
@SUJ: ***allora*** l'idea di partire dal mio paese era ***diciamo*** che //+ in realtà io ho studiato e poi'
ho lavorato come infermiere in un ospedale solo che c'era un periodo che non non pagavano gli
stipendi e poi c'era [//] c'erano molti problemi ...
certo dipendere dai genitori poi pure loro ***non è che*** avevano una possibilità +//...
quindi io ho pensato anche se ***non è che*** c'era *proprio* questa necessità ...

[@EXP: can you tell me a bit how your idea of leaving your country was born?
@SUJ: *well* the idea of leaving my country was *let's say* that //+ in reality I studied and then
I worked as a male nurse in a hospital but there was a period where they didn't didn't pay the
salaries and then there was [//] there were many problems ...
certainly to depend on your parents then they too *it's not that* they had the possibility of +// (= they didn't really have the possibility of supporting me) ...
so I thought [to leave] even though *it's not that* there was a real necessity (= it was not really necessary)]

In the passage by the Ukrainian informant, we find turn-taking devices (*allora*: [well'), reformulators (*diciamo:* [let's say]), demarcative means[9] (*certo:* [well] in the context above) and a structurally complex DMs, namely *non è che*, whose function is to focus a string of the utterance produced (meta-textual function). Tables 9.2 and 9.3 illustrate the DMs used by the Ukrainian subjects.

Concerning the Sinhalese subjects, we divided these subjects in two subgroups because of their different levels in Italian: the advanced subgroup

9 Demarcative means mark the beginning or end of a linguistic chunk.

and the basic subgroup. On the whole, both subgroups employ lexically less varied DMs. Furthermore, the functions that the basic learners assign to them are not always clear, as shown in the following extract:

Table 9.2. The Ukrainian group: Narrations[10]

Interactive function: Narrations	
Acceptation markings / Request for Confirmation (*No?, eh?, ti pare?, non è così?, esatto, ecco, giusto, certo*)	30 (8%)
Request of Attention and Verification of Correct Reception (*capisci?, sai/lo sapete, capito? eh?*)	76 (20%)
Modulations Mechanisms (*in qualche modo, praticamente, diciamo, veramente, proprio / davvero, magari, insomma, penso io*)	128 (35%)
Pause fillers (*Eh, mh, cioè, non so, come (posso) dire, come si dice, diciamo*)	88 (24%)
Turn takings markings (*Allora / ecco / vabbé, guarda*)	40 (11%)
Total	362 (65%)
Metatextual functions: Narrations	
Demarcative means (*Insomma, senti, a proposito, comunque*)	64 (38%)
Focalizers (*Ma, sì, dico / voglio dire, proprio / appunto, ecco*)	49 (29%)
Reformulators (*Cioè, diciamo, anzi, insomma, non so, mettiamo/ prendiamo*)	53 (32%)
Total	166 (30%)
Inferential functions: Narrations (*quindi / allora*)	29 (5%)

Table 9.3. The Ukrainian group: Dialogues[11]

Interactive functions: Dialogues	
Acceptation markings / Request for Confirmation (*No?, eh?, ti pare?, non è così?, esatto, ecco, giusto, certo*)	21(21%)
Request of Attention and Verification of Correct Reception (*capisci?, sai/lo sapete, capito? eh?*)	–

10 For English translations of Italian DM cf. gloss 8.

11 For English translations of Italian DM cf. gloss 8.

Table 9.3. (*Continued*)

Modulations Mechanisms (*in qualche modo, praticamente, diciamo, veramente, proprio / davvero, magari, insomma, penso io*)	41(41%)
Pause fillers (*Eh, mh, cioè, non so, come (posso) dire, come si dice, diciamo*)	37(37%)
Turn takings markings (*Allora / ecco / vabbè, guarda*)	1(1%)
Total	101(65.1%)
Metatextual functions: Dialogues	
Demarcative means (*Insomma, senti, a proposito, comunque*)	23(43.3%)
Focalizers (*Ma, sì, dico / voglio dire, proprio / appunto, ecco*)	14(26.4%)
Reformulators (*Cioè, diciamo, anzi, insomma, non so, mettiamo/ prendiamo*)	16(30%)
Total	53(34.1%)
Inferential functions: Dialogues (*quindi / allora*)	1(0.65)

(5) Marion, Sri Lankan

@EXP: e dove stai lavorando?
@SUJ: lavoro mh # Portici ... lava macchine ***poi*** venuta
prima mattina oggi adesso finito lavoro poi domani mattina andare ...

[@EXP: and where are you working?
[work.1st.S mh # Portici [a small town close to Naples] washes cars *then* come PP.F early morning today now finished work *then* tomorrow morning to-go ...]
@SUJ: I work in Portici I wash cars *then* I came here early in the morning today. Now I've finished my work then tomorrow I'll go again]

The linguistic level (concerning production) of Marion is evidently low. Furthermore, the function by which she employs *poi* in *poi venuta di prima mattina* is not clear at all.

Let's observe a different extract from another basic Sri Lankan speaker:

(6) Sunjeev, Sri Lankan

@SUJ: ... qualche volta carabiniere pure controllato a me che hanno detto 'permesso di soggiorno?' io detto 'io non c'è permesso di soggiorno ... però Hanno mi liberato non è detto niente ... se vai in Germania loro mandano via subito! ***Guarda*** come fatto carabinieri che ha detto 'vai a casa non girare la notte' perché io stava andando da mio fratello

[@SUJ: sometimes policeman also cheked to me that have.PL said greencard?' I said.PP 'I not there's greencard' but have.1st.PL me set.free.PP not is said.PP nothing ... if go.2nd.S Germany they send away immediately! *Look* how done policemen who has said 'go to home don't go around the night' because I was going to my brother's]

Sunjeev's interlanguage is more advanced than that of Marion, although still quite basic. Despite that, the function of the DM *guarda* – that Italian speakers use as request of attention – sounds slightly ambiguous, since it should go along with an adversative DM (cf. our English paraphrases of the extract: *conversely look at the way* they behaved with me ...).

In general, the Sri Lankan subgroups show a low attention for metatextual functions (global organization of the text that they are producing) but a frequent employment of inferential markings such as *quindi* and *allora*, which are among the most used by Italian native speakers. In other words, these subjects have problems with identifying the more pragmatically connotated functions of DMs. The following extract comes from one of the more advanced subjects and illustrates the use of inferential *quindi*:

(7) Susante, Sri Lankan

io non lo so parlare napoletano però qualche parola # però quando loro parlano capisco perché sono sempre qua dentro dei Quartieri Spagnoli *quindi* loro parlano e io capisco # però io non lo so parlare napoletano ... no tutti parola io conosco # e loro quando parlano napoletano subito subito parlano *quindi* non capisco

[I cannot speak Neapolitan but [just] some words # but when they speak I understand because I'm always in the Spanish Quarters[12] *so* they speak and I understand # but I cannot speak Neapolitan ... I don't know all the words # and when they speak Neapolitan ...
they speak very quickly *so* I don't understand]

12 The Spanish Quarters are one of the lower class quarters in Naples in which the Neapolitan dialect is very much spoken.

Table 9.4. The Srilankese basic group: Dialogues[13]

Interactive functions: Dialogues	
Acceptation markings / Request for Confirmation (*No?, eh?, ti pare?, non è così?, esatto, ecco, giusto, certo*)	4(1%)
Request of Attention and Verification of Correct Reception (*capisci?, sai/lo sapete, capito? eh?*)	35 (23%)
Modulations Mechanisms (*in qualche modo, praticamente, diciamo, veramente, proprio / davvero, magari, insomma, penso io*)	19 (12%)
Pause fillers (*Eh, mh, cioè, non so, come (posso) dire, come si dice, diciamo*)	88 (60%)
Turn takings markings (*Allora / ecco / vabbé, guarda*)	8 (4%)
Total	146 (86.4%)
Metatextual functions: Dialogues	
Demarcative means (*Insomma, senti, a proposito, comunque*)	11 (65%)
Focalizers (*Ma, sì, dico / voglio dire, proprio / appunto, ecco*)	2 (12%)
Reformulators (*Cioè, diciamo, anzi, insomma, non so, mettiamo/ prendiamo*)	4 (23%)
Total	17 (10%)
Inferential functions: Dialogues (*quindi / allora*)	6 (4%)

Table 9.5. The Srilankese advanced group: Dialogues[14]

Interactive Functions: Dialogues	
Acceptation markings / Request for Confirmation (*No?, eh?, ti pare?, non è così?, esatto, ecco, giusto, certo*)	1 (4%)
Request of Attention and Verification of Correct Reception (*capisci?, sai/lo sapete, capito? eh?*)	1(4%)
Modulations Mechanisms (*in qualche modo, praticamente, diciamo, veramente, proprio / davvero, magari, insomma, penso io*)	0
Pause fillers (*Eh, mh, cioè, non so, come (posso) dire, come si dice, diciamo*)	5 (20%)
Turn takings markings (*Allora / ecco / vabbé, guarda*)	18 (72%)
Total	25 (17.9%)

(*Continued*)

13 For English translations of Italian DM cf. gloss 7.

14 For English translations of Italian DM cf. gloss 7.

Table 9.5. (*Continued*)

Metatextual functions: Dialogues	
Demarcative means (*Insomma, senti, a proposito, comunque*)	18 (64.2%)
Focalizers (*Ma, sì, dico / voglio dire, proprio / appunto, ecco*)	5 (17.9%)
Reformulators (*Cioè, diciamo, anzi, insomma, non so, mettiamo/ prendiamo*)	5(17.9%)
Total	28 (20%)
Inferential functions: Dialogues (*quindi / allora*)	87 (62.1%)

Among the four groups of learners that we interviewed, the Polish one is definitively the closest to the Italian reference group, as Table 9.6 clearly illustrates.

Table 9.6. Native Italian speakers vs Polish learners

Dialogues	Italian	Polish
Interactive functions	285 (62%)	219 (56.5%)
Metatextual functions	143 (31%)	147 (37.5%)
Inferential functions	30 (7%)	23 (6%)
Narrations		
Interactive functions	139 (53%)	44 (50.6%)
Metatextual functions	122 (47%)	35 (40.2%)
Inferential functions	–	8 (9.2%)

The Italian L2 of Polish subjects is definitively very close to the Italian native productions except for – as the table shows – the presence of inferential markings.

Discussion

Interactional and meta-textual DMs

The interactional functions of DMs frequently show up both in narrations and dialogues, which differs from the meta-textual functions that, at least theoretically, should mostly appear in narrations because of the less interactive aspect of this task.

In the Polish, Ukrainian and Senegalese groups, the interactional DMs are always more frequent than the meta-textual ones in both the textual genres considered (cf. Tables 9.1, 9.2, 9.3 and 9.6); nevertheless, for the Senegalese subjects, the two categories of DMs are more balanced (57% *vs* 49%), which shows the possibility for meta-textual DMs to be very much employed even in interactive tasks when the learners' level in L2 is very high. For the SriLankan informants, the meta-textual DMs are scarcer than in all the other groups (cf. Tables 9.4 and 9.5).

These results are to be interpreted using the different aims that the two types of DMs have: *the interactive function is certainly primary* for learners in a natural environment since it makes a message effective; the meta-textual function aims at making what a speaker utters as coherent and cohesive as possible, which theoretically is not less important, but it can be less important for learners with a lower linguistic competence in L2, as their utterances tend to be shorter and less organized in textual (namely global) terms.

With respect to the SriLankans – who very rarely exploit meta-textual devices – the results concerning them cannot simply be explained by the lack of narrations for these subjects since the meta-textual markers are numerous for the Senegalese group despite the lack of narrations for the latter as well.

Inferential Markings

The percentage of the inferential DMs is particularly relevant for the Sri Lankan speakers (cf. Tables 9.4 and 9.5), who often use markings such as *quindi* and *dunque*. The function of these items is essentially *inferential*, so in contrast with other DMs that can take on several meanings according to the co(n)texts, *quindi* and *dunque* are semantically and pragmatically *more stable*. This could make them *more transparent*, which is different from DMs having a large range of functions.

As a result of what we have just observed, the low attention that our Sri Lankan subjects seem to pay to the functional domain of other DMs is probably due to their greater variability. In order, for a learner to grasp all the nuances of DMs, they need a constant and *deeply motivated interaction* with the native community; an interaction that the Sri Lankan speakers do not have. If this is the case, further studies could explore the possibility for acquisition of DMs in Italian (or other L2 languages) to appear according to an implicational scale based on their greater or lesser semantic and pragmatic transparency.

Linguistic results and socio-biographical variables

In the previous two paragraphs, we explained our results with respect to our four groups of learners by virtue of their interlanguage level, the pragmatic transparency or functional usefulness of DMs, and the type of textual genre analysed. These linguistic and paralinguistic motivations need, nevertheless, to be integrated with sociolinguistic factors.

As expected, our data show that a higher interlinguistic level goes along with a larger lexicon of the items in question and a greater appropriateness with respect to the co(n)text. This apparently obvious result becomes more significant when it is correlated with some socio-biographical variables, in particular the *plan of staying in Italy definitively*.

The Senegalese and Polish groups are made up of individuals having Italian partners and almost always plan to stay in Italy indefinitely. The Ukrainian subjects, even though rather integrated in the local Italian native community, often have middle term plans; the Sri Lankan group, despite their long or very long sojourn in Italy, do not have Italian partners and always plan to go back to their country, even when they are socially integrated.

Now, with respect to the employment of DMs, they are varied and sound native-like just in the linguistic productions of the Polish and Senegalese subjects.

Conclusions

In the present work, we analysed the types and functions of DMs in the dialogic and narrative speech of immigrant learners in the area of Naples. Our groups of learners had different interlanguage levels and source languages and mostly learned Italian in a natural environment. We presented them with two different types of tasks, dialogues and narrations, and compared the results from them with those produced by a group of native speakers of Italian. The comparison brought us to some interesting considerations of both linguistic and sociolinguistic nature.

From the viewpoint of the interlanguage theory, the employment of DM by our learners is clearly connected with the level of competence in L2: the higher the latter is, the more correct and more varied the use of DMs. This apparently obvious result is nevertheless less clear for the Sinhalese subjects. In this group, some of the informants have a low level of competence; but higher levels are not lacking, and yet the interactive and meta-textual DMs are much less frequent than for other groups of learners[15]. In contrast with these results, the inferential markings are particularly frequent in the texts of the Sri Lankans.

If the interlanguage level cannot explain this state of affairs for the Sri Lankans, the correlation of the results with some socio-biographical variables – in particular, the lack of intention to remain in Italy indefinitely – seems to explain most of it. The linguistic motivations are not to be completely excluded, since the semantic stability of some DMs could also play a role; rather, they must be integrated with extra-linguistic factors, a type of factors that are sometimes, incomprehensibly, left out in L2 studies.

Acronyms, abbreviations and symbols

#: short empty pause
##: long empty pause
[//]: self-correction
+//: self-interruption
...: cancellation of a passage
*EXP: interviewer

15 There seems to be no reason from the L1 which could justify this result (Chandralal 2010).

*SUJ: informant
1st: first person
2nd: second person
Discourse Markers: DM
F: female
Foreign Language: FL
Foreign Language Acquisition: FLA
mh: filled pause
Mother tongue or first language: L1
PL: plural
PP: past participle
S: singular
Second language: L2 [L3, etc.]
Second Language Acquisition: SLA

Bibliography

Andorno, C., 'Apprendere il lessico: elaborazione di segnali discorsivi (sì, no, così)', In Marina Chini, Paola Desideri, Maria Elena Favilla and Gabriele Pallotti, eds, *Imparare una lingua: recenti sviluppi teorici e proposte applicative* (Perugia: Guerra Edizioni, 2007), 95–122.

Andorno, C., 'Connettivi in italiano L2 fra struttura dell'enunciato e struttura dell'interazione, in Giuliano Bernini, Lorenzo Spreafico and Ada Valentini, eds, *Competenze lessicali e discorsive nell'acquisizione di lingue seconde* (Perugia: Guerra Edizioni, 2008), 481–510.

Bazzanella, C., 'I segnali discorsivi', in Lorenzo Renzi, Giampaolo Salvi and Anna Cardinaletti, eds, *Grande grammatica italiana di consultazione* (Bologna: Il Mulino, 1995), 225–257.

Borroguero Zuloaga, Margarita, 'A vueltas con los marcadores del discurso: de nuevo sobre su delimitación y sus funzione', in Angela Ferrari, Letizia Lala, and Roska Stojomeniva, eds, *Testualità, fondamenti, unità, relazioni* (Firenze: Franco Cesati, 2015), 151–170.

Carroll, M., and M. Lambert, 'Crosslinguistic Analysis of Temporal Perspectives in Text Production'. In Henriette Hendricks, ed., *The Structure of Learner Variety* (Berlin: Mouton de Gruyter, 2005), 203–230.

Carroll, M., and M. Lambert, 'Reorganizing Principles of Information Structure in Advanced L2s: a Atudy of French and German Learners of English, in Heidi Byrnes, Heather Weger-Guntharp and Katherine Sprang, eds, *Educating for Advanced Foreign Language Capacities* (Washington DC: Georgetown University Press, 2006), 54–73.

Carroll, M., and Christiane von Stutterheim, 'Typology and Information Organisation: Perspective Taking and Language Specific Effects in the Construal of Events', in Anna Giacalone Ramat, ed., *Typology and Second Language Acquisition* (Berlin: Mouton de Gruyter, 2003), 365–402.

Carroll, M., Christiane von Stutterheim and R. Nüse, 'The Thought and Language Debate: a Psycholinguistic Approach', in Thomas Pechman and Christopher Habel, eds, *Multidisciplinary Approaches to Language Production* (Berlin / New York: Mouton de Gruyter, 2004), 184–218.

Carroll, M., M. Lambert, C. von Stutterheim, and A. Rossdeutscher, 'Subordination in Narratives and Macrostructural Planning: Taking a Comparative Point of View', in Catherine Fabricius Hansen, and Wiebke Ramm, eds, *'Subordination' versus 'Coordination' in Sentence and Text* (Amsterdam: Benjamins, 2008), 161–184.

Giuliano, Patrizia, 'Contrasted and Maintained Information in a Narrative Task: Analysis of Texts in English and Italian as L1s and L2s', *EUROSLA Yearbook* 12 (2012), 30–62.

Giuliano, Patrizia, and L. Di Maio, 'Abilità descrittiva e coesione testuale in L1 e L2: lingue romanze e lingue germaniche a confronto', *Linguistica e filologia* 25 (2008), 125–205.

Giuliano, Patrizia, and S. Musto, 'The Construction of Textual Cohesion in Spanish and Italian, as Mother Tongues and as Second Languages', in *EUROSLA Yearbook 2017* (in preparation).

Grice, H. P., 'Logic and Conversation', in Peter Cole, and Jerry L. Morgan, eds, *Syntax and Semantics. Speech Acts 3* (New York: Academic Press, 1975), 58–85.

Grice, H. P., *Studies in the Way of Words* (Cambridge, MA: Harvard University Press, 1989).

Klein, W., and C. Perdue, *Utterance Structure. Developing Grammars Again* (Amsterdam: John Benjamins Publishing Company, 1992).

Klein, W., and C. Perdue, 'The Basic Variety', *Second Language Research* 13/4 (1997), 301–347.

Nigoević, M., and P. Sučić, 'Competenza pragmatica in italiano L2: l'uso dei segnali discorsivi da parte degli apprendenti croati', *Italiano LinguaDue* 3 (2011), 94–114.

Slobin, D. I., 'From "Thought and Language" to "Thinking for Speaking"' in Joseph Gumperz, and Stephen Levinson, *Rethinking Linguistic Relativity* (Cambridge: Cambridge University Press, 1996), 70–96.

Slobin, D. I., 'Language and Thought Online: Cognitive Consequences of Linguistic Relativity, in Dedre Gentner, and Susan Goldin-Meadow, eds, *Language in Mind: Advances in the Investigation of Language and Thought* (Cambridge MA: MIT Press, 2003), 157–192.

Slobin, D. I., 'Relating Events in Translation', in Dorit Ravid, and Hava Bat-Zeev Shyldkrot, eds, *Perspectives on Language and Language Development: Essays in Honor of Ruth A. Berman* (Dordrecht: Kluwer, 2004), 115–129.

Slobin, D. I., 'Learning to Think for Speaking', *Pragmatics* 1/1 (1987), 7–25.

von Stutterheim, Christiane, 'Linguistic Structure and Information Organisation. The Case of Very Advanced Learners', *EUROSLA Yearbook* 3 (Amsterdam: John Benjamins, 2003), 183–206.

von Stutterheim, Christiane, and M. Carroll, 'The Impact of Grammatical Temporal Categories on Ultimate Attainment in L2 Learning', in Heidi Byrnes, Heather Weger-Guntharp, and Katherine Sprang, eds, *Educating for Advanced Foreign Language Capacities* (Washington, DC: Georgetown University Press, 2006), 42–53.

von Stutterheim, Christiane, M. Carroll, and W. Klein, 'Two Ways of Construing Complex Temporal Structures', in Friederich Lenz, ed., *Deictic Conceptualization of Space, Time and Person* [Cognitive Linguistics Research] (Berlin: Mouton de Gruyter, 2003), 97–133.

von Stutterheim, Christiane, and R. Nüse, 'Processes of Conceptualisation in Language Production', *Linguistics* [Special Issue: Perspectives in Language Production] (2003), 851–881.

von Stutterheim, Christiane, R. Nüse and J. Murcia Serra, 'Crosslinguistic Differences in the Conceptualisation of Events', Hilde Hasselgård, Stig Johansson, Bergljpt, and Catherine Fabricius-Hansen, eds, *Information Structure in a Cross-Linguistic Perspective* (Amsterdam/New York: Rodopis, 2002), 179–198.

Notes on contributors

SIMONA ANASTASIO is a PhD student in Language Sciences at the Université Paris 8 (France) and the Università degli Studi di Napoli Federico II (Italy) (cotutelle agreement). She is currently fixed-term Professor of French L2 in the International Relations Department of the University Paris Est Marne La Vallée. In recent years, she has participated in various conferences and has published articles on her areas of research specialization, that is, first and second language acquisition. In particular, she focuses on dynamic spatial relations, inter-typological and intra-typological variations, psycholinguistics, discourse markers, reformulations and verb morphology.

IRIA BELLO VIRUEGA is a research assistant at Ruprecht-Karls-Universität Heidelberg (Germany). She received her MA in English Studies and her PhD in English Linguistics from the Universidade da Coruña (Spain). Currently she teaches undergraduate and graduate courses on Spanish and English Linguistics and Translation and her main research interests are corpus and experimental linguistics, information processing and focalization processes. Within the research group 'Discourse Particles and Cognition' (DPKog), she studies the processing of pragmatic scales and discourse markers using eye-tracking.

CAROLINA BERNALES holds a MA in Applied English Linguistics and a PhD in Second Language Acquisition from the University of Wisconsin-Madison (US). She currently works as a tenure-track assistant professor in the Linguistics Department at the Pontificia Universidad Católica de Valparaíso (Chile), where she teaches graduate and undergraduate courses in English syntax, academic writing and second language acquisition. She also serves on the editorial board of *Revista Signos. Estudios de Lingüística* (WoS). Her current research focuses on lexical processing and reading comprehension in a second language. She has published on classroom interaction and foreign language learning in peer-reviewed journals.

MARILISA BIRELLO is a lecturer in the Faculty of Education of the Universitat Autònoma de Barcelona (Spain). Her research interests include teachers' education, teachers' beliefs, and conversation analysis. She is in charge of the Department of Language Teacher Development at the School of Modern Language of the Universitat de Barcelona. Most of her teaching experience is in the area of initial teacher training and teaching of Italian as a foreign language. She is also supervising MA and PhD theses on the topics of teacher's beliefs on writing tasks and students' interaction in the classroom.

MARGARITA BORREGUERO ZULOAGA studied Spanish and Italian Philology and Philosophy at the Universidad Complutense de Madrid (Spain). She is an associate professor at the Italian Studies Department at this University and Managing Director of the Complutense Center for Spanish. She was awarded a Humboldt Fellowship at Ruprecht-Karls-Universität Heidelberg (2010–2012) and has been a visiting scholar at the Università degli Studi di Bergamo and the Università degli Studi di Torino (Italy). Her research interests are in the fields of contrastive and text linguistics, in particular information structure, discourse markers and anaphors. She has been a member of A.Ma.Dis Research Group on Acquisitional Linguistics since 2006 and is currently working on the acquisition of Italian and Spanish discourse markers. Her recent publications include *La interfaz lengua-texto. Un modelo de estructura informativa* (2015), in co-operation with Angela Ferrari.

MARIA VITTORIA CALVI is Full Professor of Spanish Linguistics and Translation (since October 2002) in the Department of Language Mediation and Intercultural Communication at the Università degli Studi di Milano (Italy). She is editor-in-chief of the journal *Cuadernos AISPI. Estudios de lenguas y literaturas hispánicas*. Her main research interests are contrastive linguistics of Spanish and Italian (*Didattica di lingue affini. Spagnolo e italiano*, 1995); Spanish and Italian in migration contexts ('The Use of Deixis in the Oral Narratives of Latin American Immigrants in Italy', 2014; 'La alternancia anche / también en el español hablado por inmigrantes hispanoamericanos en Italia', 2016); genre analysis and cross-cultural variations in professional and specialized discourse, with special attention to the language of tourism (*Lengua y comunicación en el español del turismo*, 2006; 'Léxico de especialidad y lengua del turismo', 2016; 'The Language of Tourism in New Travel Guides: Discursive Identities and Narratives' 2017).

KIM COLLEWAERT is Teaching Assistant in Spanish Linguistics at Vrije Universiteit Brussel (Belgium) and currently working on a PhD under the supervision of Prof. Dr An Vande Casteele. She studies the acquisition of Spanish as a second language, focusing on discourse cohesion. The main research lines she investigates are the use of referential mechanisms and discourse markers by SFL learners.

ROBERTA FERRONI is Professor of Italian Language and Literature in graduate and undergraduate programs at the Universidade de São Paulo (Brazil). She holds a doctorate degree in Italian Language and Literature from the same university. She has experience in teacher training and refresher courses. Her research interests involve the study of interaction in foreign language classes and interactional competence in different contexts. Her publications include numerous articles in books and in specialized journals.

PATRIZIA GIULIANO has taught for almost three years in the Department of Language Sciences at the Université Paris 8 (France), focusing on the acquisition of second languages in a 'natural environment'. Since 2001, she teaches Didactics of Modern Languages and Acquisitional Linguistics at the Università degli Studi di Napoli Federico II (Italy), where she is an associate professor. Her interests range from the acquisition of Italian as first and second language to linguistic disadvantages of socio-cultural origin and the acquisition of foreign languages both in natural and institutional environments.

CHRISTIAN KOCH studied French, Spanish and Italian philology at the Universität Siegen (Germany), where he later taught French and Spanish linguistics. Since 2014, he has been working as a research assistant at the chair of Applied Linguistics/Romance Languages at the Universität Siegen. Currently, he is preparing a PhD thesis about Romance polyglottism, particularly the outstanding ability to speak four or more Romance languages.

Other fields of interest and research are language typology, translation analysis, linguistic communication about music, Andean Spanish, as well as foreign language learning generally, especially the acquisition of pronunciation, linguistic structures in spoken language and language variety.

ELENA LANDONE is Professor of Spanish Linguistics and Didactics at the Università degli Studi di Milano (Italy). Her research focuses on issues in intercultural pragmalinguistics and she has a special interest in politeness and discourse markers and their importance in foreign language learning/teaching.

ELISA NARVÁEZ GARCÍA is a PhD candidate at the Ruprecht-Karls-Universität Heidelberg (Germany). In 2015, she received her master's degree in Iberian and Ibero-American Studies at the Katholieke Universiteit Leuven (Belgium). She works as an editorial assistant at *Boletín de lingüística* (Institute of Philology 'Andrés Bello') and is also part of the research group 'Discourse Particles and Cognition' (DPKog), headed by Prof. Óscar Loureda. Her current research focuses on the processing of causality in Spanish and English using eye tracking and complementary methods.

ROSA RUSSO holds a degree in Modern Languages and Literatures from the Università degli Studi di Napoli Federico II (Italy). She completed a PhD in Language and Cognition at the Université Paris 8 (France) in co-tutorship with the Università degli Studi di Napoli Federico II in 2017. Her main areas of research are second language acquisition, language typology, universals and linguistic variation, typological constraints in language acquisition, space and cognition, language universals and language-specific effects in language use, intra-typological contrasts, and discourse markers.

EUGENIA SAINZ is Professor of Spanish in the *Dipartimento di Studi Linguistici e Culturali Comparati* at the Università Ca' Foscari Venezia (Italy). She conducted her doctoral research at the Universidad Autónoma de Madrid (Spain). Her main research area is discourse analysis with particular attention to the syntax-pragmatic interface, procedural meanings and discourse markers in Spanish and Italian.

BRITTA THÖRLE is Professor of Applied Linguistics/Romance Languages at the Universität Siegen (Germany). After having completed her studies of

Romance and German philology at the Johannes Gutenberg-Universität Mainz (Germany) and the Université de Bourgogne (France), she worked as a research assistant at the Universität Mannheim (Germany), where she was awarded a PhD in Romance Philology. Afterwards, she was employed as Junior Professor of French and Spanish Linguistics and Foreign Language Teaching at the Christian-Albrechts-Universität zu Kiel (Germany). Her main research interests are second language acquisition from an interactional point of view, the relation between linguistic structure and interaction as well as the study of languages for special purposes and communication in organizations.

LOURDES TORRES graduated in Translation and Interpreting in English, German and Spanish at the Universidade de Vigo (Spain), where she also received her master's degree in Applied Linguistics of Spanish as a Foreign Language in 2013. She has worked as a professional translator and Spanish teacher. She is currently a PhD candidate of the Doctoral College 'Discourse Particles, Information Structure and Cognition' at the Centre for Ibero-American Studies (IAZ) at Ruprecht-Karls-Universität Heidelberg. She is also part of the research group 'Discourse Particles and Cognition' (DPKog) headed by Prof. Loureda. In her current research, she studies the processing and comprehension of the Spanish focus particle *hasta* by Spanish native speakers by means of eye tracking and complementary research methods.

AN VANDE CASTEELE is Professor in Spanish Linguistics at Vrije Universiteit Brussel (Belgium). She teaches several courses on Spanish syntax, semantics and pragmatics and on Spanish as a second language in the Bachelor and Master of Arts in Linguistics and Literary Studies. Her research interests include interlanguage pragmatic discourse analysis, the use of discourse particles, the analysis of referential mechanisms (proper names and appositive constructions), secondary predication and the acquisition of Spanish as a second language.

Index